Production Efficiency with the Stochastic Management Model

Akio Torii

Production Efficiency with the Stochastic Management Model

Springer

Akio Torii
Institute of Economic Research
Chuo University
Hachiouji, Tokyo, Japan

ISBN 978-981-95-3500-2 ISBN 978-981-95-3501-9 (eBook)
https://doi.org/10.1007/978-981-95-3501-9

This Springer imprint is published by the registered company Springer Nature Singapore Pte Ltd.
The registered company address is: 152 Beach Road, #21-01/04 Gateway East, Singapore 189721, Singapore

Preface

Technical inefficiency refers to an estimation method for production or cost functions in which it is assumed that the deviation from the frontier function includes a term with an asymmetric probability density distribution. Typically, the distribution is assumed to be positively skewed, and such deviations are interpreted as inefficiency in firms or industries. However, the relationship between the concept of technical inefficiency as a methodological assumption for estimating production functions and the broader or literal sense of inefficiency, which is understood as an actual phenomenon within firms or organizational units, has not been carefully examined. It is possible that technical inefficiency may be observed even if firms act rationally, and conversely, that inefficiencies in firm behavior may not manifest as technical inefficiency in estimates. This book estimates production functions in Japanese manufacturing under the assumption that technical inefficiency exists; that is, it employs technical inefficiency as an estimation method. However, the goal is not to accurately estimate the production function for each industry or to identify the distribution of technical inefficiency. Rather, the overall objective is to examine how we might test whether inefficiency, understood in the everyday sense of "waste" or as a problem inherent in organizational structures, is observed in Japanese manufacturing.

To this end, two theoretical models for the mechanism by which inefficiency arises are developed. Using these models, we analyze how behaviors that might be considered wasteful in production manifest as technical inefficiency, and test whether such phenomena are statistically observed in actual data. In general, merely confirming the existence of technical inefficiency as expected through the estimation of a production function that assumes such inefficiency is not sufficient to establish the presence of inefficiency as an organizational problem. This is because one cannot avoid the criticism that what is observed as inefficiency may in fact be recognized by firms and rationally managed, and thus should not be regarded as true inefficiency in a substantive sense. Thus, to demonstrate the existence of inefficiency, we must develop models that can capture behavior inconsistent with rational decision-making.

The first model is a vintage dynamic model that describes the facility renewal behavior of establishments. In industries where technological progress is present, establishments improve their productivity through facility renewal, while their relative productivity to the frontier technology declines due to the obsolescence of facilities. The nature of facility renewal decisions made by individual establishments determines the distributional characteristics of productivity within an industry. For example, if facility renewal occurs at a constant probability regardless of an establishment's level of productivity relative to the frontier production function, and the resulting productivity after renewal is equally likely to fall anywhere between the frontier level and the pre-renewal level, the productivity distribution in that industry converges asymptotically to an exponential distribution. If, instead, the probability of facility renewal is proportional to the gap between the frontier technology and actual productivity, productivity converges asymptotically to a half-normal distribution. Thus, by assuming a specific vintage model, the shape of the asymmetric distribution in technical inefficiency reflects the nature of facility renewal. If it is shown that the probability of facility renewal is inversely correlated with productivity, meaning that establishments with lower productivity are less likely to renew their facilities, then the rationality of establishment decision-making must be seriously questioned.

The second model is static and assumes that one important factor of production is unobserved, and that dispersion in this input causes apparent technical inefficiency. While capital, labor, and materials are typically considered observable inputs, managerial effort is also an important input but is not directly measurable. Some technical inefficiency models assume that productivity is affected by the level of managerial effort. Because managerial effort requires some form of cost, rational managers would seek to optimize its input. The optimal level is determined where the marginal product of effort matches its opportunity cost. Assuming that the actual input of effort is symmetrically dispersed around this optimum, and that the production function is concave, the resulting distribution of productivity is negatively skewed. In this case, technical inefficiency will be observed in the estimation of the production function. If deviations from the optimal effort input are normally distributed, the technical inefficiency term follows a distribution derived from the normal distribution, whose properties encode information about managerial input. When managerial effort is not allocated appropriately, and decisions ignore its cost and effectiveness, the resulting distribution will reflect these behaviors. One oft-cited feature of Japanese industry is the low productivity of white-collar workers, with excessively long working hours and limited consideration of cost-effectiveness. If this is true, the effects might be observable in the distributional characteristics of technical inefficiency.

As described above, a major focus of this book is to examine the distributional characteristics of the asymmetric deviations from the frontier function, which are observed as technical inefficiency. Typically, the distribution is assumed to be an asymmetric distribution, such as the half-normal distribution, as well as its truncated version, and parameters are estimated from firm-level data within a single industry or panel data capturing temporal changes. Nonparametric approaches for estimating inefficiency distributions have also been proposed, but these too rely on data from a single industry. Instead of treating inefficiency as an industry-specific feature, this book considers it as a phenomenon broadly shared across many industries within a national economy. It is based on the hypothesis that inefficiency may result from common behavioral or institutional patterns such as management culture, which can be shared across multiple industrial sectors. The tolerability of inefficiency may depend on the business culture of the country or region where firms operate. If business culture is shared among adjacent industries in the same region, inefficiency may be observed as a general tendency across many industries.

By considering inefficiency as a cross-industry tendency, the estimation of asymmetric deviations is no longer dependent on data from a single industry. It is difficult to test the distributional features of a given sample when the sample comes from only one industry. However, if technical inefficiency exhibits a consistent distributional form across many industries, then estimation methods that are different from conventional approaches become possible. This book employs a method using the moments of deviation from the frontier function up to the fourth order. Specifically, it uses the ratio of excess kurtosis to the skewness raised to the four-thirds power.

The asymmetric distributions assumed for modeling technical inefficiency typically include parameters that determine their variance, which corresponds to the magnitude of inefficiency. Some of these distributions also include additional parameters that influence their shape. Deviations from the frontier production function are modeled as the convolution of such asymmetric distributions with normally distributed random noise. To estimate the distributional characteristics of technical inefficiency, one must separate the observed, convolved deviations into the asymmetric component attributable to inefficiency and the symmetric component attributable to noise. In this context, we make use of the property that the ratio of excess kurtosis to the skewness raised to the power of four-thirds remains invariant under convolution with a normal distribution. Moreover, this ratio is not affected by the variance of the symmetric error term in the estimated production function, nor by the variance parameter representing the scale of technical inefficiency. Utilizing this property, it becomes possible to statistically test whether distributional characteristics indicative of technical inefficiency are observed across many industries. This book applies this method to input-output data from approximately 350 four-digit manufacturing industries in Japan to test for the presence of such inefficiency.

This is the core argument of the book. The author previously participated in an international project on technical inefficiency led by the late Professor R.E. Caves at Harvard University, estimating inefficiency in Japanese industry using 1977 data, as reported in Torii(1992). Later, with support from a Ministry of International Trade and Industry (MITI) project, the author gained access to 1990s data and published results in Japanese as Torii(2001). The main ideas in this book emerged during that period, but for various reasons, a full analytical report could not be completed until now. Thanks to Springer Nature, the author has finally been able to publish this work. However, the comprehensive production function estimates for Japanese manufacturing still rely on data from 1993 and 1995, now three decades old. The theoretical discussion has been thoroughly revised, and all Monte Carlo simulations have been recalculated. The author extends sincere gratitude to Springer Nature for the opportunity to publish this research, as well as to the editor, Mr. Yutaka Hirachi. The research on technical inefficiency presented here is also deeply indebted to the guidance of the late Professors R.E. Caves, Masu Uekusa (University of Tokyo), and

David G. Mayes (University of Auckland). It is deeply regrettable that this report could not be presented during their lifetimes. The delay is entirely due to the author's own limitations.

This book aims to introduce a method for testing issues related to technical inefficiency that has not been discussed in previous research. Although the method is deeply indebted to and inspired by a large body of earlier work, the author was not able to devote sufficient space to reviewing that literature. The author regrets this shortcoming, which is entirely due to personal limitations. Undoubtedly, there are many shortcomings in the theoretical arguments and statistical methods presented here, which are also the author's sole responsibility. English editing support was obtained from Editage. In addition, I made limited use of ChatGPT for linguistic purposes only, without employing it beyond that scope.

Hachiouji, Japan Akio Torii

References

Torii, Akio. 1992. "Technical Efficiency in Japanese Industries." *Industrial Efficiency in Six Nations*, pp. 31–120.

Torii, Akio. 2001. *Efficiency in Japanese Industries*. Tokyo: NTT Publishing. (in Japanese)

Contents

1 Introduction: Identifying Technical Inefficiency 1
- 1.1 Stochastic Frontier Analysis and the Wrong Skewness Problem 1
- 1.2 Technical Inefficiency and X-inefficiency 2
- 1.3 The Aim of This Book 7
- 1.4 The Method of Using the Relationship Among Residual Moments 9
- 1.5 Two Models Explaining Negatively Skewed Inefficiencies 11
  - 1.5.1 The Vintage Facility Renewal Investment Model 11
  - 1.5.2 The Model of Unobservable Managerial Inputs 12
- 1.6 The Combined Effect of the Two Models 15
- 1.7 The Structure of This Book 16
- Appendix 17
- References 19

2 A Method for Estimating and Testing the Distribution Parameters of an Asymmetric Distribution When a Large Number of Moment Estimates Are Available 21
- 2.1 Identification of Distribution Type and Calculation of Moments of Convolution with Normal Distribution 23
  - 2.1.1 Half-Normal Distribution 23
  - 2.1.2 Exponential Distribution 24
  - 2.1.3 Gamma Distribution 25
  - 2.1.4 Truncated Normal 26
  - 2.1.5 Exponential Power-Type 27
  - 2.1.6 Square Normal-Type 28
- 2.2 Distribution-Specific Moment Relationships and Their Estimation 28
  - 2.2.1 Parameter-Invariant Moment Relationships 28

2.2.2 Identification of Distribution Type and Estimation of Parameters ... 32
2.3 Properties of the Distribution Parameter Estimators: Exponential Power-Type Distribution ... 34
2.3.1 Estimation of the Model Equation Under OLS ... 35
2.3.2 Log-Log OLS Estimation ... 36
2.3.3 Further Monte Carlo Experiments ... 37
2.4 Property of the Distributional Parameter Estimators: Square Normal-Type Distribution ... 38
2.5 Conclusion and Discussion ... 41
Appendix: Calculation of Moments of Convolution of Exponential Power-Type Distribution/Square Normal-Type Distribution and Normal Distribution ... 42
Tables: Results of Monte Carlo Experiments ... 44
References ... 66

3 Dynamic Model Explaining the Asymmetric Distribution of Deviations from the Production Frontier ... 69
3.1 Vintage Inefficiency Model ... 70
3.1.1 Determination of Facility Renewal Timing Using Vintage Inefficiency Model ... 71
3.1.2 Mechanism of Technical Inefficiency Generation (Without Considering Adjustment Costs) ... 73
3.1.3 Mechanism of Technical Inefficiency Generation (Considering Adjustment Costs) ... 74
3.1.4 The Level of Inefficiency and Renewal of Facility ... 75
3.1.5 Probabilistic Process Model of Facility Renewal ... 77
3.1.6 Symmetric Distribution of Inefficiency and the Rationality of Decision ... 79
3.1.7 Power-Law Proportional Rational Facility Renewal Decision ... 81
3.2 A Management Inefficiency Model ... 84
3.3 Conclusion ... 89
Appendix: Vintage-type Technical Inefficiency and Market Structure ... 89
References ... 92

4 Technical Inefficiency and X-inefficiency ... 95
4.1 Leibenstein's X-inefficiency and the Technical Inefficiency in Econometrics ... 97
4.1.1 Leibenstein's X-inefficiency ... 97
4.1.2 Definition of Technical Inefficiency ... 101
4.1.3 Stochastic Production Frontier Model ... 102
4.2 Relation Between X-inefficiency and Technical Inefficiency ... 105
4.2.1 Existence of Technical Inefficiency That Is Not X-inefficiency ... 106

4.2.2 X-inefficiency Not Observed as Technical Inefficiency 108
4.3 "Irrational" Behavior and the Neoclassical Critique of X-inefficiency ... 112
4.3.1 Relativity of Rationality ... 112
4.3.2 Observation of X-inefficiency ... 115
4.4 Refutable Definition of X-inefficiency as an Alternative to Cause ... 117
4.4.1 Definition as Residual Inefficiency After Rational Decision-making ... 118
4.4.2 Avoidable Inefficiency That Still Occurs ... 119
4.4.3 Correlation with Market Structure ... 120
4.5 Defining X-inefficiency as Uncontrolled Inefficiency ... 122
4.6 Conclusion ... 126
References ... 128

5 X-inefficiencies Across Japanese Manufacturing Industries: Identification Based on a Vintage Capital Investment Model ... 131
5.1 Test of Technical Inefficiency ... 133
5.1.1 Validity of Econometric Models that Assume Technical Inefficiency ... 133
5.1.2 Test of the Validity of the Distribution by Lee (1983) ... 134
5.1.3 Goodness-of-Fit Test by Wang et al. (2011) ... 135
5.1.4 Without Assuming a Specific Distribution ... 136
5.2 A Model for Testing X-inefficiency ... 138
5.2.1 Basic Configuration of the Vintage Model and the Rational Adjustment of the Facility Renewal Interval ... 138
5.2.2 Rational Adjustment of Facility Renewal Interval and PDF of Controlled Inefficiency ... 140
5.2.3 Testing for Controlled Inefficiency ... 142
5.2.4 Procedure 1: Examination of Four Typical Distribution Types ... 143
5.2.5 Procedures 2 and 3: Extension of Half-Normal Distribution and Null Hypothesis to Be Tested ... 146
5.3 A Method for Testing X-inefficiency ... 149
5.3.1 Formulation of Hypotheses for Testing X-inefficiency ... 150
5.3.2 Inter-Industry Cross-Sectional Analysis ... 151
5.3.3 Employing MOLS ... 153
5.4 Test of X-inefficiency Existence in the Japanese Manufacturing Industries ... 154
5.4.1 Estimation Model of Technical Inefficiency ... 154
5.4.2 Test for the Existence of X-Inefficiency ... 159
5.4.3 Test of the Hypothesis of Half-Normal and Exponential Distribution ... 167

5.4.4 Identification of X-Inefficiency Using the Vintage Model 170
5.5 Conclusion and Discussion 174
Appendix: Proof of Proposition 5 177
References 177

6 X-inefficiencies in the Japanese Manufacturing Industries II: Identifying X-inefficiencies assuming the Existence of Inefficiency Unobserved Production Factors 179
6.1 A Model Assuming an Unobserved Production Factor 180
6.1.1 Input–Output Model with Controlled, Unobserved Production Factor 181
6.1.2 Characteristics of Managerial Resource Input 184
6.1.3 Absence of Control over Managerial Resources 187
6.2 Method for Testing the Existence of X-inefficiency 191
6.2.1 Square Normal-Type Distribution 192
6.2.2 Test Using the Relation Between Moments 193
6.3 The Existence of X-inefficiency in the Japanese Manufacturing Industries 196
6.3.1 Relationship Between Moments 196
6.3.2 Test for the Presence of X-Inefficiency 197
6.4 Conclusion 202
References 204

Abbreviations

CDF	Cumulative Distribution Function
COLS	Corrected OLS
DEA	Data Envelopment Analysis
DFA	Distribution Free Analysis
DMU	Decision Making Unit
FDH	Free Disposal Hull
JSIC	Japan Standard Industrial Classification
LM	Lagrange Multiplier
ML	Maximum Likelihood
MLE	Maximum Likelihood Estimator
MOLS	Modified OLS
OLS	Ordinary Least Squares
PDF	Probability Density Function
QC	Quality Control
QMP	Quality Management Practice
SFA	Stochastic Frontier Analysis
TFA	Thick Frontier Approach

Chapter 1
Introduction: Identifying Technical Inefficiency

1.1 Stochastic Frontier Analysis and the Wrong Skewness Problem

Technical efficiency in stochastic production frontier models, as introduced by Aigner et al. (1977) and Meeusen and van Den Broeck (1977), refers to a method of estimating the production function or cost function that assumes the deviation between the frontier production (or cost) function and the observed outputs includes a term with an asymmetric probability density distribution. Define the input–output relation of an establishment j in industry i as:

$$y_j = f_i(\boldsymbol{x}_j; \boldsymbol{\beta}_i) + v_j - u_j \tag{1.1}$$

where $\boldsymbol{x}_j$ is an input vector, y_j is a scalar output of the establishment, $f_i(\cdot)$ is a production frontier function, and $\boldsymbol{\beta}_i$ is the vector of production function parameters. Note that for variables indexed by j, which indicate establishment-level data, the subscript i is omitted for simplicity. Specifically, the subscript j refers to the j-th establishment within industry i. The term v_j represents a symmetric error term, which is commonly assumed to follow a normal distribution in most studies. On the other hand, u_j, representing technical inefficiency, is often modeled using positively skewed asymmetric distributions such as the half-normal, truncated normal, or exponential distribution. This modeling approach is widely known as Stochastic Frontier Analysis (SFA).

Thus, technical inefficiency is a theoretical framework that hypothesizes how inefficiencies in firms or organizations affect the production input–output relationship. It is designed and implemented to capture inefficiency distinct from allocative efficiency, which refers to a decrease in productivity caused by selection error in the composition of the input vector $\boldsymbol{x}_j$. Indeed, most papers discussing SFA refer to Farrell (1957) or Debreu (1951), both of whom defined technical efficiency in their interpretation of deviations from the production or cost frontier. For instance, this

A. Torii, *Production Efficiency with the Stochastic Management Model*,
https://doi.org/10.1007/978-981-95-3501-9_1

can be seen in papers such as Aigner et al. (1977), Meeusen and van Den Broeck (1977), Coelli et al. (2005), Lovell et al. (1993), and Greene (2008), among others.

However, the relationship between technical inefficiency in the estimation of production (or cost) functions and the inefficiencies present in firms or, more generally, in organizations has not been adequately explored. No solid reasons have been provided to explain why inefficiencies within firms or organizations should lead to positively skewed distributions, or why asymmetric deviations from the estimated frontier, rather than symmetric ones, should necessarily be interpreted as evidence of inefficiency.

Indeed, residuals from frontier functions are often observed to be positively skewed, which is known as the wrong skewness problem.[1] Since the residuals from the estimated frontier functions are analyzed as the result of the convolution of v_j (which has zero skewness) and $-u_j$ (which is negatively skewed), the error term $v_j - u_j$ is expected to exhibit negative skewness. Papadopoulos and Parmeter (2024) present a comprehensive review of the discussion on this theme. A naive inference introduced in the paper regarding why inefficiency brings a positively skewed distribution is that "market forces make efficiency a factor of survival, so more firms will tend to be closer to low levels of inefficiency." As departures from this inference, the paper summarizes situations where the convolved deviations suffer a wrong skewness problem. These include idiosyncratic cases where a mass of highly inefficient firms can survive, where part of the distribution of inefficient firms is truncated, where heterogeneous firms are grouped into a single industry, where symmetric and asymmetric error terms are correlated, where an important production factor is missing from the production function, and where random noise unexpectedly exhibits skewness. The very fact that these highly diverse factors have been pointed out separately suggests that negatively skewed deviations from the frontier under market forces have yet to be examined from a unified perspective.

1.2 Technical Inefficiency and X-inefficiency

It can certainly be argued that, under competitive market conditions, inefficient firms are more likely to be eliminated; to avoid this outcome, firms are likely to seek to reduce the degree of inefficiency; as a result, the productivity distribution may take a form with its mode located at a low level of inefficiency, and the skewness of the productivity distribution may be negative; in other words, the distribution of the degree of inefficiency may exhibit positive skewness. Here, the term "productivity" refers not to the conventional measure of output per unit of input, but rather to a relative measure of output compared to what is achievable at the frontier given a level of inputs. Throughout this chapter, "productivity" will be used exclusively in this sense for the sake of simplicity and to avoid repeated explanations. However,

[1] Olson et al. (1980) first reported this issue observed in Monte Carlo simulation results as Type I failure.

conversely, if we observe that the deviation from the frontier shows a negatively skewed distribution, there has been no clear reason given for concluding that this skewness is proof that inefficiency exists. Can we conclude that the distribution of productivity will never show negative skewness in a situation where each firm is operating efficiently and making rational decisions?

When posing such questions, the terms "efficiency" or "inefficiency" are often used in nuanced and multifaceted ways. First, inefficiency may mean that a firm's productivity is simply lower than that of other firms or business establishments. This typically includes cases where lower productivity is observed at a certain point in time. Second, inefficiency may instead suggest a more intrinsic quality of the firm's performance that persists over time, rather than a temporary decline in productivity. In what follows, we will examine the relationship between negative skewness in productivity distribution and inefficiency for each of these cases.

In the first case, when inefficiency is defined as a downward deviation in relative productivity at a specific point in time, the negative skewness of the deviation distribution contributes to a lower average productivity due to the extended left tail, which corresponds to negative deviations from the frontier. In Torii (1992), the author demonstrated that in an industry experiencing steady technological progress, if each establishment makes an investment to embody the latest technology with a probability proportional to the gap between its current productivity and the frontier productivity level, the resulting productivity distribution follows a half-normal distribution. Consider an industry undergoing continuous technological advancement, where establishments that invest in their facilities at a later point can benefit from more advanced and cost-efficient technologies. Because embodying such technologies entails substantial investment costs, rational establishments cannot renovate continuously, but instead choose a positive and optimal interval between successive investments. Although each establishment reaches the frontier at the moment it adopts the latest technology, its productivity begins to decline immediately and continues to decrease at a constant rate relative to the frontier until the next investment in facilities. Therefore, because establishments do not continuously keep up with frontier technology, the time-averaged productivity falls below the frontier level, leading to inefficiency in the first sense. Consequently, rational establishments adopt an investment policy that yields a time-averaged productivity below the frontier, with the extent of the deviation depending on investment cost. The observed productivity forms a distribution that, through the use of SFA, can be identified as including a non-negative technical inefficiency term with a tail extending in the positive direction.

The following mechanism explains why inefficiency forms a skewed distribution that can be observed through SFA. Suppose that, for a given establishment j, the optimal investment interval that maximizes long-run profit is determined such that the establishment renews its facilities when its inefficiency relative to the frontier reaches a value of $\bar{u}_j$, taking into account its establishment-specific costs. If the establishment follows this investment schedule, its degree of inefficiency over time will be uniformly distributed over the interval $[0, \bar{u}_j]$, as inefficiency increases monotonically from 0 to $\bar{u}_j$ and then resets periodically. Due to differences in establishment-specific costs, the optimal investment threshold $\bar{u}_j$ will vary across establishments, resulting in a certain degree of dispersion in the inefficiency thresholds observed in the population. Considering that many establishments in the industry follow such productivity (inefficiency) dynamics, we examine the distribution of inefficiency levels across the entire industry. At lower levels of inefficiency, that is, levels closer to the frontier, any establishment can exhibit such low inefficiency immediately after making a renewal investment. Therefore, the probability density at these levels is likely to be high. In contrast, at higher levels of inefficiency, the number of establishments capable of exhibiting such high inefficiency decreases as the inefficiency level increases. This is because, if an establishment's renewal threshold $\bar{u}_j$ is smaller than a given inefficiency level, the establishment will never allow its inefficiency to reach that level before making a renewal investment, and thus always maintains a lower inefficiency level. As the inefficiency level increases, fewer establishments allow inefficiency to reach such high levels before renewing investment. Accordingly, the probability density declines. Thus, the inefficiency distribution becomes a decreasing function of inefficiency and exhibits positive skewness, as observed through SFA.

The distribution of productivity across establishments thus exhibits negative skewness, reflecting deviations from the frontier production function. But should this be regarded as technical inefficiency in Farrell's sense? Is it appropriate to define technical inefficiency based on deviations from the frontier at a single point in time? If technical inefficiency is empirically identified through the distribution of such deviations in an industry's input–output data, can we say that the objective of SFA has been achieved? In fact, if firms are maximizing profits by selecting optimal investment intervals that maximize their time-averaged productivity, it is reasonable to regard them as embodying frontier technology. If this perspective is not accepted, even a rational and efficiently operating firm may be misclassified as technically inefficient. In such a context, "technical" inefficiency may risk being understood merely as a definitional artifact, rather than as a reflection of economically meaningful inefficiency.

In the second sense of inefficiency, let us consider cases where inefficiency reflects an inherent characteristic of the firm. Many methodological studies on the estimation of technical inefficiency through SFA refer to Farrell's (1957) definition of technical inefficiency as the estimation target. However, empirical studies that aim to estimate the level of technical inefficiency within specific industries often cite not only Farrell's (1957) definition but also Leibenstein's (1966, 1976, 1987) concept of X-inefficiency as the theoretical basis for measured inefficiency.[2] Meeusen and van Den Broeck (1977) also refer to Leibenstein (1966). Leibenstein (1976) argued that incorporating psychological or behavioral factors into microeconomics, which traditionally focused on rational decision-making, would enable a broader analysis of firm behavior. He introduced the concept of X-inefficiency to explain inefficiencies arising from firm behavior that cannot be captured under the assumption of full rationality as posited in traditional neoclassical microeconomics. The fact that many empirical studies cite X-inefficiency as a theoretical basis for observed technical

---

[2] For example, see Chen (2007), Piacenza (2006), Rahman et al. (2012), Perelman and Pestieau (1994), among many others.

inefficiency suggests that their authors either presume that negative deviations from the frontier reflect the presence of X-inefficiency or expect that industries containing firms whose decisions deviate from the assumptions of rational behavior will exhibit negatively skewed distributions of deviations from the frontier. However, neither of these presumptions has been explicitly discussed in the literature. Thus, the relationship between X-inefficiency and the observed positive skewness in the distribution of technical inefficiency remains unclear.

This book notes that X-inefficiency and the technical inefficiency observed in SFA, characterized by a positively skewed distribution u_j, do not have a direct relationship. That is, the existence of one does not logically imply the existence of the other. First, consider again the argument based on the simple vintage model discussed earlier in relation to the first sense of inefficiency. This refers to the case in which inefficiency is interpreted simply as a relative inferiority in productivity at a given point in time. In that discussion, we argued that establishments making rational and efficient decisions choose an optimal, positive interval for renewal investments. As a result, their time-averaged productivity falls below the productivity level based on frontier technology. Assuming an appropriate stochastic process, technical inefficiency is then observed through SFA as a non-negative term whose distribution exhibits positive skewness. Such establishments, however, are making rational decisions within the framework of traditional microeconomics. Therefore, even if technical inefficiency is observed, they are not X-inefficient. This demonstrates that technical inefficiency may still be observed through SFA even in the absence of X-inefficiency.

On the other hand, when firms exhibit X-inefficient behavior, their direct outcomes do not necessarily follow an asymmetric distribution. For example, consider a case where the degree of inefficiency forms a symmetric distribution centered around a certain positive value. When Leibenstein's concept of X-inefficiency manifests in various aspects of corporate activities, as introduced in Chap. 4, it can be understood as emerging within the characteristics of worker behavior. These small, incremental effects, accumulated over numerous daily activities, are likely to influence corporate performance. Therefore, it is reasonable to expect that the effects of X-inefficiency may exhibit a symmetrical distribution. The convolution of symmetric inefficiency and symmetric random noise also results in a symmetric distribution. For technical inefficiency to be observed as a positively skewed distribution, a mechanism such as the one inferred by Papadopoulos and Parmeter (2024) would be required. That is, the mechanism suggests that competitive market pressure leads firms to reduce inefficiency in order to survive, resulting in a positively skewed distribution of inefficiency levels, with its mode located near the frontier. This mechanism may appear universal at first glance. However, the effect of market pressure on the distribution of inefficiency is not necessarily straightforward. For example, consider the half-normal distribution, which is often assumed for technical inefficiency. Its skewness remains constant at the value $\sqrt{2}(4-\pi)/(\pi-2)^{1.5} \approx 0.9952$, regardless of the value of the variance parameter σ_v^2. Therefore, even if the inefficiency of all establishments were halved due to competitive pressure, the skewness would remain unchanged. In general, the skewness of a distribution is invariant under the transformation $u' = au$. This implies the natural result that a symmetric distribution does not become asymmetric merely through a uniform scaling transformation such as $u' = au$.

One possible scenario is that, in the absence of competitive pressure, an establishment exhibits inefficiency at a fixed level $\bar{u}_j$, but under competitive pressure, its inefficiency is managed so as to be reduced and distributed uniformly over the interval $[0, \bar{u}_j]$. In this case, the probability density function of inefficiency necessarily becomes downward-sloping, resulting in a positively skewed distribution. Conversely, consider a situation where, in the absence of competitive pressure, the inefficiency levels follow a symmetric distribution with tails on both sides. If competitive pressure eliminates establishments with inefficiency above a certain threshold, and if newly entering firms that replace them inherit the same inefficiency distribution as the surviving ones, the resulting distribution becomes a truncated version of the original symmetric distribution. Since the truncation occurs at a high level of inefficiency, the resulting distribution exhibits negative skewness. Thus, for market competition to affect the inefficiency levels of establishments in such a way that a positively skewed distribution is observed, specific and restrictive assumptions must be satisfied.

Furthermore, Papadopoulos and Parmeter (2024) provide various examples in which such mechanisms do not operate, resulting in the "wrong skewness problem" appearing as a characteristic of the population. For instance, in industries that are heavily protected from competitive pressure by public regulation, the elimination mechanism does not function, and there is no reason to expect the degree of inefficiency to follow a positively skewed distribution. In such cases, technical inefficiency may not be detected through SFA.

Taken together with the argument presented in the previous paragraph, this shows that technical inefficiency and X-inefficiency do not have an inclusive relationship in which one encompasses the other. The existence of technical inefficiency does not imply the presence of X-inefficiency, nor does the presence of X-inefficiency necessarily imply that inefficiency will be observed as technical inefficiency.[3]

[3] Even if the competitive pressure mechanism is working as expected, it is difficult to identify the presence of productivity declines due to X-inefficiency from the negatively skewed productivity distribution observed as a result. This is because, even in the absence of X-inefficiency, symmetric deviations from the frontier can arise due to random noise, and the portion of these deviations that fall in the negative direction may be subject to the same selection pressure as inefficiency-related deviations. As a result, productivity exhibits negative skewness. In this case, it is impossible to distinguish, based solely on the skewed productivity distribution, whether the observed productivity decline includes declines due to X-inefficiency or whether it is solely the result of random factors with no contribution from X-inefficiency. To make this distinction, it would be necessary to assume that the probability of elimination due to competitive pressure differs between productivity declines caused by random noise and those caused by X-inefficiency, even if the magnitude of the productivity decline is the same. However, is this assumption feasible? If productivity declines due to random noise are short-term, while those due to X-inefficiency persist over the long term, the probability of elimination may indeed be higher in the latter case. In that scenario, a negatively skewed productivity distribution would be observed only when X-inefficiency is present. However, we do not have a general theory regarding the relationship between the origins of inefficiency and elimination through competition. Productivity declines stemming from purely technical reasons, such as resource constraints, may be difficult to address through firm efforts, and it is possible that

Furthermore, the existence of the wrong skewness problem in SFA indicates that even if the expected skewness direction is observed, its interpretation is not straightforward. Even if residuals with negative skewness from the production frontier are observed as predicted in a particular industry, it is not guaranteed that the mechanisms causing wrong skewness in other industries are not operating in that industry. The inefficiency term u_j may be correlated with the symmetric deviation term v_j, and the distribution may be truncated. Without accounting for these potential effects, it is impossible to accurately estimate the degree of inefficiency. It is possible that the predicted skewness was observed despite the absence of inherent technical inefficiency in the population.

1.3 The Aim of This Book

When interpreting technical inefficiency observed in the estimation of a frontier production or cost function, we must acknowledge the challenges discussed above, particularly the uncertainty about what exactly is being observed and how it can be interpreted within the framework of economics. Furthermore, unless these issues are clarified, the estimation itself may remain problematic. The statistical model, which represents deviations from the frontier function as a convolution of a symmetric error term v_j and an asymmetric inefficiency term u_j, requires that regression residuals be decomposed into v_j and u_j based on certain statistical distinctions. As long as the economic meaning of these statistical distinctions remains unclear, this difficulty cannot be avoided. From this perspective, the existence of the wrong skewness problem symbolically represents the numerous inherent issues within SFA. As a statistical technique, SFA has developed to consider that technical inefficiency manifests under various circumstances, allowing for more accurate estimation according to those circumstances. However, until it is clarified what kind of phenomenon is being captured economically or within an economic framework, SFA cannot be considered complete even as an estimation method.

This difficulty seems similar to the problem of interpreting the low productivity of individual establishments, firms, or Decision Making Units (DMUs) at a single point in time as an indicator of the degree of their technical inefficiency or X-inefficiency. The estimation method presented by Aigner et al. (1977) is ultimately for the variance of the error terms v_j and u_j, as well as the method for estimating the frontier function. Since the residuals are convoluted, it is inherently impossible to disentangle the individual residuals into v_j and u_j for each DMU. The widely used conditional expectation $\hat{u}_j = \mathbb{E}[u_j|\hat{\epsilon}_j]$ serves as an estimate of inefficiency, where $\hat{\epsilon}_j \equiv y_j -$

---

competitive elimination targets productivity declines due specifically to random noise. Firms might overcome productivity disadvantages due to organizational issues through effort, but it would be difficult to overcome the symmetrical productivity disadvantages that arose uncontrolled. In such cases, it would be impossible to distinguish the presence of X-inefficiency using SFA, which assumes negatively skewed deviations from the frontier.

$f_i(\boldsymbol{x}_j; \hat{\boldsymbol{\beta}}_i)$, but, as Wang and Schmidt (2009) demonstrate, its distribution differs from that of u_j and reflects shrinkage toward the mean inefficiency, $\mathbb{E}[u_j]$. However, empirical studies estimating technical inefficiency for specific industries often focus on inefficiency estimates $\mathbb{E}[u_j|\hat{\epsilon}_j]$ for each DMU to derive policy implications. For example, in Chen (2007), the efficiency estimates for individual DMUs are presented in a table, and the relationship between these efficiency estimates and the attributes of each DMU is analyzed using variance analysis. This approach is a typical model of empirical analysis estimating technical inefficiency for a specific industry. Although the level of technical inefficiency is ultimately estimated as a characteristic across an entire industry, the main focus of empirical analysis is the deviation from the frontier for each DMU.

In the context of the wrong skewness problem, the positive or negative skewness of the distribution of the deviation from the frontier $v_j - u_j$ is the issue. This refers to the skewness of the distribution of the sample group resulting from convolution, and not to the skewness of the inefficiency term u_j itself. For this reason, as discussed in Sect. 5 of Papadopoulos and Parmeter (2024), when the wrong skewness problem arises, various potential sources of unexpected skewness in the sample are considered, such as irregularities in the population distribution of v_j or distortions resulting from a limited sample size. This line of inquiry, which focuses on individual realizations and attempts to identify the underlying causes, is similar to the approach taken in the empirical studies discussed in the previous paragraph, where the estimated efficiency of each individual DMU is emphasized.

If it is accepted that, when evaluating the results of empirical analyses of specific industries using SFA, emphasis should be placed not on the deviations of individual DMUs from the frontier but rather on the insights these analyses provide regarding the overall tendency of technical inefficiency across the industry, then, based on the same logic, one might argue that the empirical results obtained for individual industries should not be directly interpreted as final conclusions. Instead, since these results are largely affected by noise due to convolution, they should be evaluated for the implications they offer about tendencies in the population from which they are drawn. The analysis in this book is based on the premise that the residual distribution from the frontier function in any single industry merely represents a sample from the population. Accordingly, it aims to derive implications about the broader tendencies of inefficiency across a wide span of industries rather than focusing solely on individual industry results. In particular, this analysis seeks to provide insights into the origins of technical inefficiency and to suggest the potential presence of X-inefficiency.

While the observed technical inefficiency may not directly indicate the presence of X-inefficiency, it is unlikely to be entirely unrelated. If certain characteristics of technical inefficiency are consistently observed across a wide range of industries, and if those characteristics can be interpreted as offering economic insights into the existence of X-inefficiency, then this book aims to pursue precisely that possibility.

1.4 The Method of Using the Relationship Among Residual Moments

So, specifically, how does this book intend to achieve this aim? The approach taken here is to use a simple ratio of the kurtosis to the skewness raised to the power of 4/3, calculated from the deviations from the frontier function. That is, the method utilizes central moments up to the fourth order. Meanwhile, the MOLS method, which has frequently been used in SFA, relies on the third central moment of residuals, as the positive skew of the asymmetric inefficiency component directly reflects the degree of deviation from the frontier. Generally, higher-order moments are strongly influenced by values in the tails of the distribution and are often said to be less representative of the main body of the data.[4] Moreover, the sampling variability of such moments tends to be large. However, the ratio of kurtosis to skewness raised to the 4/3 power has properties that compensate for these weaknesses when applied to extract common features across many industries.[5]

Consider the convolution $u + v$, where u is an arbitrary random variable and $v \sim N(0, \sigma_v^2)$ is normally distributed. Let M_2, M_3, and M_4 be the second-, third-, and fourth-order central moments of this convolution. If kurtosis and skewness are defined as $M_4/M_2^2 - 3$ and $M_3/M_2^{3/2}$, respectively, then the ratio of kurtosis to skewness raised to the 4/3 power is given by:

$$\frac{\text{kurtosis}}{\text{skewness}^{\frac{4}{3}}} = \frac{M_4 - 3M_2^2}{M_3^{4/3}}.$$

Both the numerator and the denominator of this ratio are independent of the variance σ_v of the noise term v, and depend solely on the population moments of u. This is an intuitively expected property, given that for a normal distribution, $M_4 - 3M_2^2 = M_3 = 0$. A formal proof is provided in the appendix to this chapter. In other words, this ratio is neutral with respect to convolution with a normal distribution, and reflects only the distributional properties of u. As such, when analyzing this function of moments, it is not necessary to decompose the convolution into its individual components v and u.

Furthermore, when comparing the various asymmetric distributions that have been assumed in SFA for modeling technical inefficiency, we observe a common property. Distributions such as the half-normal and exponential have fixed shapes, with variance determined by a scale parameter, whereas distributions like the gamma distribution additionally have a shape parameter that controls the form of the distribution. For the former types of asymmetric distributions, the ratio of $M_4 - 3M_2^2$ to $|M_3|^{4/3}$ takes a constant value: specifically, $8(\pi - 3)/(2^{2/3}(4 - \pi)^{4/3})$ for the half-normal distribution and $3/2^{1/3}$ for the exponential distribution. In the case of the

[4] See Wheeler (2011).

[5] Recently, De Michele and De Bartolo (2025) analyzed a ratio similar to the one based on excess kurtosis, although their focus was on the ratio of raw kurtosis (defined without subtracting 3) to skewness raised to the power of 4/3.

gamma distribution, the ratio takes the value $3/(2(m+1))^{1/3}$, where m is the shape parameter of the gamma distribution. For details on the derivation, see Chap. 2. It is important to note that these ratio values do not contain the parameters that determine the variance of each distribution. More precisely, the ratio of the moment functions $M_4 - 3M_2^2$ to $|M_3|^{4/3}$ for the convolution $u + v$ does not depend on the variance of the symmetric distribution v or the variance of the asymmetric distribution u. Only parameters that describe the shape of the distribution remain.

From this, if the frontier production functions and their residuals can be obtained for a wide range of industries, and if it is reasonable to assume a common mechanism that generates technical inefficiency across these industries, then it is also natural to expect that the shape of the distribution of inefficiency is common to all. In that case, a hypothesis test on the shape of the distribution can be conducted by testing the value of the coefficient K that satisfies

$$M_4 - 3M_2^2 - K \cdot |M_3|^{4/3} = 0.$$

However, when estimating this ratio from actual sample data, it is well known that both the sample kurtosis and the sample skewness have large variances; moreover, they are not statistically independent. As a result, obtaining an unbiased estimator of their ratio is extremely difficult. Methods such as the delta method or Fieller's theorem are available for constructing confidence intervals for this type of ratio. However, as suggested by the presence of the wrong skewness problem, sample skewness can take both positive and negative values and may often be close to zero. In such cases, even with these methods, it is difficult to obtain confidence intervals narrow enough to support a meaningful hypothesis test. For this reason, this book adopts a practical approach by using simple linear regression across industries to estimate the ratio as a regression coefficient, with full awareness of the bias that may arise. Because such bias is expected, we rely on detailed Monte Carlo experiments to examine the properties of the estimator and use it with caution.

In this test, the hypothesis being evaluated is not about the distributional shape of each industry, but rather about the presence of a common distributional characteristic across a wide range of industries. Naturally, different industries are subject to varying levels of random disturbances due to environmental factors such as the market conditions for inputs and outputs. Moreover, the levels of inefficiency may differ depending on the degree of competition, entry barriers, and other structural conditions. This method allows for the identification of common properties that persist despite these industry-specific differences. For instance, suppose there exists a general pattern in the manifestation of technical inefficiency that is not dependent on industry-specific management environments or technological conditions, and that this pattern is reflected in the properties of the residual moments. Or, suppose that some aspect of X-inefficiency arises commonly across many industries due to regional corporate culture, and that this, too, is reflected in the characteristics of the residual moments. In such cases, the proposed method enables the confirmation of these types of common features.

1.5 Two Models Explaining Negatively Skewed Inefficiencies

The method described here, which is based on the use of residual moments, is intended to examine the mechanism through which technical inefficiency is generated. This book develops two types of theoretical models to describe the generation of inefficiency: a dynamic model and a static model. Using these models, we explore how behaviors or choices within firms or organizations that may be regarded as wasteful can be reflected in the distributional characteristics of technical inefficiency. Furthermore, by estimating production frontiers for various manufacturing industries in Japan and analyzing the sample moments of residuals for each industry, we examine whether the characteristics suggested by the theoretical models can be observed as a common tendency across a wide range of industries.

1.5.1 The Vintage Facility Renewal Investment Model

One of the models is the vintage facility renewal investment model introduced in Sect. 1.2. Rather than treating technical inefficiency at each establishment as a static and deterministic outcome, it is viewed as dynamically evolving, with traces of its generation mechanism to be identified in the distribution of technical inefficiency itself. In industries experiencing technological progress, establishments can improve productivity through facility renewal investments. At the same time, as existing facilities become obsolete at a certain rate relative to the latest technology, productivity gradually declines in comparison to the frontier. The distributional characteristics of productivity are determined by the nature of each establishment's decision-making regarding facility renewal.

This model is not necessarily limited to industries where productivity heavily depends on facility investments. It can be applied to situations where productivity tends to decline relative to frontier technology at a constant rate, and where it can be improved through managerial decision-making. Consider an establishment whose production process consists of many subprocesses. Suppose that inefficiency arises probabilistically in each subprocess, and that the overall productivity of the establishment is determined by the aggregate productivity of all subprocesses. If the establishment can recognize the presence of inefficiency, with the probability of recognition depending on the degree of inefficiency, it is likely to take corrective action. In such cases, inefficiency should be analyzed as a dynamically varying factor. Torii (1992) shows that when slacks probabilistically arise in various business processes within a firm, and when the firm is aware of the probabilistic nature of these slacks but cannot identify their specific source, attempts to resolve the inefficiency through audits cause the level of efficiency to change dynamically via a mechanism similar to that of the vintage model.

Furthermore, this dynamic mechanism operates in a complementary manner to the mechanism of selection through market competition. The outcome in which firms or organizations achieve higher productivity through facility renewal investments is functionally equivalent to the result of inefficient firms being eliminated by competitive market forces, while firms with lower inefficiency or those embodying frontier technology enter the market. Therefore, when the mechanisms of market selection and entry are active, the vintage model is expected to capture more dynamic fluctuations in productivity.

Assuming the vintage model as described, the asymmetric distributional shape of technical inefficiency can be interpreted as reflecting general tendencies in facility renewal investment observed across a wide range of industries. For instance, since the shape of the distribution differs depending on whether facility renewal occurs at a rate proportional to the degree of inefficiency or independently of it, one can infer characteristics of investment decision-making from the observed distributional shape. If, even after accounting for variations in facility renewal costs and demand conditions across establishments, which may lead to different optimal renewal intervals, no consistent pattern is observed in the distribution of technical inefficiency that would be expected under some form of rational decision-making, then it becomes difficult to avoid questioning the rationality of facility renewal decisions at the establishment level. For example, if, under the influence of market competition, the probability of facility renewal is found to be negatively correlated with the degree of productivity shortfall from the frontier, meaning that establishments with lower productivity are less likely to invest in renewal, this would raise doubts about the assumption of rational managerial behavior.

1.5.2 The Model of Unobservable Managerial Inputs

The other model considers the case where the dispersion in the input levels of an important but unobservable production factor generates a seemingly negative skew in observed productivity, creating the appearance of technical inefficiency as an independent disturbance term. This model does not explain the generation process of inefficiency itself, but rather explains why inefficiency characterized by an asymmetric distribution is observed in the residual term of the production function.

In manufacturing industries, the typical production factors are capital and labor. When estimating a production function with gross output as the dependent variable, material inputs are also included as production factors. In addition to these, managerial effort is often considered an important production factor. For example, Delis and Tsionas (2018) estimate the effect of this factor using the share function estimation, positing that management practices, despite being unobserved, are a crucial production factor. Similarly, Papadopoulos (2021) assumes that managerial input affects production but operates independently from the technical inefficiency term due to its unobserved nature, thereby estimating the effect of managerial input. What distinguishes managerial effort from other inputs is that its input level cannot be directly and explicitly observed. Nevertheless, it is believed to have a significant impact on production relationships.

The model constructed here, similar to the models in previous studies analyzing managerial input, assumes that the input of unobserved managerial effort affects productivity. However, unlike the previous models, it emphasizes that the unobservability of managerial input causes asymmetric residuals when estimating the production function, resulting in effects that are observed as technical inefficiency.

Consider the characteristics of managerial resource input. Managerial efforts to improve an enterprise's productivity have been extensively analyzed under the concept of QMP. Flynn et al. (1995) identified key components of QMP, including top management support, workforce management, quality information, supplier involvement, product design, process management, and customer involvement. International comparative studies, such as Samson and Terziovski (1999), Zhang (2000), and Phan et al. (2011), confirm that these components are commonly observed across countries. Each establishment is expected to allocate its limited managerial resources optimally across these activities to enhance overall productivity.

It is therefore reasonable to assume that a stable production function can be specified, with managerial input included as one of its core input factors. When scarce managerial resources are used effectively, the marginal product of managerial input can reasonably be expected to be positive. Furthermore, when establishments make rational choices among QMP components by comparing their marginal products, it is reasonable to assume that the marginal product of managerial input diminishes as the level of input increases. Accordingly, it is plausible to assume that the production function is concave with respect to managerial input, as is standard in production theory.

Even under the same industry conditions and when governed by the same production function, the actual forms of managerial input are likely to vary across establishments. Differences in managers lead to differences in behavioral tendencies, and regional variation results in variation in employee characteristics. Therefore, the appropriate form of managerial effort should differ depending on these individual characteristics. It is easy to imagine how complex it is to determine how much of an establishment's resources should be allocated to QMP activities aimed at improving productivity. Furthermore, although the costs of managerial resources devoted to such activities should be accounted for, the actual cost is highly person-specific and will naturally vary across managers and establishments. Unlike other input factors, such as capital and labor, one must take into account that there is no well-functioning factor market for managerial input. Therefore, even if establishments are subject to the same production function, the amount of managerial input allocated across establishments is likely to be widely dispersed.

How does such dispersion in input levels affect output? See Fig. 1.1 for illustration. These figures illustrate a situation where firms within an industry are assumed to have already selected their respective optimal capital-labor ratios. The focus is on variation in unobserved managerial input, which is symmetrically distributed around a central value z_0. In the figures, the horizontal axis represents unobserved managerial input, while the vertical axis represents observed labor productivity. The lower figure illustrates the case where the marginal product of managerial input at z_0 is zero, while the upper figure illustrates the case where it is positive. When managerial inputs are dispersed, the observed output naturally also becomes dispersed. As illustrated in the figures, the concavity of the production function with respect to managerial input leads to an asymmetric distribution of productivity, where the degree of asymmetry depends on the value of the marginal product at z_0.

Thus, if dispersion in an unobserved but important input factor leads to an asymmetric component in the residual term of the estimated production function, then the way in which that input affects productivity should be reflected in the shape of the distribution. Moreover, just as in the case of the vintage facility replacement model, the characteristics of this distribution are expected to be identifiable through the relationship of excess kurtosis to the skewness raised to the three-fourths power,

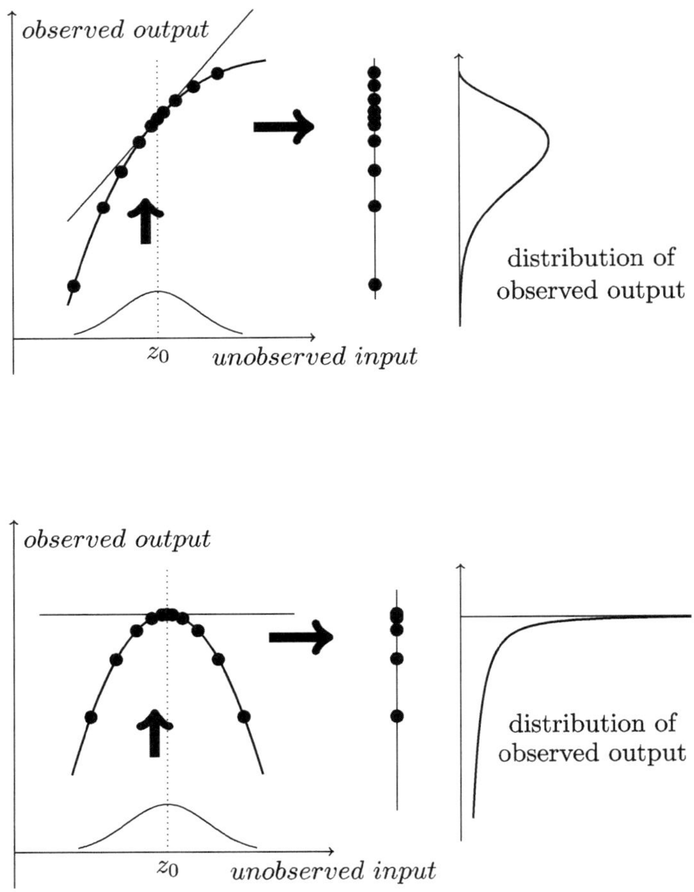

Fig. 1.1 Dispersed input generates asymmetrically distributed output

that is, in terms of the moments up to the fourth order. If, for example, the implications suggested by this relationship between moments were never observed under rational decision-making by managers regarding the input of managerial effort with cost considerations, then it would be necessary to question the rationality of such decision-making itself.

1.6 The Combined Effect of the Two Models

Here, we introduced two models of firm behavior that result in a residual distribution exhibiting negative skewness, observed as technical inefficiency through SFA. In this book, it is explained that the characteristics of how each mechanism operates are reflected in differences in the relationships among the second-, third-, and fourth-order central moments of residuals from the frontier production function. These relationships among the residual moments are observed as tendencies across many industries, utilizing the neutrality of the convolution with random noise. Even though circumstances and environments differ across industries, characteristics of the rationality of firm behavior manifest as a feature in the residual moments. So, what impact would there be on the relationships among residual moments if the two different mechanisms were operating simultaneously? In reality, it may be the case that only one of them is at work, or both may be functioning at the same time. It is also possible that they are interacting with other, entirely unknown mechanisms beyond the two described here. Since the workings of the two models described here are significantly different, we must check whether there is any mutual interference in the way they manifest when reflected as relationships among the residual moments.

The relationships among the residual moments are specifically expressed as a constant ratio between $M_4 - 3M_2^2$ and $|M_3|^{4/3}$. The value of this ratio is key to identifying the mechanism that results in the asymmetric distribution shape. If the two mechanisms independently cause deviations from the asymmetric productivity frontier, then, as proven in Proposition 2 in the Appendix, the ratio indicating the relationship among the moments becomes a weighted average with 4/3 power scaling when the distributions of the two deviations are convolved. Since this is expressed as an average, there is no interference between the mechanisms.

Each of the two mechanisms identifies specific circumstances in which managerial decisions can be inferred to be irrational, as they result in reduced productivity and appear as X-inefficiency. Such circumstances are characterized by the value of the ratio of excess kurtosis to the skewness raised to the 4/3 power, calculated from the residuals of the frontier production function, falling within a certain range. The ranges of ratio values for the two mechanisms, within which the existence of X-inefficiency cannot be ruled out, have been shown to overlap. *A priori*, it is not possible to determine which of the two mechanisms more strongly governs the relationship among the residual moments. However, if the observed relationship among the residual moments reflects similar rationality characteristics under both mechanisms, then the reliability of interpreting the results of empirical analysis would be enhanced.

The models explaining the two mechanisms behind the existence of technical inefficiency might seem specialized and applicable to only specific industries. However, the vintage model is a dynamic model that can generally be applied to situations where the productivity of individual DMUs is gradually lost over time but, with a certain probability, is updated in discrete jumps to match the productivity level defined by frontier technology. On the other hand, the model of unobserved managerial resources is a static model applicable in situations where factors affecting production are dispersed, and managers need to take some form of action. Therefore, it is expected that these two models together could cover a substantial portion of inefficiency resulting from irrational managerial decisions.

1.7 The Structure of This Book

The structure of this book is explained as follows. Chapter 2 presents a method for identifying a distribution shape that can be considered uniform across the entire population, given that the population is divided into several subsets where the distribution shape is the same but the distribution parameters differ for each subset. This method uses the second-, third-, and fourth-order central moments of the samples constituting each subset. The distribution shape under analysis is a convolution of a specific asymmetric distribution and a symmetric normal distribution. The estimation method is described explicitly, and Monte Carlo experiments are conducted for testing specific distributions. These results provide the basis for setting up and performing tests throughout this book.

Chapter 3 demonstrates that the observed asymmetric distribution of technical inefficiency can be interpreted as the asymptotic distribution of a specific stochastic process. It shows that asymmetric technical inefficiency can be observed as the steady-state distribution of a dynamic process that generates inefficiency. The explanation focuses particularly on the vintage model.

Chapter 4 discusses the issue of observing "X-inefficiency" in corporate management, as introduced by Leibenstein. It shows that observing technical inefficiency does not empirically prove the existence of X-inefficiency, and even if X-inefficiency does exist, it does not necessarily manifest as technical inefficiency. Furthermore, it demonstrates that if X-inefficiency is defined by its causes, as Leibenstein did, it becomes impossible to empirically prove its existence. Therefore, this chapter proposes to redefine X-inefficiency as "inefficiency in the absence of control" or "uncontrolled inefficiency," which serves as a second-best approach for conducting empirical analysis.

Chapter 5 presents a method for testing the existence of X-inefficiency, defined as uncontrolled inefficiency, under the hypothesis that differences in productivity are observed due to variations in the vintage of facility investments at each establishment. Using data from Japanese manufacturing, this chapter conducts the test and demonstrates that the hypothesis of the existence of X-inefficiency cannot be rejected.

Chapter 6 introduces a model that, instead of using the vintage model, assumes the existence of an important unobserved production factor. It suggests that technical inefficiency is observed in the estimation of the production function because this production factor cannot be explicitly accounted for. Based on this model, the chapter presents a method for testing whether the production factor is controlled or not. Similar to Chap. 5, the test is conducted using data from Japanese manufacturing, and it again demonstrates that the hypothesis of the existence of X-inefficiency cannot be rejected.

Appendix

Proposition 1 *Assume that the stochastic variables u and v are independent and v follows the normal distribution $N(0, \sigma_v^2)$, and denote $M_k(x)$ $(k = 2, 3, 4)$ as the population central moments of a stochastic variable x. Then,*

$$M_4(u+v) - 3M_2^2(u+v)^2 = M_4(u) - 3M_2^2(u),$$

and

$$|M_3(u+v)|^{\frac{4}{3}} = |M_3(u)|^{\frac{4}{3}}.$$

Proof

As

$$\begin{aligned}
M_4(u+v) &= \mathbb{E}[(u+v-\mu_1(u+v))^4] \\
&= \mu_4(u+v) - 4\mu_3(u+v)\mu_1(u) + 6\mu_2(u+v)\mu_1^2(u) \\
&\quad - 4\mu_1(u+v)\mu_1^3(u) + \mu_1^4(u) \\
&= \mu_4(u) + 6\mu_2(u)\mu_2(v) + \mu_4(v) - 4\left(\mu_3(u) + 3\mu_1(u)\mu_2(v)\right)\mu_1(u) \\
&\quad + 6\left(\mu_2(u) + \mu_2(v)\right)\mu_1^2(u) - 4\mu_1(u)\mu_1^3(u) + \mu_1^4(u) \\
&= \mu_4(u) + 6\mu_2(u)\mu_2(v) + \mu_4(v) - 4\mu_3(u)\mu_1(u) + 6\mu_2(u)\mu_1^2(u) \\
&\quad - 6\mu_2(v)\mu_1^2(u) - 3\mu_1^4(u)
\end{aligned}$$

and

$$M_2(u+v) = \mu_2(u) - \mu_1^2(u) + \mu_2(v),$$

where $\mu_k(x) \equiv \mathbb{E}[x^k]$, then,

$$
\begin{aligned}
&M_4(u+v) - 3M_2^2(u+v) \\
&\quad = \mu_4(u) - 4\mu_3(u)\mu_1(u) + 12\mu_2(u)\mu_1^2(u) - 6\mu_1^4(u) - 3\mu_2^2(u) \\
&\quad + \left(\mu_4(v) - 3\mu_2^2(u)\right) \\
&\quad = \mu_4(u) - 4\mu_3(u)\mu_1(u) + 12\mu_2(u)\mu_1^2(u) - 6\mu_1^4(u) - 3\mu_2^2(u).
\end{aligned}
$$

While,

$$
\begin{aligned}
&M_4(u) - 3M_2^2(u) \\
&\quad = \mu_4(u) - 4\mu_3(u)\mu_1(u) + 6\mu_2(u)\mu_1^2(u) - 3\mu_1^4(u) - 3\left(\mu_2(u) - \mu_1^2(u)\right)^2 \\
&\quad = \mu_4(u) - 4\mu_3(u)\mu_1(u) + 12\mu_2(u)\mu_1^2(u) - 6\mu_1^4(u) - 3\mu_2^2(u)
\end{aligned}
$$

In the same way,

$$
\begin{aligned}
M_3(u+v) &= \mathbb{E}\left[(u+v-\mathbb{E}[u+v])^3\right] \\
&= \mu_3(u+v) - 3\mu_2(u+v)\mu_1(u) + 3\mu_1(u+v)\mu_1^2(u) - \mu_1^3(u) \\
&= \mu_3(u) + 3\mu_1(u)\mu_2(v) - 3\left(\mu_2(u) + \mu_2(v)\right)\mu_1(u) + 2\mu_1^3(u) \\
&= \mu_3(u) - 3\mu_2(u)\mu_1(u) + 2\mu_1^3(u) \\
&= \mathbb{E}\left[(u-\mathbb{E}[u])^2\right] = M_3(u).
\end{aligned}
$$

□

Proposition 2
Assume that the stochastic variables u_1 and u_2 are independent, and denote $M_k(x)$ $(k = 2, 3, 4)$ as the population central moments of a stochastic variable x. Then,

$$
K(u_1+u_2)|M_3(u_1+u_2)|^{\frac{4}{3}} = K(u_1)|M_3(u_1)|^{\frac{4}{3}} + K(u_2)|M_3(u_2)|^{\frac{4}{3}}
$$

where

$$
K(x) \equiv \frac{M_4(x) - 3M_2(x)^2}{|M_3(x)|^{\frac{4}{3}}}
$$

Proof

$$
\begin{aligned}
M_2(u_1+u_2) =& M_2(u_1) + M_2(u_2) \\
M_3(u_1+u_2) =& M_3(u_1) + M_3(u_2) \\
M_4(u_1+u_2) =& \mathbb{E}\left[(u_1+u_2-\mathbb{E}[u_1+u_2])^4\right] \\
=& \mathbb{E}\left[(u_1-\mathbb{E}[u_1])^4\right] + 4\mathbb{E}\left[(u_1-\mathbb{E}[u_1])^3\right]\mathbb{E}[u_2-\mathbb{E}[u_2]] \\
&+ 6\mathbb{E}\left[(u_1-\mathbb{E}[u_1])^2\right]\mathbb{E}\left[(u_2-\mathbb{E}[u_2])^2\right] \\
&+ 4\mathbb{E}[u_1-\mathbb{E}[u_1]]\,\mathbb{E}\left[(u_2-\mathbb{E}[u_2])^3\right] + \mathbb{E}\left[(u_2-\mathbb{E}[u_2])^4\right] \\
=& M_4(u_1) + 6M_2(u_1)M_2(u_2) + M_4(u_2)
\end{aligned}
$$

Then,

$$
\begin{aligned}
& M_4(u_1+u_2) - 3M_2(u_1+u_2)^2 \\
& \quad = M_4(u_1) + M_4(u_2) + 6M_2(u_1)M_2(u_2) - 3\left(M_2(u_1) + M_2(u_2)\right)^2 \\
& \quad = M_4(u_1) - 3M_2(u_1)^2 + M_4(u_2) - 3M_2(u_2)^2
\end{aligned}
$$

So,

$$
\begin{aligned}
& \frac{M_4(u_1+u_2) - 3M_2(u_1+u_2)^2}{|M_3(u_1+u_2)|^{\frac{4}{3}}} |M_3(u_1+u_2)|^{\frac{4}{3}} \\
& = \frac{M_4(u_1) - 3M_2(u_1)^2}{|M_3(u_1)|^{\frac{4}{3}}} |M_3(u_1)|^{\frac{4}{3}} + \frac{M_4(u_2) - 3M_2(u_2)^2}{|M_3(u_2)|^{\frac{4}{3}}} |M_3(u_1)|^{\frac{4}{3}}
\end{aligned}
$$

□

References

Aigner D, Lovell CAK, Schmidt P (1977) Formulation and estimation of stochastic frontier production function models. J Econ 6 (1):21–37

Chen C-F (2007) Applying the stochastic frontier approach to measure hotel managerial efficiency in Taiwan. Tour Manage 28(3):696–702

Coelli TJ, Rao DSP, O'donnell CJ, Battese GE (2005) An introduction to efficiency and productivity analysis. Springer science & business media

De Michele C, De Bartolo S (2025) Skewness-Kurtosis: small samples and power-law behavior. arXiv:2506.16906

Debreu G (1951) The coefficient of resource utilization. Econ: J Econ Soc, 273–292

Delis MD, Tsionas MG (2018) Measuring management practices. Int J Prod Econ 199:65–77

Farrell MJ (1957) The measurement of productive efficiency. J Royal Statis Soc: Series A (General) 120(3):253–281

Flynn B, Schroeder RG, Sakakibara S (1995) The impact of quality management practices on performance and competitive advantage. Decision Sci 26(5):659–691

Greene W (2008) The econometric approach to efficiency analysis. In: The measurement of productive efficiency and productivity change

Leibenstein H (1966)Allocative efficiency vs."X-efficiency". Am Econ Rev 56(3):392–415

Leibenstein H (1976) Beyond economic man: a new foundation for microeconomics. Harvard University Press

Leibenstein H (1987) Inside the firm: the inefficiencies of hierarchy. Harvard University Press

Lovell CAK et al (1993)Production frontiers and productive efficiency. In: The measurement of productive efficiency: techniques and applications, pp 3, 67

Meeusen W, van Broeck JD (1977) Efficiency estimation from Cobb-Douglas production functions with composed error. Int Econ Rev, 435–444

Olson JA, Schmidt P, Waldman DM (1980) A Monte Carlo study of estimators of stochastic frontier production functions. J Econ 13(1):67–82

Papadopoulos A (2021) Measuring the effect of management on production: a two-tier stochastic frontier approach. Emp Econ 60(6):3011–3041

Papadopoulos A, Parmeter CF (2024) The wrong skewness problem in stochastic frontier analysis: a review. J Prod Anal 61(2):121–134
Perelman S, Pestieau P (1994) A comparative performance study of postal services: a productive efficiency approach. Annal d'Economie et de Statistique, 187–202
Phan AC, Abdallah AB, Matsui Y (2011) Quality management practices and competitive performance: empirical evidence from Japanese manufacturing companies. Int J Prod Econ 133(2):518–529
Piacenza M (2006) Regulatory contracts and cost efficiency: stochastic frontier evidence from the Italian local public transport. J Prod Anal 25(3):257–277
Rahman KMM, Mia M, Bhuiyan MKJ (2012) A stochastic frontier approach to model technical efficiency of rice farmers in Bangladesh: an empirical analysis. The Agricult 10(2):9–19
Samson D, Terziovski M (1999) The relationship between total quality management practices and operational performance. J Operat Manag 17(4):393–409
Torii A (1992) Technical efficiency in Japanese industries. Indust Eff Six Nations, 31–120
Torii A (2001) Efficiency in Japanese industries. NTT Publishing, Tokyo (in Japanese)
Wang WS, Schmidt P (2009) On the distribution of estimated technical efficiency in stochastic frontier models. J Econ 148(1):36–45
Wheeler DJ (2011) Problems with skewness and kurtosis, Part One. Retrieved from Quality Digest Web site: www.qualitydigest.com
Zhang Z (2000) Developing a model of quality management methods and evaluating their effects on business performance. Total Qual Manag 11(1):129–137

Chapter 2
A Method for Estimating and Testing the Distribution Parameters of an Asymmetric Distribution When a Large Number of Moment Estimates Are Available

This chapter and Chap. 3 lay the methodological foundation for the analysis conducted in this book. The primary objective of this book is to "develop a method for testing the existence of X-inefficiencies using input–output data from business establishments." As detailed in Chaps. 5 and 6, this study confirms the presence of X-inefficiency in Japan's manufacturing industry by analyzing the mechanism through which it arises. This study argues that the generation mechanism of X-inefficiency can be traced using input–output data from business establishments. This mechanism directly influences both the types of distributions that characterize inefficiency and their associated parameters. Consequently, identifying the distribution type of the inefficiency term in econometric analysis is equivalent to investigating the underlying mechanism of its generation. This chapter focuses on the testing methodology for determining the distribution type of this inefficiency.

In conventional distribution type identification, when a sufficiently large sample generated under a specific mechanism is available, the population distribution and its parameters are estimated simultaneously. In another common approach, a single distribution family is assumed *a priori* based on theoretical considerations or other prior knowledge, and its parameters are then estimated. Departing from these conventional approaches, this chapter analyzes an alternative method in which the population, representing the entire manufacturing industry, is divided into several subsets (corresponding to individual industries). A common distribution family is assumed to apply across the entire population, while each subset is further assumed to have its own parameters to characterize the distribution more precisely. Using the second-, third-, and fourth-order central moments of the samples from each subset, this chapter presents a method for identifying the common distribution family that applies to the entire population.

In the estimation of technical inefficiency using SFA, various distribution types, such as the half-normal distribution, truncated normal distribution, exponential distribution, gamma distribution, and others, are commonly used as candidates for the inefficiency term. In this chapter, we consider these various distribution types and

A. Torii, *Production Efficiency with the Stochastic Management Model*,
https://doi.org/10.1007/978-981-95-3501-9_2

generalized distribution types as candidates for the distribution type that generates technical inefficiency and present and implement methods for identification, parameter estimation, and testing. The random variable that represents inefficiency is not observed directly but only in the sample values generated by the convolution of the inefficiency terms that follow these distributions and the symmetric error terms generated by the normal distribution. Therefore, the estimation of the distribution type and its parameters must be conducted using samples drawn from this noise-affected convolution distribution.

This chapter further analyzes the properties of the distribution parameter estimators of the following two distributions:

$$\rho(u) = \frac{(1+p)^{\frac{p}{1+p}}\theta^{\frac{1}{1+p}}}{\Gamma\left(\frac{1}{1+p}\right)} \exp\left(-\frac{\theta}{1+p}u^{1+p}\right) \tag{2.1}$$

for $u \geq 0$, which generalize the half normal and exponential distributions within the exponential power family, and the distribution:

$$\rho(u) = \frac{\exp\left(-\frac{\left(\sqrt{u+\frac{a^2}{4b}}-\frac{a}{2}\right)^2}{2b^2\sigma_u^2}\right) + \exp\left(-\frac{\left(\sqrt{u+\frac{a^2}{4b}}+\frac{a}{2}\right)^2}{2b^2\sigma_u^2}\right)}{2\sqrt{2\pi}b\sigma_u\sqrt{u+\frac{a^2}{4b}}} \tag{2.2}$$

for $u > -a^2/(4b)$, that is the distribution of $u = ax + bx^2$, where x is a normally distributed random variable, $x \sim N\left(0, \sigma_u^2\right)$, and $\rho(u)$ is the density function of the random variable u. Here, $p, \theta, \sigma_u, a, b$ are parameters, including distribution parameters and other general parameters. Note that σ_u^2 is a distribution parameter that governs the dispersion of u, and it should not be interpreted as the variance of u itself. Distribution (2.1) is hereafter named the "exponential power-type distribution," and distribution (2.2) is named the "square normal-type distribution." In later chapters, hypotheses testing for the parameters in these distributions will play an important role. In the case of an exponential power-type distribution, the hypothesis is $p > 0$; in the case of a square normal-type distribution, the hypothesis is $a = 0$. The Monte Carlo experiments are specifically designed to test these hypotheses. Although these distribution types are not particularly new, to the best of our knowledge, they have never been used for estimating technical inefficiency.

The structure of this chapter is as follows. In Sect. 2.1, we identify the distribution types to be examined for identification and present the moment estimates as functions of the distribution parameters. In Sect. 2.2, we introduce the equation that generally holds as a relationship among the moments presented in Sect. 2.1. Furthermore, for cases in which the moments of the inefficiency term are calculated for a sufficient number of industries, we discuss a method for identifying the distribution type by statistically estimating this equation. In Sect. 2.3, we analyze the properties of the estimators for the exponential power-type distribution using Monte Carlo simulations, with particular attention to the nature of bias, as a preparatory step for the hypothesis testing presented in Chap. 5. Similarly, in Sect. 2.4, we analyze the properties of the estimators for the square normal-type distribution, also using Monte Carlo simulations, as preparation for the hypothesis testing in Chap. 6.

2.1 Identification of Distribution Type and Calculation of Moments of Convolution with Normal Distribution

The input–output production relationship with technical inefficiency is formulated and estimated using the stochastic frontier function model introduced in Chap. 1:

$$y_j = f_i\left(\boldsymbol{x}_j; \boldsymbol{\beta}_i\right) + v_j - u_j. \tag{1.1}$$

In this section, for the following analysis, the distribution of the convolution $\epsilon_j = v_j - u_j$ with the symmetric error term $v_j \sim N\left(0, \sigma_v^2\right)$, which is normally distributed, and the values of its second-, third-, and fourth-order central moments are presented for various distributions that have been assumed in the literature as possible distribution types for the random inefficiency variable u_j. Additionally, for the exponential power-type distribution and the square normal-type distribution introduced here, the second-, third-, and fourth-order central moments of the convolution distribution with the normal distribution of v are calculated.

2.1.1 *Half-Normal Distribution*

The density function is

$$\rho(u) = \frac{1}{\sigma_u}\sqrt{\frac{2}{\pi}}\, e^{-\frac{u^2}{2\sigma_u^2}}$$

for $u \geq 0$, where σ_u is the scale parameter.

This was the most common distribution in the earlier literature that assumed technical inefficiency. This is because of the ease of handling the convolution of normal and half-normal distributions. This may also be due to an intuitive sense of confidence in the distributions derived from the normal distribution. However, there is no direct relationship between the justification for assuming a normal distribution for a random variable as an accumulation of arbitrary random variations and the justification for assuming a half-normal distribution for an asymmetric distribution of technical inefficiency. For example, the cumulative effects of various inefficiencies generated by various factors within firms or organizations may lead to a symmetric normal distribution. However, even when the presence of absorbing and reflecting boundaries in the domain is assumed, significantly more specific assumptions are required for the distribution to converge to an asymmetric half-normal distribution.

The density function of the convolution $\epsilon = v - u$ with the normal distribution, $v \sim N(0, \sigma_v^2)$, is:

$$\frac{\sqrt{2}}{\sqrt{\pi}\sqrt{\sigma_u^2+\sigma_v^2}} e^{-\frac{\epsilon^2}{2\left(\sigma_u^2+\sigma_v^2\right)}} \left(1 - \Phi\left(\frac{\epsilon}{\sqrt{\sigma_u^2+\sigma_v^2}} \frac{\sigma_u}{\sigma_v}\right)\right),$$

where $\Phi(\cdot)$ denotes the cumulative distribution function (CDF) of the standard normal distribution.

The second-, third-, and fourth-order central moments of the convolution are:

$$\sigma_v^2 + \frac{\pi-2}{\pi}\sigma_u^2,$$

$$-\sqrt{\frac{2}{\pi}}\frac{4-\pi}{\pi}\sigma_u^3,$$

$$3\sigma_v^4 + 6\frac{\pi-2}{\pi}\sigma_v^2\sigma_u^2 + \frac{3\pi^2-4\pi-12}{\pi}\sigma_u^4,$$

respectively.

2.1.2 Exponential Distribution

The density function is:

$$\rho(u) = \frac{e^{-u/\mu}}{\mu}$$

for $u \geq 0$, where μ is the scale parameter. This distribution, like the half-normal distribution, is also commonly used.

Half-normal and exponential distributions were employed as inefficiency distributions in earlier studies. Stevenson (1980) argued that these distributions are used only because of their asymmetry and monotonic decrease with respect to the level of inefficiency; that is, the peak of the distribution occurs at the point where the inefficiency level is zero.[1] He argued that there is no inherent reason why human behavior should necessarily peak at zero inefficiency; that is, efficient behavior does not have to be the most likely.

The density function of the convolution with the normal distribution is:

$$\frac{1}{\eta} e^{\frac{2\epsilon\eta+\sigma_v^2}{2\eta^2}} \left(1 - \Phi\left(\frac{\sigma_v^2+\epsilon\eta}{\eta\sigma_v}\right)\right).$$

[1] See Teigen (1995).

The second-, third-, and fourth-order central moments of the convolution are:

$$\sigma_v^2 + \eta^2, \quad -2\eta^3, \quad 3\sigma_v^4 + 6\sigma_v^2\eta^2 + 9\eta^4,$$

respectively.

2.1.3 Gamma Distribution

The density function is:

$$\rho(u) = \frac{u^m}{\Gamma(m+1)\alpha^{m+1}} e^{-\frac{u}{\alpha}}$$

for $u \geq 0$, where m and α are the shape and scale parameters, respectively. It should be noted that the parameterization of the Gamma distribution is not uniquely standardized in the literature. Some definitions use a shape and scale form with exponent u^{m-1}. In this paper, we adopt the above parameterization.

Stevenson's (1980) alternatives to the half-normal and other distributions are the gamma and truncated normal distributions, both of which have nonzero modes. Both distributions have two parameters: the magnitude of the variance and shape of the distribution. Compared to the half-normal and exponential distributions, which have only one degree of freedom, the gamma distribution has multiple degrees of freedom and is more likely to match the actual distribution. However, the gamma distribution is challenging to handle in practice, except when the shape parameter takes a specific integer value. As a result, it is rarely used in empirical analyses, with a few exceptions, such as Greene (1990). The gamma distribution reduces to the exponential distribution when the shape parameter $m = 0$, and can therefore be regarded as a generalization of the exponential distribution.

The gamma distribution describes the distribution of the cumulative time until a fixed number of events occurs in a Poisson process. Oikawa (2016) argues that when managers adjust managerial variables that determine productivity using Bayesian learning, the resulting technical inefficiency follows a gamma distribution.[2]

The density function of the convolution with the normal distribution is:

$$\frac{\sigma_v^m e^{\frac{\left(\epsilon\alpha+\sigma_v^2\right)^2}{2\sigma_v^2\alpha^2}}}{\sqrt{2\pi}\Gamma(m+1)\alpha^{m+1}} \int_{\frac{\epsilon\alpha+\sigma_v^2}{\sigma_v\alpha}}^{\infty} \left(t - \frac{\epsilon\alpha+\sigma_v^2}{\sigma_v\alpha}\right)^m e^{-\frac{t^2}{2}} dt.$$

[2] Tsionas (2017) points out that Oikawa's (2016) conclusion depends heavily on the specific assumptions of the setting. In Tsionas (2023), the distribution of technical inefficiency arising from learning under more general conditions is discussed in greater detail.

The second-, third-, and fourth-order central moments of the convolution are:

$$
\begin{aligned}
&\sigma_v^2 + (m+1)\alpha^2, \\
&-2(m+1)\alpha^3, \\
&3\alpha_v^4 + 6(m+1)\sigma_v^2\alpha^2 + 3(m+1)(m+3)\alpha^4,
\end{aligned}
$$

respectively.

2.1.4 *Truncated Normal*

The density function is:

$$
\rho(u) = \frac{e^{-\frac{(u-\mu)^2}{2\sigma_u^2}}}{\sqrt{2\pi}\sigma_u\left(1 - \Phi\left(-\frac{\mu}{\sigma_u}\right)\right)}
$$

for $u \geq 0$, where μ and σ_u are the location and scale parameters, respectively.

Truncated normal distribution is also proposed by Stevenson (1980). This distribution is a generalization of the half-normal distribution and has two parameters: a location parameter (where to cut) and a scale parameter indicating the magnitude of the variance. Compared with the gamma distribution, it is easier to handle in a quantitative manner, and various convolutions with a normal distribution can be calculated relatively easily. However, the truncated normal distribution is less well-founded than the gamma distribution when analyzing the mechanisms of technical inefficiency generation as the result of autonomous stochastic processes, which is the primary focus of this book. For example, even when absorbing or reflecting boundaries are introduced into a Brownian motion, it is unlikely that the resulting distribution would converge to a truncated normal distribution except under specific and restrictive circumstances. [3]

[3] It is commonly assumed that phenomena expected to follow a normal distribution but subjected to external constraints, such as regulatory or institutional restrictions, might naturally result in a truncated normal distribution. This is because external constraints, such as those imposed by regulations, often limit the range of observations, creating a theoretical truncation at certain boundaries. For instance, these constraints could include situations where certain observations are missing from the sample due to legal or institutional factors or cannot be observed due to measurement limitations.

However, in practice, truncated normal distributions are rarely observed as the natural outcome of social or economic phenomena. In most cases, they are assumed *a priori* in empirical analyses, based on theoretical reasoning derived from prior analytical models, and then applied to real-world data without explicit validation of their appropriateness for the observed phenomena. This is particularly true in the context of SFA, where the truncated normal distribution is frequently employed as a prior assumption.

This discrepancy can be explained by the fact that when external constraints are imposed, economic agents often adapt their behavior to minimize the impact of those constraints. Such adaptive behavior leads to distortions or departures from the theoretical boundaries where truncation would occur, resulting in distributions that are not well-represented by a truncated normal form. For

The density function of the convolution with the normal distribution is:

$$\frac{e^{-\frac{(\epsilon+\mu)^2}{2\sigma^2}}}{\sqrt{2\pi}\sigma}\frac{1-\Phi\left(\frac{\sigma\left(\epsilon\sigma_u^2-\mu\sigma_v^2\right)}{2\sigma_u\sigma_v}\right)}{1-\Phi\left(-\frac{\mu}{\sigma_u}\right)}.$$

The second-, third-, and fourth-order central moments of the convolution are:

$$\begin{aligned}
&\sigma_v^2+\left(1-R_0^2\right)\sigma_u^2-\mu\sigma_u R_0,\\
&-R_0\sigma_u\left(\mu^2+3R_0\mu\sigma_u+\sigma_u^2\left(-1+2R_0^2\right)\right),\\
&-R_0\mu\sigma_u\left(\mu^2+4R_0\mu\sigma_u+3\sigma_u^2\left(1+2R_0^2\right)+6\sigma_v^2\right)\\
&\quad+\sigma_u^4\left(3-2R_0^2-3R_0^4\right)+3\sigma_v^2\left(2\sigma_u^2\left(1-R_0^2\right)+\sigma_v^2\right),
\end{aligned}$$

respectively, where

$$R_0\equiv\frac{e^{-\frac{\mu^2}{2\sigma_u^2}}}{\sqrt{2\pi}\left(1-\Phi\left(-\frac{\mu}{\sigma_u}\right)\right)},\quad \sigma^2\equiv\sigma_u^2+\sigma_v^2.$$

2.1.5 *Exponential Power-Type*

The density function is given by (2.1). When $p=1$, the density function is

$$\rho(x)=\sqrt{\frac{2\theta}{\pi}}\exp\left(-\frac{\theta}{2}x^2\right)$$

which is the half-normal distribution, $\left(\sigma_u^2=1/\theta\right)$, and when $p=0$, $\rho(x)=\theta\exp(-\theta x)$, which is an exponential distribution. Thus, this is a generalized distribution of half-normal and exponential distributions.

---

an example of this phenomenon, see Yu et al. (2006), which demonstrates how regulatory thresholds influence observed distributions through managerial actions, resulting in significant departures from a simple truncated normal shape.

In contrast, when considering physical phenomena rather than economic ones, where agents do not exhibit adaptive responses, truncated normal distributions are more commonly observed. For instance, Elteto and Molnar (1999) provide an example in the context of network traffic, where the distribution of delays or traffic loads conforms naturally to a truncated normal form due to physical constraints in the system.

The second-, third-, and fourth-order central moments of the convolution are:

$$\sigma_v^2 + \left(\frac{1+p}{\theta}\right)^{\frac{2}{1+p}} \frac{g_3 g_1 - g_2^2}{g_1^2},$$

$$-\left(\frac{1+p}{\theta}\right)^{\frac{3}{1+p}} \frac{g_4 g_1^2 - 3g_3 g_2 g_1 + 2g_2^3}{g_1^3},$$

$$6\sigma_v^4 + \left(\frac{1+p}{\theta}\right)^{\frac{4}{1+p}} \frac{g_5 g_1^3 - 4g_4 g_2 g_1^2 + 6g_3 g_2^2 g_1 - 3g_2^4}{g_1^4}$$

$$-3\left(\frac{1+p}{\theta}\right)^{\frac{2}{1+p}} \frac{g_3 g_1 - g_2^2}{g_1^2}.$$

where $g_j \equiv \Gamma(j/(1+p))$. The calculations of these moments are presented in the Appendix.

2.1.6 *Square Normal-Type*

The density function is given by Eq. (2.2). The probability density function (2.2) represents a distribution derived from the normal distribution. The second-, third-, and fourth-order central moments of the convolution are:

$$\left(a^2 + 2b^2\sigma_u^2\right)\sigma_u^2 + \sigma_v^2,$$

$$-2b\sigma_u^4(3a^2 + 4b^2\sigma_u^2),$$

$$3\sigma_u^4\left(a^4 + 20a^2b^2\sigma_u^2 + 20b^4\sigma_u^4\right) + 6\sigma_u^2\sigma_v^2\left(a^2 + 2b^2\sigma_u^2\right) + 3\sigma_v^4,$$

respectively. The calculations of these moments are presented in the Appendix.

2.2 Distribution-Specific Moment Relationships and Their Estimation

2.2.1 *Parameter-Invariant Moment Relationships*

Lee (1983) presented a method for identifying the distribution of technical inefficiency. However, only the distributions within the Pearson family were tested, excluding exponential power-type distributions and square normal-type distributions, except in special cases. In tests for the existence of technical inefficiency conducted by researchers other than Lee (1983), the normality of the distribution of deviations from the frontier function is commonly tested. Specifically, the null hypothesis in these papers assumes that the deviations follow a standard normal distribution, without requiring an explicit assumption about technical inefficiency. For example, Schmidt and Lin (1984) suggested a test based on the skewness of the regression residuals. If we assume that technical inefficiency is half-normally distributed, the skewness is expressed as a function of the symmetric error term parameter σ_v and the distribution parameter σ_u of the asymmetric technical inefficiency:

$$-\sqrt{\frac{2}{\pi}}\frac{4-\pi}{\pi}\sigma_u^3 \Big/ \left(\sigma_v^2+\frac{\pi-2}{\pi}\sigma_u^2\right)^{\frac{3}{2}}.$$

In addition, with the assumption of exponential distribution, the skewness is:

$$-\frac{2\eta^3}{\left(\sigma_v^2+\eta^2\right)^{\frac{3}{2}}}.$$

As skewness is negative in both cases, it is not possible to distinguish between the two simply by observing the skewness that is significantly negative. In other words, these tests are not sufficiently powerful for identifying distributions. To identify the distribution, information on the values of the parameters, σ_u, σ_v, and η must be given *a priori*.[4]

This fact that "unless the values of the parameters are given *a priori*, it is not possible to identify the symmetric error term and the asymmetric technical inefficiency term" has important implications on how we identify the distribution of technical inefficiency. This suggests that the problem can not only be avoided but also resolved by using an equation that does not depend on these parameters in the test. Indeed, when using up to third-order moments, it is impossible to form an equation that is independent of the parameters. Therefore, it is not possible to identify the distribution by simply using skewness. However, if parameters up to fourth order are used, it is possible to form a parameter-independent equation.

This property can be verified in the case of the half-normal distribution. The second-, third-, and fourth-order central moments of the convolution of a half-normal distribution representing technical inefficiency and a normal distribution representing the general error term have already been derived in Sect. 2.1. By eliminating the two parameters, σ_u and σ_v, from these moment expressions, we can confirm through calculation that the following relationship holds among the moments:

$$M_4-3M_2^2=\frac{8(\pi-3)}{2^{\frac{2}{3}}(4-\pi)^{\frac{4}{3}}}\,|M_3|^{\frac{4}{3}},$$

[4] Wang et al. (2011) proposed a bootstrap-based goodness-of-fit test to evaluate the assumed distribution of technical inefficiency by directly testing the residual distributions. However, their method does not comprehensively test a broad family of distributions; it focuses on specific distributional assumptions, such as the half-normal and exponential distributions. For a detailed explanation, refer to Subsect. 5.1.3.

where M_2, M_3, and M_4 denote the second-, third-, and fourth-order central moments, respectively. Note that this equation holds independently of the parameter values σ_u and σ_v. Therefore, a statistical test based on this relationship can be conducted even when the values of these parameters are not known *a priori*.

When the deviation u due to technical inefficiency has an exponential distribution, the relation between the moments is:

$$M_4 - 3M_2^2 = \frac{3}{\sqrt[3]{2}} |M_3|^{\frac{4}{3}},$$

which is different from the above relation only in terms of the coefficient of $|M_3|^{\frac{4}{3}}$. A test of the value of this coefficient can distinguish the distribution of technical inefficiencies.

By setting the coefficient of $|M_3|^{\frac{4}{3}}$ as K_h, the relationship between the moments can be expressed in the form of Eq. (2.3) in either case.

$$M_4 - 3M_2^2 = K_h |M_3|^{\frac{4}{3}}. \tag{2.3}$$

The value K_h can be calculated for the other distributions introduced in Sect. 2.1. First, in the case of the gamma distribution, $K_h = 3/\sqrt[3]{2(m+1)}$ is given. The value is not a constant but remains a shape parameter because the gamma distribution has two parameters: one that indicates the size of the variance and the other that determines the shape of the distribution. The parameter that indicates the dispersion of the distribution can be eliminated; however, the parameter that indicates the shape of the distribution remains. Thus, in general, a single value of K_h corresponds to one specific distribution shape. This property enables us to test hypotheses about the shape of the distribution. In this test, any symmetric random noise is absorbed into the magnitude of σ_v, and the testing equation itself does not depend on the value of σ_v; the same relationship holds regardless of its size. Therefore, the test remains robust even in the presence of symmetric noise. The relationship between the moments up to the fourth order shown here holds not only for distribution types used to model inefficiency, such as half-normal distributions, but also for convolutions with a normal distribution that exhibits a symmetric error term. See discussion in Sect. 1.4.

For the case of truncated normal distribution, the value of K_h is given:

$$K_h = \frac{-R_1^3 - 7R_1^2 - 12R_1 - 6 + (3R_1 + 4)R_1^2/m^2}{\left(R_1^2 + 3R_1 + 2 - R_1^2/m^2\right)^{4/3}}, \tag{2.4}$$

where $R_1 \equiv me^{\frac{m^2}{2}} \int_{-m}^{\infty} e^{-t^2/2} dt$, and $m = \mu/\sigma_u$. As in the case of gamma distribution, there remains the shape parameter, m. Considering the level of K_h as a function of this shape parameter m, it becomes a monotonically decreasing function of m as

Fig. 2.1 Value of K_h for truncated normal distribution

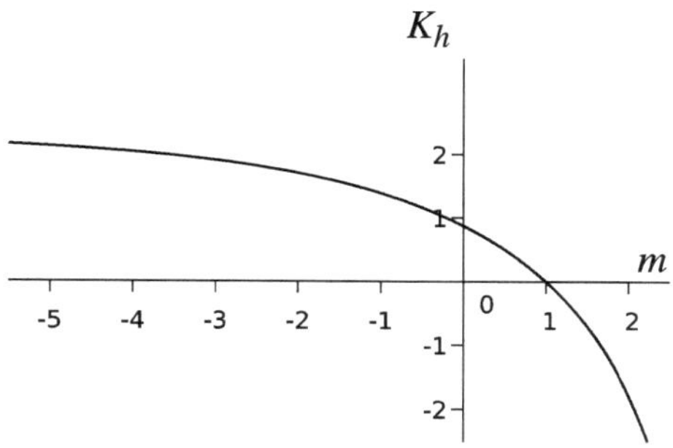

shown in Fig. 2.1.[5] When m takes a negative value with a sufficiently large absolute magnitude, which corresponds to a truncated normal distribution that is cut off at the far tail of the normal distribution, the value of K_h converges to $3/\sqrt[3]{2}$.[6] This indicates that a truncated distribution cut off at the far tail of the normal distribution can be approximated by an exponential distribution.[7] Thus, the value of K_h for the truncated normal distribution lies within a range whose upper bound is the value of K_h for the exponential distribution.

We now examine the moment relationships for the exponential power-type and square normal-type distributions. First, in the case of the exponential power-type distribution, the relationship among moments can be expressed in the same form as Eq. (2.3). The constant K_h is given by:

---

[5] Figure 2.1, showing the value of Eq. (2.4), and Fig. 2.2 , showing the value of Eq. (2.5), are plotted based on numerical calculations. The author has not yet succeeded in showing analytically that Eqs. (2.4) and (2.5) are monotonically decreasing functions of m and p, respectively.

[6] As the value of m approaches negative infinity, the asymptotic expansion of R_1 shows that it can be approximated as:

$$-1+\frac{1}{m^2}-\frac{3}{m^4}+\frac{15}{m^6}-\frac{105}{m^8}+\cdots.$$

Substituting this into the expression for K_h, we obtain an expression of the form:

$$(6m^{24}+801m^{22}+\cdots)/\left(2m^{18}-30m^{16}+\cdots\right)^{4/3}.$$

Thus, when m is sufficiently large, this value converges to $3/2^{\frac{1}{3}}$.

[7] When $\mu \to -\infty$, $\int_{-\mu/\sigma}^{\infty} e^{-t^2/2}dt$ is asymptotically expanded as $-\sigma\exp(-\mu^2/(2\sigma^2))/\mu$. Therefore, when $\mu \to -\infty$, the density function of a truncated normal distribution,

$$\exp\left(-\frac{(x-\mu)^2}{2\sigma^2}\right)\Big/\left(\sigma\int_{-\mu/\sigma}^{\infty}\exp\left(-\frac{t^2}{2}\right)dt\right)$$

is asymptotically approximated by

$$-\mu\exp\left(-\frac{x^2-2x\mu}{2\sigma^2}\right)\Big/\sigma^2=-\exp\left(\frac{x}{\sigma^2}\left(\mu-\frac{x}{2}\right)\right)\mu\Big/\sigma^2.$$

When $|\mu| \gg x$, this distribution is approximated by an exponential distribution $-\exp(-\mu x/\sigma^2)\mu/\sigma^2$.

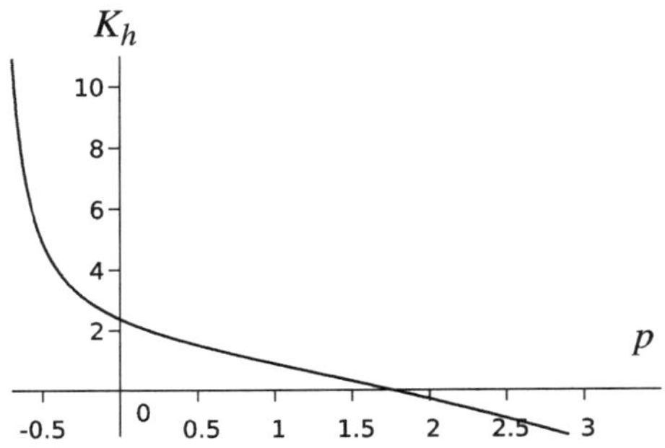

Fig. 2.2 Value of K_h for exponential power-type distribution

$$K_h = \frac{g_5 g_1^3 - 4 g_4 g_2 g_1^2 + 12 g_3 g_2^2 g_1 - 6 g_2^4 - 3 g_3^2 g_1^2}{\left(g_4 g_1^2 - 3 g_3 g_2 g_1 + 2 g_2^3\right)^{4/3}}, \tag{2.5}$$

where $g_j \equiv \Gamma(j/(1+p))$. The value of K_h is a monotonic decreasing function of p over the domain $p > -1$, taking values in the range $[-\infty, +\infty]$, as shown in Fig. 2.2. Therefore, if an econometric analysis yields an estimate of K_h that satisfies Eq. (2.3), the corresponding value of p can be uniquely determined.

Similarly, in the case of a square normal-type distribution, the relationship between moments can be written as in Eq. (2.3). The constant K_h takes the value:

$$K_h = 3\left(1 + \frac{a^2}{b^2\sigma_u^2}\right) \Big/ \left(1 + \frac{3a^2}{4b^2\sigma_u^2}\right)^{4/3} \leq 3. \tag{2.6}$$

The value of K_h takes a maximum value of 3 when $a = 0$, and it is a monotonically decreasing function of $a^2/(b^2\sigma_u^2) > 0$ in the region $a > 0$.

2.2.2 *Identification of Distribution Type and Estimation of Parameters*

Subsection 2.2.1 demonstrates that for most of the distribution types considered for technical inefficiency, the central moments up to the fourth order of the random variable generated by convolution with a normal distribution satisfy the relationship given in Eq. (2.3), with the variance-related parameters eliminated. When a distribution type has only a parameter indicating the magnitude of variance, a single coefficient K_h corresponds to that distribution. In contrast, when a distribution type includes a shape parameter in addition to the variance parameter, the coefficient K_h becomes a function of the shape parameter.

Suppose a variable indicating the performance of an economic activity is observed, and technical inefficiency is suspected. The observed performance is assumed to result from a convolution with a normally distributed error term. Furthermore, suppose that a sufficiently large number of distinct sample sets of this variable are available, allowing regression analysis across the sets. If each sample corresponds to an establishment, each sample set can be interpreted as representing a distinct industry. The following analysis considers the case in which many such industries are available. For each sample set, the second- (M_{2i}), third- (M_{3i}), and fourth-order (M_{4i}) central moments of the variable are computed where i indexes the sample set. If the following relationship:

$$M_{4i} - 3M_{2i}^2 = K_h \, |M_{3i}|^{\frac{4}{3}} + \epsilon_i$$

is estimated using an appropriate estimation method, the resulting estimate $\widehat{K}_h$ can be used to test the distribution type and/or its shape parameter, where ϵ_i denotes the estimation error. If the tested distribution type has only a variance parameter, the hypothesis concerning the distribution type can be tested across all samples. Conversely, if the distribution type has a shape parameter in addition to a variance parameter, a hypothesis regarding the value of the shape parameter can be tested under the assumption that the distribution type is consistent across samples. In both cases, it is important to note that the variance parameter may differ across sample sets, as the moment relationship above holds regardless of the magnitude of the variance parameter. This is because the relationship between the moments in Eq. (2.3) remains invariant with respect to the variance parameter.

The value of K_h can be expressed as the ratio of excess kurtosis to the absolute value of skewness raised to the power of $4/3$. The rationale for conducting hypothesis testing in the form of a regression coefficient test, rather than directly testing the value of this ratio, was briefly discussed in Chap. 1. As described in the context of the *wrong skewness problem*, although the third central moment is theoretically expected to take a negative value when technical inefficiency is present, it often takes a positive value in practice, contrary to this expectation. This suggests that the third central moment is close to zero in many samples. Consequently, the ratio becomes highly unstable, leading to serious problems in statistical inference. As will be shown using real data in Chap. 5, excess kurtosis also tends to behave similarly, owing to the constancy of the ratio. Therefore, using the reciprocal of K_h does not mitigate the issue either. For this reason, the present study adopts an approach that tests K_h through the estimated coefficient in the regression analysis.

Using the above procedures, it is possible to test the validity of assuming either the half-normal or exponential distribution. For the gamma and truncated normal distributions, one can estimate the value of the shape parameter or test hypotheses regarding that parameter. In the case of the half-normal and exponential distributions, the following hypotheses can be tested directly:

$$K_h = \frac{8(\pi - 3)}{2^{\frac{2}{3}}(4 - \pi)^{\frac{4}{3}}}, \qquad K_h = \frac{3}{\sqrt[3]{2}}.$$

For the gamma distribution, the shape parameter m can be estimated from the following relationship:

$$K_h = 3/\sqrt[3]{2(m+1)}\ .$$

For the truncated normal distribution, the value of the shape parameter m can be estimated from Eq. (2.4).

In the remainder of this chapter, the analysis is restricted to the exponential power-type distribution and the square normal-type distribution. The properties of the distribution parameter estimators, which are calculated based on the OLS estimates of the regression coefficients described above, are examined through Monte Carlo simulations. This restriction of the target distributions is intended to facilitate the specific hypothesis tests conducted in the following chapters. Notably, since the exponential power-type distribution encompasses both the half-normal and exponential distributions depending on the value of its shape parameter, tests for the validity of these two distributions are also addressed within the same framework. Although similar analyses are feasible for the gamma and truncated normal distributions, they are not included here, as they are not directly relevant to the primary objectives of this study, as explained in later chapters.

2.3 Properties of the Distribution Parameter Estimators: Exponential Power-Type Distribution

If technical inefficiency follows an exponential power-type distribution, the coefficient K_h is, in theory, a function of the parameter p, as given in Eq. (2.5). However, the statistical properties of the estimator of K_h, which is obtained using ordinary least squares (OLS) across a finite number of industries based on the moments of regression residuals calculated from finite samples within each industry, are not known. In this section, we examine the nature of this estimator using a Monte Carlo simulation. Specifically, we generate random variables that follow the probability density function given in Eq. (2.1), with θ fixed at 4.[8]

Next, random variables v are independently generated from the normal distribution $N(0, \sigma_v^2)$, and the differences $v - u$ are computed. This process is repeated N times to obtain N samples, which constitute one virtual industry. A total of 300 such virtual industries are generated. For each virtual industry (denoted as industry i), the second-, third-, and fourth-order central moments are calculated and denoted as m_{2i}, m_{3i}, and m_{4i}, respectively. We fix the number of virtual industries at 300 so as to correspond to the actual number of industries in Japan, which are used in the regression analysis and subsequent hypothesis testing presented in later chapters.

[8] The parameter $\theta = 4$ is fixed for technical reasons related to random number generation, but this does not affect the estimation of the regression coefficients. As noted above, the estimated relationship is independent of the absolute value of the parameter indicating the magnitude of the variance. What matters for the estimation is the relative magnitude of the variance of the stochastic error term being convoluted. Since this stochastic error term is varied across settings, there is no problem with fixing θ at a constant value.

2.3.1 Estimation of the Model Equation Under OLS

For the samples of moments obtained in the above procedure, we first consider estimating the regression coefficient K_h using OLS directly. Specifically, across these hypothetical industries, we conduct an OLS analysis with the intercept fixed at 0:

$$m_{4i} - 3\,(m_{2i})^2 = K_h \cdot \mathrm{sign}(-m_{3i})\,|m_{3i}|^{\frac{4}{3}} + \epsilon_i, \tag{2.7}$$

where sign(x) denotes the sign function, defined as 1 if $x > 0$, -1 if $x < 0$, and 0 if $x = 0$. The regression equation is formulated in a way that allows for linear extension in cases where the third moment of the residual term is positive, which may occur due to sample-dependent variations in the error structure. This extension addresses situations that cannot be captured by the original specification of the model. The OLS regression procedure is repeated 10,000 times to obtain the mean and variance of the estimated value of K_h. This simulation process is performed for $p = 1.5$, 1.0, 0.5, 0.0, -0.5, and for cases $\sigma_v = 0.05, 0.1, 0.25, 0.5, 1.0, 2.0$, assuming that the hypothetical industry consists of $N = 50$, 100, 200, 500, 1000, 3000, 30000 establishments. The results are summarized in Tables 2.1, 2.2, 2.3, 2.4, 2.5, 2.6, and 2.7.

These tables show that although the moment estimator appears to be consistent, for the estimates to asymptotically converge to the true value, the individual hypothetical industry must consist of at least a sample of several thousand establishments. In the case of a typical industry with an average of approximately 100 establishments, bias is unavoidable. The author could not find a way to obtain unbiased estimators of K_h. The direction of the bias is not a monotonic function of the sample size. When the value of the parameter σ_v, which indicates the magnitude of the random noise, is below a certain value, the estimates are stable.

The Monte Carlo experiment assumes a constant value of θ. This value defines the magnitude of the variance in the distribution of inefficiency. If we assume a half-normal distribution, then $1/\theta$ corresponds to the magnitude of the parameter σ_u^2.[9] From the tables, it is observed that the estimates of K_h remain stable when $\sigma_v < 0.25$. In many cases, as the magnitude of random noise increases beyond this threshold, the estimate begins to deviate significantly from the theoretical value and approaches zero. Thus, if the variance of the asymmetric technical inefficiency term is smaller than that of the symmetric error term, the estimated value of K_h can be expected to be close to zero. This is because the symmetric error term also exhibits variation in higher-order moments, and this variation acts as noise. When σ_v is sufficiently large relative to σ_u, this noise renders the relationship between

[9] Note, however, that this is different from the actual variance in the case of a half-normal distribution. It is merely a parameter of the distribution function. When assuming a half-normal distribution, the form is customarily written following the style of the normal distribution as $\sqrt{2/\pi} \cdot 1/\sigma_u \cdot \exp\left(-u^2/(2\sigma_u^2)\right)$. Accordingly, there is a discrepancy between the distribution parameter σ_u^2 and the actual variance of the distribution, which is given by $(\pi - 2)/\pi \cdot \sigma_u^2$. The moments for a general value of p are provided in Subsect. 2.1.5.

the moments of the asymmetric error term unobservable.[10] Therefore, if the null hypothesis that the estimated relationship between moments yields $K_h = 0$ is not rejected, this indicates that the variance of the symmetric error term is relatively large in comparison to that of the asymmetric error term.

However, it is important to note that a small estimated value of K_h may arise either when σ_v is large or when the parameter p is large. Accordingly, while observing a large estimate of K_h allows us to infer that p is likely small, a small estimate of K_h could be the result of either a large σ_v or a large p, making it difficult to distinguish between the two cases. Nevertheless, as shown in Tables 2.1, 2.2, 2.3, 2.4, 2.5, 2.6, and 2.7, within the expected range of the parameter p, such as in the case of the half-normal or exponential distributions, the distinction between these cases remains identifiable as long as the value of σ_v is not excessively large. Specifically, when both p and σ_v are small, a sufficiently high estimate of K_h is observed. Even when p is large, if σ_v is sufficiently small, the estimated value of K_h is still expected to be a significantly positive number.

2.3.2 *Log-Log OLS Estimation*

The regression equation used to obtain the estimated value of K_h is not limited to direct OLS. It is also possible to transform the regression equation to be estimated into the form given in Eq. (2.8).

$$\log\left(m_{4i} - 3m_{2i}^2\right) = \log\left(K_h\right) + \frac{4}{3}\log\left(-m_{3i}\right) + \epsilon_i, \tag{2.8}$$

This logarithmic transformation is introduced to mitigate potential imbalance in the explanatory variable when using OLS. However, since $m_{4i} - 3m_{2i}^2$ or $-m_{3i}$, or both, may take on negative values in finite samples, samples for which either of these values is negative are excluded from the estimation to ensure the log transformation is well-defined. Care is taken to ensure that this sample restriction does not introduce selection bias into the estimation results.[11] This process is equivalent to estimating the intercept in an OLS regression of $\log(m_{4i} - 3(m_{2i})^2)$ on $\log((-m_{3i})^{4/3})$, with

[10] When σ_v^2 dominates the variance of the asymmetric terms, both moment functions, $m_4 - 3m_2^2$ and $\text{sign}(m_3) \cdot |m_3|^{4/3}$, converge to zero, as a consequence of the properties of the underlying normal distribution. With a sufficiently large sample size, the sample skewness and sample kurtosis, calculated from a sample drawn from a normally distributed population, are almost uncorrelated, though not independent. See Shenton and Bowman (1977) and Doornik and Hansen (2008). Therefore, the ratio of these moment functions is expected to converge to zero. This property is confirmed in each of the tables.

[11] An alternative approach is to add a positive constant to the moment function before taking the logarithm. We experimented with this method, but found that it introduced substantial bias due to nonlinear distortion, and therefore did not adopt it.

the slope fixed at one, using only the subsample for which both $m_{4i} - 3(m_{2i})^2$ and $-m_{3i}$ are positive.[12]

To obtain the properties of the estimators by using this method, another Monte Carlo experiment must be performed. The results of the estimation of the value of $\log(K_h)$, in the same setting as in the previous Monte Carlo experiment, are presented in Tables 2.8, 2.9, 2.10, 2.11, 2.12, 2.13, and 2.14.

As shown in the previous section, the Monte Carlo experiment corresponding to regression Eq. (2.7) indicates that when $\sigma_v > 0.25$, the estimate of K_h deviates significantly from its theoretical value due to the dominance of the symmetric random noise term over the moment structure of the asymmetric technical inefficiency term. The Monte Carlo experiment using Eq. (2.8) yields a similar result. When $\sigma_v < 0.25$, the estimates are relatively stable, although slightly biased. However, when $\sigma_v > 0.25$, the symmetric random noise dominates once again, causing the estimated value of $\log(K_h)$ to deviate substantially from its theoretical value. Unlike in the case of Eq. (2.7), the theoretical value of $\log(K_h)$ expected when p is relatively small does not differ from that expected when σ_v is large. This makes it difficult to distinguish between the two cases based on the estimated value alone. On the other hand, when p is relatively large and σ_v is small, the theoretical value of $\log(K_h)$ is expected to be negative, and such negative estimates are observed only under those conditions.

These observations imply that the two estimation equations provide complementary identification capabilities. The method based on Eq. (2.8) alone is not sufficient for reliably estimating K_h, and should be used as a supplement to the method based on Eq. (2.7). Moreover, the fact that the directions of bias differ between the two approaches further highlights the complementary roles of the two methods.

2.3.3 *Further Monte Carlo Experiments*

This book empirically examines X-inefficiency in the Japanese manufacturing sector, using 4-digit Japan Standard Industrial Classification (JSIC) industries as relatively homogeneous units for production function estimation. As noted in Chap. 5, each industry typically yields a sample of around 100 establishments. To conduct hypothesis testing on the values of K_h across these industries, we conduct additional, detailed Monte Carlo experiments assuming a sample size of 100, which roughly corresponds to the number of establishments in a typical Japanese industry. The results are summarized in Tables 2.15, 2.16, 2.17, 2.18, 2.19, 2.20, and 2.21. Tables 2.15 and 2.16 present the OLS estimates of K_h for a wider range of p values, while Tables 2.17 and 2.18 report the 2.5% and 97.5% quantiles for two-sided tests, and Table 2.19 shows the 95% quantile for one-sided tests. Tables 2.20 and 2.21 summarize the estimated skewness values, which are considered to indicate the relative magnitude of the asym-

[12] Samples for which not only $m_{4i} - 3m_{2i}^2$ but also $-m_{3i}$ is negative are excluded, because under the assumption that the constant K_h is positive, cases in which $m_{4i} - 3m_{2i}^2 < 0$ correspond to those in which $m_{3i} > 0$.

metric variance component compared to σ_v. As discussed in the previous subsection, when the value of σ_v is large relative to the variance of the asymmetric term, the relationship between moments becomes unobservable due to being overwhelmed by noise from the symmetric error term. The extent of this noise is reflected in the skewness values; therefore, skewness serves as an indicator of whether the moment conditions are likely to be preserved in each sampled industry. If necessary, it can also be used as a filtering criterion. The results presented in these tables are used in Chap. 5.

Furthermore, as discussed in Chap. 5, the presence of X-inefficiency is tested by examining whether the null hypothesis $p > 0$ can be rejected. To explore this in greater detail, especially in the case where $p = 0$, additional Monte Carlo experiments are conducted. The results, shown in Tables 2.22, 2.23, and 2.24, include OLS estimates of K_h across different sample sizes, the 2.5% and 97.5% quantiles, and the 95% quantile for one-sided testing. Table 2.25, as noted earlier, also provides skewness estimates for this specific setting.

As shown by the results of the Monte Carlo experiments, when each virtual industry has a sufficiently large sample size and the variance of the random noise, σ_v, is sufficiently small relative to the variance of the asymmetric term, the estimated value of K_h, though biased, exhibits a small standard deviation. This enables the bias to be estimated through regression analysis, allowing for the construction of a bias-corrected estimate of K_h. Since this procedure goes beyond the scope of this book, it is not addressed here. A formula for bias correction based on this approach is derived in Torii (2001).

2.4 Property of the Distributional Parameter Estimators: Square Normal-Type Distribution

In the case of the square normal-type distribution, as with the exponential power-type distribution, it is generally not possible to analytically derive the statistical properties of the estimators when the coefficient K_h is obtained via OLS across multiple sample groups. This distribution refers to that of u, where $u = ax + bx^2$ and $x \sim N(0, \sigma_u^2)$. When the square normal-type distribution is assumed for the technical inefficiency term in later chapters, the primary objective becomes testing the null hypothesis $a = 0$ regarding the distribution parameters. Therefore, in this section, we use the Monte Carlo method to examine the relationship among the sample central moments observed under the condition $a = 0$. According to the theoretical relationship among sample central moments predicted for the square normal-type distribution (Eq. 2.6), the value of K_h is 3 when $a = 0$. Accordingly, the theoretical value of K_h in the Monte Carlo experiment presented below is 3.

First, a random number is generated from the χ_1^2 distribution and scaled by $\sigma_u/\sqrt{2}$, resulting in a variable with variance σ_u^2. Next, a value is generated from the normal distribution $N(0, \sigma_v^2)$, and the scaled value obtained in the first step is subtracted from it. In the Monte Carlo experiments below, we need to assess how the relative magnitude of the variance of the technical inefficiency term u to that of the symmetric error term v affects the estimator of K_h. Therefore, the parameter b is set to $1/\sqrt{2}$ so that the variance of u becomes σ_u^2 under the restriction $a = 0$, rather than the variance of x. This procedure is repeated N times to obtain N samples, which together constitute one virtual industry. A total of 300 such virtual industries are created. For each virtual industry i, the second-, third-, and fourth-order sample central moments are calculated and denoted as m_{2i}, m_{3i}, and m_{4i}, respectively. Then, across these virtual industries, the coefficient K_h is estimated using OLS with the intercept fixed at zero, based on the regression (2.7).

This estimation is repeated 10,000 times to obtain the mean and variance of the K_h estimates. This procedure is conducted for various values of σ_v ranging from 0.01 to 8.0, while fixing the value of σ_u at 1.0. For each case, the samples consist of $N = 50, 100, 150, 200, 500, 1000, 3000$ virtual industries. The results are summarized in Tables 2.26 and 2.27.

As the random noise increases, the estimated value of K_h gradually decreases. In particular, when σ_v/σ_u exceeds 1, K_h rapidly diminishes as σ_v/σ_u exceeds 1, and takes a value close to 0 when σ_v/σ_u exceeds 5.

These tables show that, as in the case of the exponential power-type distribution, bias in the estimates is inevitable in the case of the square-normal distribution, depending on the number of samples. In general, the larger the value of σ_v, which indicates the magnitude of the random noise, the more the estimate of K_h tends to be downward biased. However, when σ_v is smaller than σ_u, which is fixed at 1.0 and represents the variance of the asymmetric term, the estimates of K_h appear to be stable. Figure 2.3 summarizes the estimated values of K_h for various values of σ_v. When the random noise is relatively small, the estimated value of K_h is around $3.1 \sim 3.2$, although this value depends on the sample size. As random noise increases from zero, the estimate of K_h remains stable initially but gradually begins to decrease

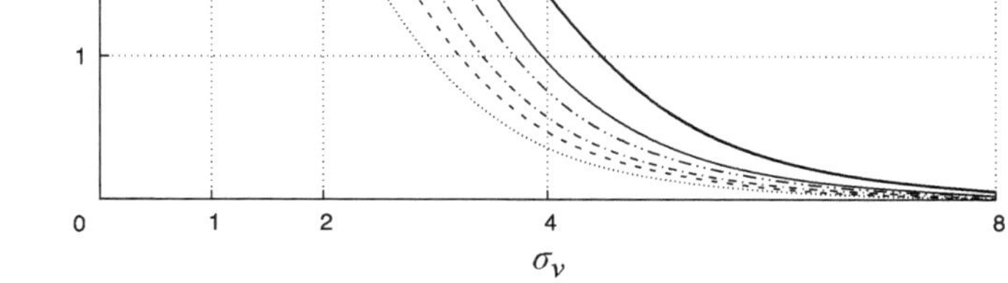

Fig. 2.3 Estimates of K_h by OLS (Square normal-type distribution with $a = 0$)

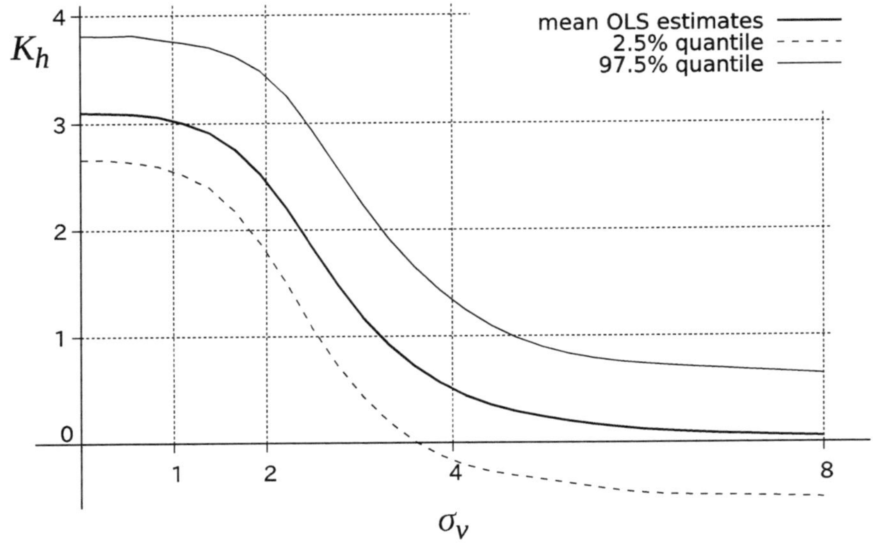

Fig. 2.4 95% confidence intervals of OLS estimates of K_h (Square normal-type distribution with $a = 0$). *Note* The case sample size is 100

after a certain point. In particular, when the ratio σ_v/σ_u exceeds 1, the estimate of K_h declines significantly.

Tables 2.28 and 2.29 report the 2.5% and 97.5% quantiles for two-sided tests, and Table 2.30 reports the 95% quantile. Figure 2.4 illustrates the 95% empirical confidence intervals of OLS estimates of K_h for a sample size of 100, as a function of σ_v. The intervals are constructed based on the 2.5% and 97.5% quantiles of the distribution of OLS estimates obtained from 10,000 simulation trials.

Tables 2.31 and 2.32 present the results of Monte Carlo experiments based on regression Eq. (2.8), while Tables 2.33 and 2.34 report the estimated 2.5% and 97.5% quantiles, and Table 2.35 shows the estimated 95% quantile. According to the results in Tables 2.31, 2.32, 2.33, 2.34, and 2.35, the estimates of $\log(K_h)$ obtained from the coefficients of the log-log OLS regression using specification (2.8) are downward biased when the symmetric error term σ_v is small. This bias diminishes as the number of establishments in the sample increases. The bias arises from the fact that, when the sample size is small, both the sample skewness and sample kurtosis tend to be downward biased. Since the logarithmic transformation increases the weight of observations with smaller values in the regression, the samples subject to such bias receive greater weight, which results in the type of bias observed in the tables.

These results are used in Chap. 6, where the existence of X-inefficiency is tested using data from Japanese manufacturing industries to examine the overall tendency across industries. The test is conducted under the assumption that technical inefficiency follows a square normal-type distribution, based on the model described in Chap. 6.

2.5 Conclusion and Discussion

In this chapter, we developed a statistical method aimed at identifying X-inefficiency in the Japanese manufacturing industry. This method provides the basis for the hypothesis testing conducted in the later chapters. The observed performance of an establishment with X-inefficiency is assumed to follow a distribution formed by the convolution of an asymmetric distribution and a symmetric error term. As distributions for describing inefficiency, we considered what are referred to here as the exponential power-type distribution and the square normal-type distribution. We then analyzed the properties of these distributions after convolution with a normal distribution for use in subsequent statistical tests. In addition, we presented a method for identifying the distribution type that is assumed to be common across the entire population. It is applicable when the population is divided into multiple subsets, where the distribution type remains the same but the distribution parameters vary between subsets. The method relies on the property that, for all distribution types previously used to describe technical inefficiency, the second-, third-, and fourth-order central moments of the convolution with a normal distribution satisfy a relationship that does not involve the parameters of the normal distribution and the variance-related parameter of the original asymmetric distribution. To the best of our knowledge, this approach has not been used in previous research for the purpose of identifying or testing the form of the distribution of technical inefficiency.[13]

Most prior analyses of technical inefficiency have been conducted within individual industries. The absence of discussion regarding the method presented in this chapter may be due to the fact that distributional analysis has rarely been carried out across a wide range of industries within the manufacturing sector. With the methods presented in this chapter, a specific distribution can be expressed either as a single value or as a function of the parameters that characterize it. This makes the approach highly useful for estimation and hypothesis testing to identify distributional form.

However, there are some limitations to this method. First, it only targets situations in which the population is divided into a number of subsets, and the distribution type is the same across the population; however, the distribution parameters are known to be different for each subset. For example, this method is not applicable if each industry has a different mechanism for generating inefficiencies and therefore a different distribution type for the inefficiencies generated. If the distribution to be tested has only one parameter that indicates a difference in variance (for example, in the case of a half-normal distribution), the method presented in this chapter tests the hypothesis that the value of K_h is a certain value, and thus the correctness of the hypothesis can be examined. However, when the distribution has a parameter indicating the shape of the distribution, such as in the case of an exponential power-type distribution, it is possible to test whether the shape parameter lies within a specific range, but it is

[13] For example, Rahman and Gokhale (1996) analyzed the properties of moment-based and maximum likelihood estimators for the exponential power distribution using Monte Carlo simulation. However, the estimation method employed in the present study is entirely different. The author is not aware of any application of this method in other fields.

not possible to determine whether the original distribution is indeed an exponential power-type distribution.

Second, since the estimators to be tested were calculated using moments up to the fourth order of the regression residuals, the nature of the sample distribution could not be analyzed directly. The tests were designed in a manner consistent with the econometric analysis presented in later chapters, and they relied heavily on the results of repeated Monte Carlo simulations.

Appendix: Calculation of Moments of Convolution of Exponential Power-Type Distribution/Square Normal-Type Distribution and Normal Distribution

First, $\mathbb{E}\left(u^i\right)$ $(i = 1, 2, 3, 4)$ is obtained for a random variable u following an exponential power-type distribution (2.1).

$$\mathbb{E}\left(u^i\right) = \int_0^{\infty} \rho(u) u^i du = \left(\frac{1+p}{\theta}\right)^{\frac{i}{1+p}} \frac{g_{1+i}}{g_1},$$

where $g_j = \Gamma(j/(1+p))$. For the random variable $v \sim N\left(0, \sigma_v^2\right)$, $\mathbb{E}(v^i)$ are

$$\mathbb{E}(v) = \mathbb{E}\left(v^3\right) = 0, \quad \mathbb{E}\left(v^2\right) = \sigma_v^2, \quad \mathbb{E}\left(v^4\right) = 3\sigma_v^4.$$

Then, for the random variable $\epsilon = v - u$,

$$\mathbb{E}(\epsilon) = \mathbb{E}(v) - \mathbb{E}(u) = -\left(\frac{1+p}{\theta}\right)^{\frac{1}{1+p}} \frac{g_2}{g_1},$$

$$\begin{aligned}
\mathbb{E}\left(\epsilon^2\right) &= \mathbb{E}\left(v^2\right) - 2\mathbb{E}(v)\mathbb{E}(u) + \mathbb{E}\left(u^2\right) = \sigma_v^2 + \left(\frac{1+p}{\theta}\right)^{\frac{2}{1+p}} \frac{g_3}{g_1}, \\
\mathbb{E}\left(\epsilon^3\right) &= \mathbb{E}\left(v^3\right) - 3\mathbb{E}\left(v^2\right)\mathbb{E}(u) + 3\mathbb{E}(v)\mathbb{E}\left(u^2\right) - \mathbb{E}(u^3) \\
&= -3\sigma_v^2 \left(\frac{1+p}{\theta}\right)^{\frac{1}{1+p}} \frac{g_2}{g_1} - \left(\frac{1+p}{\theta}\right)^{\frac{3}{1+p}} \frac{g_4}{g_1}, \\
\mathbb{E}\left(\epsilon^4\right) &= \mathbb{E}\left(v^4\right) - 4\mathbb{E}\left(v^3\right)\mathbb{E}(u) + 6\mathbb{E}\left(v^2\right)\mathbb{E}\left(u^2\right) - 4\mathbb{E}(v)\mathbb{E}\left(u^3\right) + \mathbb{E}(u^4) \\
&= 3\sigma_v^4 + 6\sigma_v^2 \left(\frac{1+p}{\theta}\right)^{\frac{2}{1+p}} \frac{g_3}{g_1} + \left(\frac{1+p}{\theta}\right)^{\frac{4}{1+p}} \frac{g_5}{g_1}.
\end{aligned}$$

Using these results, the central moments of random variables ϵ are

$$\begin{aligned}
\mathbb{E}\left(\epsilon - \overline{\epsilon}\right)^2 &= \mathbb{E}\left(\epsilon^2\right) - \mathbb{E}(\epsilon)^2 = \sigma_v^2 + \left(\frac{1+p}{\theta}\right)^{\frac{2}{1+p}} \frac{g_3 g_1 - g_2^2}{g_1^2}, \\
\mathbb{E}\left(\epsilon - \overline{\epsilon}\right)^3 &= \mathbb{E}\left(\epsilon^3\right) - 3\mathbb{E}\left(\epsilon^2\right)\mathbb{E}(\epsilon) + 2\mathbb{E}(\epsilon)^2
\end{aligned}$$

$$
\begin{aligned}
&= -\left(\frac{1+p}{\theta}\right)^{\frac{3}{1+p}} \frac{g_4 g_1^2 - 3g_3 g_2 g_1 + 2g_2^3}{g_1^3}, \\
\mathbb{E}(\epsilon-\bar{\epsilon})^4 &= \mathbb{E}\left(\epsilon^4\right) - 4\mathbb{E}\left(\epsilon^3\right)\mathbb{E}(\epsilon) + 6\mathbb{E}\left(\epsilon^2\right)\mathbb{E}(\epsilon)^2 - 3E(\epsilon)^4, \\
&= 6\sigma_v^4 + \left(\frac{1+p}{\theta}\right)^{\frac{4}{1+p}} \frac{g_5 g_1^3 - 4g_4 g_2 g_1^2 + 6g_3 g_2^2 g_1 - 3g_2^4}{g_1^4} \\
&\quad + 3\left(\frac{1+p}{\theta}\right)^{\frac{2}{1+p}} \frac{g_3 g_1 - g_2^2}{g_1^2}\sigma_v^2.
\end{aligned}
$$

For a square normal-type distribution, the same procedures are applied. First, for the random variable $u = ax + bx^2$ derived from the normal distribution $x \sim N\left(0, \sigma_u^2\right)$,

$$
\begin{aligned}
&\mathbb{E}(x) = \mathbb{E}\left(x^3\right) = \mathbb{E}\left(x^5\right) = \mathbb{E}\left(x^7\right) = 0, \quad \mathbb{E}\left(x^2\right) = \sigma_u^2, \\
&\mathbb{E}\left(x^4\right) = 3\sigma_u^4, \quad \mathbb{E}\left(x^6\right) = 15\sigma_u^6, \quad \mathbb{E}\left(x^8\right) = 105\sigma_u^8.
\end{aligned}
$$

Then,

$$
\begin{aligned}
\mathbb{E}(u) &= a\mathbb{E}(x) + b\mathbb{E}\left(x^2\right) = b\sigma_u^2, \\
\mathbb{E}\left(u^2\right) &= a\mathbb{E}\left(x^2\right) + 2ab\mathbb{E}\left(x^3\right) + b^2\mathbb{E}\left(x^4\right) = a^2\sigma_u^2 + 3b^2\sigma_u^4, \\
\mathbb{E}\left(u^3\right) &= a\mathbb{E}\left(x^3\right) + 3a^2b\mathbb{E}\left(x^4\right) + 3ab^2\mathbb{E}\left(x^5\right) + b^3\mathbb{E}\left(x^6\right) = 9a^2b\sigma_u^4 + 15b^3\sigma_u^6, \\
\mathbb{E}\left(u^4\right) &= a^4\mathbb{E}\left(x^4\right) + 4a^3b\mathbb{E}\left(v^5\right) + 6a^2b^2\mathbb{E}\left(x^6\right) + 4ab^3\mathbb{E}\left(x^7\right) + b^4\mathbb{E}(x^8) \\
&= 3a^4b\sigma_u^4 + 90a^2b^2\sigma_u^6 + 105b^4\sigma_u^8.
\end{aligned}
$$

Therefore,

$$
\begin{aligned}
\mathbb{E}(\epsilon) &= \mathbb{E}(v) - \mathbb{E}(u) = -b\sigma_u^2, \\
\mathbb{E}\left(\epsilon^2\right) &= \mathbb{E}\left(v^2\right) - 2\mathbb{E}(v)\mathbb{E}(u) + \mathbb{E}\left(u^2\right) = a^2\sigma_u^2 + 3b^2\sigma_u^4 + \sigma_v^2, \\
\mathbb{E}\left(\epsilon^3\right) &= E\left(v^3\right) - 3\mathbb{E}\left(v^2\right)\mathbb{E}(u) + 3\mathbb{E}(v)\mathbb{E}\left(u^2\right) - \mathbb{E}(u^3) \\
&= -9a^2b\sigma_u^4 - 15b^3\sigma_u^6 - 3b\sigma_u^2\sigma_v^2, \\
\mathbb{E}\left(\epsilon^4\right) &= \mathbb{E}\left(v^4\right) - 4\mathbb{E}\left(v^3\right)\mathbb{E}(u) + 6\mathbb{E}\left(v^2\right)\mathbb{E}\left(u^2\right) - 4\mathbb{E}(v)\mathbb{E}\left(u^3\right) + \mathbb{E}(u^4) \\
&= 3a^4\sigma_u^4 + 90a^2b^2\sigma_u^6 + 105b^4\sigma_u^8 + 6(a^2\sigma_u^2 + 3b^2\sigma_u^4)\sigma_v^2 + 3\sigma_v^4.
\end{aligned}
$$

Using these results, the moments of random variables ϵ are

$$\begin{aligned}
\mathbb{E}\,(\epsilon-\overline{\epsilon})^2 &= \mathbb{E}\left(\epsilon^2\right)-\mathbb{E}(\epsilon)^2=\left(a^2+2b^2\sigma_u^2\right)\sigma_u^2+\sigma_v^2,\\
\mathbb{E}\,(\epsilon-\overline{\epsilon})^3 &= \mathbb{E}\left(\epsilon^3\right)-3\mathbb{E}\left(\epsilon^2\right)\mathbb{E}(\epsilon)+2\mathbb{E}(\epsilon)^2=-2b\sigma_u^4(3a^2+4b^2\sigma_u^2),\\
\mathbb{E}\,(\epsilon-\overline{\epsilon})^4 &= \mathbb{E}\left(\epsilon^4\right)-4\mathbb{E}\left(\epsilon^3\right)\mathbb{E}(\epsilon)+6\mathbb{E}\left(\epsilon^2\right)\mathbb{E}(\epsilon)^2-3\mathbb{E}(\epsilon)^4\\
&= 3\sigma_u^4\left(a^4+20a^2b^2\sigma_u^2+20b^4\sigma_u^4\right)+6\sigma_u^2\sigma_v^2\left(a^2+2b^2\sigma_u^2\right)+3\sigma_v^4.
\end{aligned}$$

Tables: Results of Monte Carlo Experiments

Table 2.1 OLS estimates of K_h (The case sample size is 50)

p	Theoretical value of K_h	σ_v					
		0.05	0.1	0.25	0.5	1.0	2.0
1.5	0.300	0.593 (0.117)	0.615 (0.126)	0.738 (0.191)	0.521 (0.279)	0.123 (0.311)	0.020 (0.319)
1.0	0.875	1.077 (0.126)	1.086 (0.137)	1.097 (0.192)	0.699 (0.293)	0.147 (0.323)	0.030 (0.319)
0.5	1.500	1.638 (0.152)	1.637 (0.160)	1.567 (0.203)	0.979 (0.310)	0.194 (0.328)	0.034 (0.319)
0	2.381	2.350 (0.203)	2.337 (0.206)	2.220 (0.241)	1.392 (0.376)	0.226 (0.350)	0.033 (0.320)
−0.5	4.917	3.142 (0.176)	3.125 (0.179)	2.959 (0.252)	1.480 (0.658)	0.141 (0.354)	0.023 (0.319)

Note Averages based on 10,000 trials. Standard deviations are shown in parentheses

Table 2.2 OLS estimates of K_h (The case sample size is 100)

p	Theoretical value of K_h	σ_v					
		0.05	0.1	0.25	0.5	1.0	2.0
1	0.300	0.499 (0.078)	0.526 (0.086)	0.672 (0.139)	0.591 (0.238)	0.152 (0.295)	0.027 (0.296)
1.0	0.875	1.030 (0.082)	1.045 (0.089)	1.090 (0.138)	0.808 (0.242)	0.182 (0.292)	0.035 (0.290)
0.5	1.500	1.652 (0.106)	1.656 (0.114)	1.640 (0.154)	1.139 (0.258)	0.229 (0.299)	0.038 (0.294)
0	2.381	2.533 (0.176)	2.529 (0.182)	2.460 (0.220)	1.674 (0.336)	0.280 (0.314)	0.045 (0.292)
−0.5	4.917	3.897 (0.238)	3.887 (0.240)	3.717 (0.298)	1.987 (0.687)	0.166 (0.325)	0.021 (0.292)

Note Averages based on 10,000 trials. Standard deviations are shown in parentheses

Table 2.3 OLS estimates of K_h (The case sample size is 200)

p	Theoretical value of K_h	σ_v					
		0.05	0.1	0.25	0.5	1.0	2.0
1.5	0.300	0.415 (0.051)	0.434 (0.056)	0.561 (0.097)	0.607 (0.203)	0.165 (0.266)	0.032 (0.268)
1.0	0.875	0.970 (0.052)	0.980 (0.056)	1.032 (0.092)	0.865 (0.195)	0.212 (0.266)	0.034 (0.270)
0.5	1.500	1.605 (0.065)	1.611 (0.070)	1.621 (0.103)	1.251 (0.204)	0.269 (0.273)	0.036 (0.269)
0	2.381	2.549 (0.125)	2.549 (0.129)	2.521 (0.165)	1.872 (0.267)	0.332 (0.281)	0.041 (0.270)
−0.5	4.917	4.557 (0.284)	4.549 (0.288)	4.382 (0.337)	2.435 (0.660)	0.187 (0.300)	0.019 (0.268)

Note Averages based on 10,000 trials. Standard deviations are shown in parentheses

Table 2.4 OLS estimates of K_h (The case sample size is 500)

p	Theoretical value of K_h	σ_v					
		0.05	0.1	0.25	0.5	1.0	2.0
1.5	0.300	0.348 (0.029)	0.358 (0.032)	0.434 (0.059)	0.554 (0.158)	0.191 (0.250)	0.035 (0.254)
1.0	0.875	0.915 (0.029)	0.920 (0.031)	0.953 (0.052)	0.878 (0.145)	0.256 (0.252)	0.033 (0.258)
0.5	1.500	1.546 (0.036)	1.549 (0.038)	1.560 (0.056)	1.335 (0.142)	0.336 (0.252)	0.044 (0.258)
0	2.381	2.471 (0.070)	2.473 (0.072)	2.471 (0.090)	2.046 (0.178)	0.416 (0.258)	0.046 (0.259
−0.5	4.917	5.020 (0.259)	5.021 (0.265)	4.903 (0.320)	2.971 (0.539)	0.232 (0.281)	0.020 (0.256)

Note Averages based on 10,000 trials. Standard deviations are shown in parentheses

Table 2.5 OLS estimates of K_h (The case sample size is 1000)

p	Theoretical value of K_h	σ_v					
		0.05	0.1	0.25	0.5	1.0	2.0
1.5	0.300	0.323 (0.020)	0.328 (0.022)	0.371 (0.041)	0.486 (0.127)	0.211 (0.253)	0.036 (0.263)
1.0	0.875	0.892 (0.019)	0.895 (0.021)	0.915 (0.036)	0.874 (0.111)	0.292 (0.249)	0.043 (0.262)
0.5	1.500	1.519 (0.023)	1.522 (0.025)	1.530 (0.036)	1.383 (0.104)	0.399 (0.250)	0.047 (0.265)
0	2.381	2.419 (0.043)	2.420 (0.043)	2.423 (0.056)	2.138 (0.123)	0.512 (0.253)	0.046 (0.264)
−0.5	4.917	5.027 (0.205)	5.026 (0.206)	4.965 (0.255)	3.306 (0.405)	0.278 (0.280)	0.024 (0.263)

Note Averages based on 10,000 trials. Standard deviations are shown in parentheses

Table 2.6 OLS estimates of K_h (The case sample size is 3000)

p	Theoretical value of K_h	σ_v					
		0.05	0.1	0.25	0.5	1.0	2.0
1.5	0.300	0.304 (0.011)	0.306 (0.012)	0.322 (0.023)	0.388 (0.086)	0.250 (0.258)	0.037 (0.295)
1.0	0.875	0.876 (0.011)	0.877 (0.012)	0.885 (0.020)	0.866 (0.071)	0.377 (0.252)	0.047 (0.293)
0.5	1.500	1.500 (0.013)	1.501 (0.013)	1.504 (0.019)	1.437 (0.063)	0.564 (0.238)	0.054 (0.297)
0	2.381	2.376 (0.021)	2.376 (0.022)	2.378 (0.028)	2.252 (0.071)	0.787 (0.243)	0.068 (0.297)
−0.5	4.917	4.823 (0.138)	4.825 (0.141)	4.815 (0.181)	3.794 (0.271)	0.424 (0.300)	0.031 (0.297)

Note Averages based on 10,000 trials. Standard deviations are shown in parentheses

Table 2.7 OLS estimates of K_h (The case sample size is 30000)

p	Theoretical value of K_h	σ_v					
		0.05	0.1	0.25	0.5	1.0	2.0
1.5	0.300	0.296 (0.004)	0.296 (0.004)	0.298 (0.007)	0.307 (0.030)	0.282 (0.210)	0.060 (0.404)
1.0	0.875	0.869 (0.003)	0.869 (0.004)	0.870 (0.006)	0.868 (0.024)	0.648 (0.181)	0.089 (0.407)
0.5	1.500	1.490 (0.004)	1.490 (0.004)	1.491 (0.006)	1.483 (0.021)	1.119 (0.157)	0.133 (0.402)
0	2.381	2.353 (0.006)	2.353 (0.006)	2.353 (0.008)	2.338 (0.022)	1.738 (0.161)	0.157 (0.402)
−0.5	4.917	4.620 (0.029)	4.621 (0.029)	4.620 (0.035)	4.448 (0.078)	1.593 (0.311)	0.055 (0.411)

Note Averages based on 10,000 trials. Standard deviations are shown in parentheses

Table 2.8 Log-log OLS estimates of $\log(K_h)$ (The case sample size is 50)

p	Theoretical $\log(K_h)$	σ_v					
		0.05	0.1	0.25	0.5	1.0	2.0
1.5	−1.204	−0.673 (0.101)	−0.599 (0.101)	−0.085 (0.130)	0.419 (0.188)	0.575 (0.223)	0.601 (0.235)
1.0	−0.134	−0.485 (0.079)	−0.438 (0.081)	−0.043 (0.110)	0.413 (0.178)	0.569 (0.221)	0.598 (0.233)
0.5	0.405	−0.239 (0.062)	−0.215 (0.065)	0.056 (0.092)	0.427 (0.163)	0.569 (0.220)	0.596 (0.233)
0.0	0.868	0.097 (0.048)	0.093 (0.051)	0.256 (0.080)	0.485 (0.155)	0.574 (0.218)	0.596 (0.233)
−0.5	1.593	0.525 (0.034)	0.509 (0.048)	0.589 (0.106)	0.596 (0.186)	0.594 (0.228)	0.602 (0.235)

Note Averages based on 10,000 trials. Standard deviations are shown in parentheses

Table 2.9 Log-log OLS estimates of $\log(K_h)$ (The case sample size is 100)

p	Theoretical $\log(K_h)$	σ_v = 0.05	0.1	0.25	0.5	1.0	2.0
1.5	−1.204	−0.788 (0.091)	−0.718 (0.091)	−0.166 (0.111)	0.603 (0.177)	0.857 (0.22)	0.898 (0.23)
1.0	−0.134	−0.490 (0.068)	−0.456 (0.070)	−0.091 (0.091)	0.588 (0.160)	0.849 (0.216)	0.898 (0.228)
0.5	0.405	−0.106 (0.050)	−0.107 (0.053)	0.073 (0.072)	0.607 (0.145)	0.848 (0.212)	0.898 (0.230)
0.0	0.868	0.352 (0.035)	0.322 (0.038)	0.359 (0.062)	0.689 (0.134)	0.858 (0.208)	0.893 (0.229)
−0.5	1.593	0.816 (0.023)	0.760 (0.032)	0.816 (0.085)	0.880 (0.165)	0.893 (0.221)	0.906 (0.228)

Note Averages based on 10,000 trials. Standard deviations are shown in parentheses

Table 2.10 Log-log OLS estimates of $\log(K_h)$ (The case sample size is 200)

p	Theoretical $\log(K_h)$	σ_v = 0.05	0.1	0.25	0.5	1.0	2.0
1.5	−1.204	−0.943 (0.082)	−0.875 (0.083)	−0.356 (0.096)	0.684 (0.161)	1.082 (0.211)	1.150 (0.225)
1.0	−0.134	−0.482 (0.057)	−0.464 (0.059)	−0.203 (0.074)	0.661 (0.145)	1.073 (0.209)	1.147 (0.223)
0.5	0.405	0.060 (0.037)	0.040 (0.040)	0.065 (0.058)	0.680 (0.127)	1.067 (0.203)	1.143 (0.226)
0.0	0.868	0.561 (0.022)	0.537 (0.025)	0.451 (0.046)	0.805 (0.116)	1.080 (0.201)	1.148 (0.222)
−0.5	1.593	1.020 (0.017)	0.986 (0.021)	0.972 (0.066)	1.097 (0.149)	1.137 (0.216)	1.155 (0.228)

Note Averages based on 10,000 trials. Standard deviations are shown in parentheses

Table 2.11 Log-log OLS estimates of $\log(K_h)$ (The case sample size is 500)

p	Theoretical $\log(K_h)$	σ_v = 0.05	0.1	0.25	0.5	1.0	2.0
1.5	−1.204	−1.157 (0.073)	−1.101 (0.073)	−0.655 (0.083)	0.638 (0.140)	1.303 (0.203)	1.422 (0.223)
1.0	−0.134	−0.394 (0.041)	−0.407 (0.044)	−0.332 (0.060)	0.600 (0.122)	1.289 (0.199)	1.418 (0.219)
0.5	0.405	0.253 (0.021)	0.235 (0.023)	0.132 (0.041)	0.631 (0.102)	1.280 (0.190)	1.416 (0.221)
0.0	0.868	0.714 (0.015)	0.706 (0.016)	0.624 (0.028)	0.826 (0.089)	1.299 (0.187)	1.413 (0.220)
−0.5	1.593	1.205 (0.015)	1.194 (0.016)	1.127 (0.043)	1.305 (0.125)	1.393 (0.202)	1.429 (0.221)

Note Averages based on 10,000 trials. Standard deviations are shown in parentheses

Table 2.12 Log-log OLS estimates of $\log(K_h)$ (The case sample size is 1000)

p	Theoretical $\log(K_h)$	σ_v					
		0.05	0.1	0.25	0.5	1.0	2.0
1.5	−1.204	−1.298 (0.064)	−1.252 (0.066)	−0.875 (0.076)	0.468 (0.123)	1.423 (0.195)	1.589 (0.221)
1.0	−0.134	−0.287 (0.027)	−0.308 (0.030)	−0.361 (0.049)	0.427 (0.102)	1.401 (0.185)	1.581 (0.216)
0.5	0.405	0.325 (0.014)	0.318 (0.015)	0.237 (0.028)	0.492 (0.082)	1.386 (0.180)	1.580 (0.215)
0.0	0.868	0.776 (0.011)	0.772 (0.012)	0.733 (0.018)	0.769 (0.070)	1.412 (0.174)	1.581 (0.217)
−0.5	1.593	1.307 (0.013)	1.301 (0.014)	1.249 (0.027)	1.400 (0.106)	1.551 (0.197)	1.603 (0.220)

Note Averages based on 10,000 trials. Standard deviations are shown in parentheses

Table 2.13 Log-log OLS estimates of $\log(K_h)$ (The case sample size is 3000)

p	Theoretical $\log(K_h)$	σ_v					
		0.05	0.1	0.25	0.5	1.0	2.0
1.5	−1.204	−1.398 (0.048)	−1.390 (0.052)	−1.176 (0.066)	−0.006 (0.096)	1.526 (0.178)	1.817 (0.210)
1.0	−0.134	−0.186 (0.013)	−0.193 (0.014)	−0.278 (0.030)	0.041 (0.074)	1.483 (0.168)	1.806 (0.208)
0.5	0.405	0.373 (0.008)	0.371 (0.008)	0.348 (0.013)	0.280 (0.055)	1.456 (0.158)	1.804 (0.210)
0.0	0.868	0.825 (0.007)	0.824 (0.007)	0.812 (0.010)	0.716 (0.043)	1.499 (0.150)	1.803 (0.208)
−0.5	1.593	1.419 (0.011)	1.417 (0.011)	1.399 (0.015)	1.446 (0.074)	1.746 (0.183)	1.840 (0.213)

Note Averages based on 10,000 trials. Standard deviations are shown in parentheses

Table 2.14 Log-log OLS estimates of $\log(K_h)$ (The case sample size is 30,000)

p	Theoretical $\log(K_h)$	σ_v					
		0.05	0.1	0.25	0.5	1.0	2.0
1.5	−1.204	−1.250 (0.013)	−1.257 (0.015)	−1.340 (0.033)	−0.951 (0.071)	1.204 (0.129)	2.170 (0.198)
1.0	−0.134	−0.146 (0.004)	−0.147 (0.004)	−0.153 (0.007)	−0.271 (0.039)	1.067 (0.114)	2.146 (0.196)
0.5	0.405	0.396 (0.002)	0.396 (0.003)	0.394 (0.004)	0.364 (0.016)	0.996 (0.097)	2.129 (0.192)
0.0	0.868	0.851 (0.002)	0.851 (0.002)	0.850 (0.003)	0.841 (0.010)	1.142 (0.087)	2.137 (0.191)
−0.5	1.593	1.510 (0.005)	1.510 (0.005)	1.508 (0.006)	1.498 (0.019)	1.909 (0.130)	2.250 (0.207)

Note Averages based on 10,000 trials. Standard deviations are shown in parentheses

Table 2.15 OLS estimates of K_h (The case sample size is 100): part I

p	Theoretical value of K_h	σ_v					
		0.05	0.1	0.25	0.5	1.0	2.0
2.0	−0.292	−0.012 (0.081)	0.037 (0.091)	0.327 (0.147)	0.450 (0.248)	0.127 (0.288)	0.023 (0.295)
1.7	0.068	0.293 (0.078)	0.329 (0.087)	0.526 (0.142)	0.524 (0.247)	0.138 (0.291)	0.024 (0.290)
1.5	0.300	0.499 (0.078)	0.526 (0.086)	0.672 (0.139)	0.591 (0.238)	0.152 (0.295)	0.027 (0.296)
1.3	0.529	0.706 (0.078)	0.728 (0.086)	0.831 (0.137)	0.670 (0.240)	0.156 (0.293)	0.028 (0.298)
1.1	0.759	0.921 (0.080)	0.936 (0.088)	1.002 (0.137)	0.758 (0.244)	0.172 (0.293)	0.031 (0.294)
1.0	0.875	1.030 (0.082)	1.045 (0.089)	1.090 (0.138)	0.808 (0.242)	0.182 (0.292)	0.035 (0.290)
0.9	0.992	1.146 (0.085)	1.157 (0.091)	1.189 (0.139)	0.863 (0.243)	0.192 (0.294)	0.034 (0.290)
0.8	1.113	1.263 (0.090)	1.274 (0.096)	1.291 (0.141)	0.919 (0.246)	0.196 (0.296)	0.040 (0.293)
0.7	1.237	1.386 (0.094)	1.392 (0.099)	1.400 (0.144)	0.989 (0.247)	0.213 (0.301)	0.033 (0.292)
0.6	1.365	1.515 (0.099)	1.520 (0.104)	1.515 (0.149)	1.063 (0.255)	0.218 (0.299)	0.034 (0.295)
0.5	1.501	1.656 (0.106)	1.656 (0.114)	1.640 (0.154)	1.139 (0.258)	0.229 (0.299)	0.038 (0.294)
0.4	1.644	1.798 (0.115)	1.799 (0.121)	1.771 (0.162)	1.230 (0.267)	0.239 (0.297)	0.035 (0.289)
0.3	1.800	1.957 (0.126)	1.958 (0.132)	1.921 (0.172)	1.331 (0.278)	0.251 (0.307)	0.041 (0.293)
0.2	1.970	2.131 (0.141)	2.129 (0.145)	2.083 (0.184)	1.434 (0.295)	0.265 (0.306)	0.039 (0.293)
0.1	2.161	2.319 (0.154)	2.319 (0.163)	2.259 (0.198)	1.543 (0.309)	0.277 (0.308)	0.035 (0.292)

Note Averages based on 10,000 trials. Each cell shows the mean of K_h estimates with its standard deviation in parentheses

Table 2.16 OLS estimates of K_h (The case sample size is 100): part II

p	Theoretical value of K_h	σ_v					
		0.05	0.1	0.25	0.5	1.0	2.0
0.0	2.381	2.533 (0.176)	2.529 (0.182)	2.460 (0.220)	1.674 (0.336)	0.280 (0.314)	0.045 (0.292)
−0.1	2.643	2.773 (0.200)	2.766 (0.202)	2.680 (0.242)	1.802 (0.365)	0.280 (0.317)	0.033 (0.297)

(continued)

Table 2.16 (continued)

p	Theoretical value of K_h	σ_v					
		0.05	0.1	0.25	0.5	1.0	2.0
−0.2	2.966	3.038 (0.222)	3.031 (0.226)	2.925 (0.263)	1.943 (0.415)	0.267 (0.323)	0.034 (0.295)
−0.3	3.390	3.320 (0.240)	3.310 (0.245)	3.194 (0.282)	2.051 (0.468)	0.258 (0.332)	0.035 (0.300)
−0.4	3.985	3.621 (0.248)	3.609 (0.253)	3.468 (0.295)	2.111 (0.562)	0.225 (0.334)	0.027 (0.300)
−0.5	4.918	3.897 (0.238)	3.887 (0.240)	3.717 (0.298)	1.987 (0.687)	0.166 (0.325)	0.021 (0.292)
−0.6	6.644	4.140 (0.202)	4.115 (0.213)	3.861 (0.335)	1.446 (0.801)	0.094 (0.315)	0.014 (0.286)
−0.7	10.922	4.308 (0.165)	4.274 (0.178)	3.412 (0.746)	0.466 (0.584)	0.026 (0.298)	0.006 (0.294)
−0.8	30.569	4.373 (0.144)	3.756 (0.781)	0.321 (0.581)	0.021 (0.293)	0.011 (0.291)	0.012 (0.291)

Note Averages based on 10,000 trials. Each cell shows the mean of K_h estimates with its standard deviation in parentheses

Table 2.17 2.5% and 97.5% quantiles of OLS estimates of K_h (The case sample size is 100): part I

p	Theoretical value of K_h	σ_v					
		0.05	0.1	0.25	0.5	1.0	2.0
2.0	−0.292	−0.172 0.147	−0.137 0.217	0.048 0.621	−0.013 0.961	−0.427 0.708	−0.565 0.604
1.7	0.068	0.141 0.447	0.165 0.508	0.258 0.820	0.066 1.034	−0.426 0.715	−0.546 0.587
1.5	0.300	0.348 0.651	0.361 0.699	0.414 0.964	0.135 1.080	−0.424 0.728	−0.563 0.617
1.3	0.529	0.555 0.865	0.560 0.899	0.573 1.114	0.206 1.152	−0.410 0.736	−0.559 0.610
1.1	0.759	0.770 1.079	0.770 1.117	0.748 1.291	0.299 1.267	−0.401 0.766	−0.542 0.604
1.0	0.875	0.875 1.197	0.877 1.226	0.848 1.381	0.361 1.325	−0.401 0.741	−0.547 0.615
0.9	0.992	0.987 1.317	0.985 1.345	0.935 1.484	0.408 1.362	−0.376 0.788	−0.546 0.602
0.8	1.113	1.093 1.445	1.098 1.475	1.040 1.589	0.472 1.431	−0.394 0.776	−0.527 0.618

(continued)

Table 2.17 (continued)

p	Theoretical value of K_h	σ_v					
		0.05	0.1	0.25	0.5	1.0	2.0
0.7	1.237	1.211 1.580	1.210 1.596	1.143 1.708	0.532 1.510	−0.378 0.822	−0.541 0.615
0.6	1.365	1.332 1.734	1.329 1.833	1.251 1.603	0.608 1.603	−0.363 0.817	−0.553 0.613
0.5	1.501	1.456 1.866	1.450 1.892	1.368 1.981	0.674 1.712	−0.350 0.841	−0.532 0.617
0.4	1.644	1.587 2.034	1.578 2.051	1.485 2.117	0.763 1.810	−0.342 0.830	−0.523 0.602
0.3	1.800	1.728 2.219	1.716 2.229	1.624 2.291	0.851 1.943	−0.340 0.869	−0.531 0.624
0.2	1.970	1.879 2.418	1.871 2.431	1.767 2.483	0.930 2.083	−0.318 0.886	−0.539 0.614
0.1	2.161	2.041 2.634	2.028 2.657	1.916 2.678	1.003 2.214	−0.311 0.897	−0.535 0.613

Note Averages based on 10,000 trials. Each cell shows the 2.5% quantile of K_h estimates on the first line, and the 97.5% quantile on the second line

Table 2.18 2.5% and 97.5% quantiles of OLS estimates of K_h (The case sample size is 100): part II

p	Theoretical value of K_h	σ_v					
		0.05	0.1	0.25	0.5	1.0	2.0
0.0	2.381	2.220 2.885	2.204 2.912	2.077 2.940	1.094 2.404	−0.316 0.914	−0.541 0.647
−0.1	2.643	2.408 3.170	2.404 3.173	2.259 3.198	1.172 2.625	−0.319 0.942	−0.557 0.623
−0.2	2.966	2.624 3.454	2.623 3.467	2.458 3.466	1.251 2.898	−0.335 0.941	−0.541 0.615
−0.3	3.390	2.857 3.762	2.850 3.769	2.678 3.756	1.242 3.079	−0.369 0.948	−0.559 0.632
−0.4	3.985	3.134 4.049	3.113 4.055	2.900 4.013	1.147 3.323	−0.388 0.940	−0.564 0.617
−0.5	4.918	3.404 4.273	3.390 4.267	3.097 4.221	0.822 3.452	−0.453 0.831	−0.546 0.603
−0.6	6.644	3.665 4.411	3.623 4.408	3.108 4.354	0.214 3.265	−0.506 0.735	−0.548 0.577
−0.7	10.922	3.859 4.476	3.796 4.466	1.674 4.381	−0.364 2.026	−0.552 0.609	−0.563 0.593
−0.8	30.569	3.946 4.493	1.579 4.508	−0.447 1.964	−0.545 0.606	−0.565 0.598	−0.552 0.591

Note Averages based on 10,000 trials. Each cell shows the 2.5% quantile of K_h estimates on the first line, and the 97.5% quantile on the second line

Table 2.19 95% quantiles of OLS estimates of K_h (The case sample size is 100)

p	Theoretical value of K_h	σ_v					
		0.05	0.1	0.25	0.5	1.0	2.0
2.0	−0.292	0.121	0.188	0.571	0.868	0.595	0.497
1.7	0.068	0.423	0.476	0.768	0.942	0.610	0.494
1.5	0.300	0.625	0.669	0.907	0.991	0.628	0.511
1.3	0.529	0.837	0.870	1.060	1.065	0.630	0.508
1.1	0.759	1.054	1.086	1.236	1.166	0.659	0.502
1.0	0.875	1.167	1.194	1.326	1.234	0.654	0.511
0.9	0.992	1.287	1.312	1.428	1.269	0.680	0.501
0.8	1.113	1.412	1.436	1.532	1.331	0.674	0.515
0.7	1.237	1.545	1.561	1.652	1.418	0.709	0.514
0.6	1.365	1.684	1.696	1.776	1.496	0.715	0.516
0.5	1.501	1.830	1.848	1.914	1.594	0.728	0.516
0.4	1.644	1.993	2.006	2.052	1.687	0.726	0.506
0.3	1.800	2.173	2.183	2.225	1.816	0.752	0.524
0.2	1.970	2.376	2.380	2.406	1.956	0.766	0.513
0.1	2.161	2.589	2.599	2.610	2.084	0.775	0.508
0.0	2.381	2.834	2.852	2.847	2.261	0.791	0.528
−0.1	2.643	3.110	3.109	3.109	2.454	0.794	0.519
−0.2	2.966	3.399	3.404	3.383	2.700	0.797	0.519
−0.3	3.390	3.710	3.708	3.676	2.889	0.801	0.535
−0.4	3.985	4.007	4.008	3.947	3.129	0.792	0.518
−0.5	4.918	4.246	4.238	4.168	3.244	0.703	0.504
−0.6	6.644	4.396	4.390	4.314	2.974	0.602	0.479
−0.7	10.922	4.470	4.457	4.315	1.626	0.508	0.481
−0.8	30.569	4.487	4.466	1.467	0.497	0.485	0.484

Note Averages based on 10,000 trials. Each cell shows the 95% quantile of K_h estimates

Table 2.20 Skewness of OLS residuals (The case sample size is 100): part I

p	σ_v					
	0.05	0.1	0.25	0.5	1.0	2.0
2.0	−0.586 (0.197)	−0.525 (0.203)	−0.285 (0.220)	−0.086 (0.235)	−0.016 (0.235)	0.004 (0.238)
1.7	−0.661 (0.208)	−0.596 (0.216)	−0.321 (0.227)	−0.098 (0.235)	−0.017 (0.240)	−0.005 (0.241)
1.5	−0.721 (0.221)	−0.642 (0.223)	−0.348 (0.231)	−0.109 (0.238)	−0.019 (0.239)	−0.005 (0.235)
1.3	−0.792 (0.236)	−0.703 (0.236)	−0.377 (0.244)	−0.116 (0.240)	−0.025 (0.238)	−0.002 (0.240)
1.1	−0.866 (0.255)	−0.766 (0.248)	−0.413 (0.252)	−0.126 (0.244)	−0.027 (0.237)	−0.003 (0.235)

(continued)

Table 2.20 (continued)

p	σ_v					
	0.05	0.1	0.25	0.5	1.0	2.0
1.0	−0.906 (0.265)	−0.805 (0.262)	−0.427 (0.259)	−0.128 (0.244)	−0.021 (0.239)	−0.001 (0.239)
0.9	−0.955 (0.275)	−0.850 (0.272)	−0.452 (0.265)	−0.130 (0.248)	−0.025 (0.238)	−0.001 (0.239)
0.8	−1.005 (0.289)	−0.889 (0.287)	−0.464 (0.269)	−0.138 (0.251)	−0.025 (0.241)	−0.002 (0.237)
0.7	−1.067 (0.305)	−0.933 (0.298)	−0.481 (0.278)	−0.140 (0.249)	−0.021 (0.239)	−0.005 (0.236)
0.6	−1.128 (0.325)	−0.989 (0.312)	−0.510 (0.288)	−0.144 (0.253)	−0.028 (0.238)	−0.006 (0.239)
0.5	−1.196 (0.345)	−1.047 (0.338)	−0.527 (0.298)	−0.155 (0.255)	−0.030 (0.239)	−0.006 (0.240)
0.4	−1.268 (0.366)	−1.109 (0.366)	−0.547 (0.313)	−0.156 (0.261)	−0.025 (0.241)	−0.002 (0.241)
0.3	−1.352 (0.392)	−1.180 (0.392)	−0.571 (0.332)	−0.165 (0.260)	−0.029 (0.240)	−0.003 (0.235)
0.2	−1.449 (0.434)	−1.252 (0.417)	−0.591 (0.344)	−0.166 (0.264)	−0.030 (0.241)	−0.001 (0.238)
0.1	−1.563 (0.479)	−1.329 (0.458)	−0.608 (0.375)	−0.162 (0.272)	−0.025 (0.242)	−0.004 (0.242)

Note Averages based on 10,000 trials. Each cell shows the mean and standard deviation of the skewness. Standard deviations are in parentheses

Table 2.21 Skewness of OLS residuals (The case sample size is 100): part II

p	σ_v					
	0.05	0.1	0.25	0.5	1.0	2.0
0.0	−1.679 (0.526)	−1.427 (0.516)	−0.629 (0.398)	−0.163 (0.272)	−0.027 (0.242)	−0.009 (0.236)
−0.1	−1.809 (0.596)	−1.501 (0.572)	−0.623 (0.412)	−0.153 (0.282)	−0.024 (0.243)	−0.005 (0.233)
−0.2	−1.980 (0.680)	−1.598 (0.638)	−0.617 (0.457)	−0.151 (0.280)	−0.022 (0.240)	−0.003 (0.241)
−0.3	−2.148 (0.763)	−1.676 (0.734)	−0.602 (0.496)	−0.125 (0.279)	−0.014 (0.243)	−0.004 (0.239)
−0.4	−2.344 (0.911)	−1.721 (0.864)	−0.522 (0.521)	−0.109 (0.521)	−0.017 (0.240)	−0.003 (0.241)
−0.5	−2.528 (1.078)	−1.639 (0.995)	−0.399 (0.498)	−0.077 (0.273)	−0.011 (0.239)	−0.004 (0.236)
−0.6	−2.465 (1.298)	−1.299 (1.099)	−0.233 (0.459)	−0.043 (0.258)	−0.004 (0.244)	−0.002 (0.237)

(continued)

Table 2.21 (continued)

p	σ_v					
	0.05	0.1	0.25	0.5	1.0	2.0
−0.7	−1.688 (1.469)	−0.592 (0.896)	−0.080 (0.318)	−0.012 (0.247)	−0.000 (0.239)	−0.002 (0.237)
−0.8	−0.271 (0.769)	−0.054 (0.336)	−0.003 (0.240)	0.001 (0.239)	−0.003 (0.238)	0.001 (0.239)

Note Averages based on 10,000 trials. Each cell shows the mean and standard deviation of the skewness of K_h estimates. Standard deviations are in parentheses

Table 2.22 OLS estimates of K_h (The case $p = 0$)

Sample size	σ_v					
	0.05	0.1	0.25	0.5	1.0	2.0
50	2.350 (0.203)	2.337 (0.206)	2.220 (0.241)	1.392 (0.376)	0.226 (0.350)	0.033 (0.320)
80	2.497 (0.188)	2.492 (0.195)	2.400 (0.232)	1.585 (0.351)	0.265 (0.326)	0.038 (0.301)
100	2.533 (0.176)	2.529 (0.182)	2.460 (0.220)	1.674 (0.336)	0.280 (0.314)	0.045 (0.292)
120	2.553 (0.163)	2.548 (0.170)	2.490 (0.206)	1.736 (0.324)	0.294 (0.308)	0.038 (0.284)
150	2.555 (0.145)	2.555 (0.152)	2.515 (0.191)	1.796 (0.296)	0.312 (0.296)	0.039 (0.279)
200	2.549 (0.125)	2.549 (0.129)	2.521 (0.165)	1.872 (0.267)	0.332 (0.281)	0.041 (0.270)
250	2.534 (0.107)	2.535 (0.114)	2.515 (0.141)	1.923 (0.242)	0.349 (0.277)	0.043 (0.265)
300	2.518 (0.096)	2.522 (0.104)	2.507 (0.127)	1.954 (0.223)	0.363 (0.273)	0.038 (0.262)
400	2.492 (0.079)	2.493 (0.082)	2.490 (0.106)	2.006 (0.199)	0.392 (0.265)	0.048 (0.255)
500	2.471 (0.070)	2.473 (0.072)	2.471 (0.090)	2.046 (0.178)	0.416 (0.258)	0.046 (0.259)
700	2.443 (0.053)	2.446 (0.056)	2.446 (0.073)	2.092 (0.148)	0.462 (0.255)	0.045 (0.258)
1000	2.419 (0.043)	2.420 (0.043)	2.423 (0.056)	2.138 (0.123)	0.512 (0.253)	0.046 (0.264)
2000	2.387 (0.027)	2.388 (0.028)	2.390 (0.036)	2.216 (0.086)	0.670 (0.249)	0.055 (0.277)
3000	2.376 (0.021)	2.376 (0.022)	2.378 (0.028)	2.252 (0.071)	0.787 (0.243)	0.068 (0.297)

Note Averages based on 10,000 trials. Standard deviations are shown in parentheses

Table 2.23 2.5% and 97.5% quantiles of OLS estimates of K_h (The case $p = 0$)

Sample size	σ_v					
	0.05	0.1	0.25	0.5	1.0	2.0
50	1.985 2.748	1.963 2.754	1.791 2.731	0.739 2.213	−0.433 0.912	−0.584 0.676
80	2.157 2.872	2.146 2.889	1.997 2.911	0.986 2.365	−0.337 0.942	−0.562 0.640
100	2.219 2.889	2.204 2.899	2.072 2.924	1.106 2.441	−0.316 0.924	−0.526 0.618
120	2.253 2.879	2.241 2.898	2.134 2.938	1.188 2.471	−0.293 0.908	−0.521 0.590
150	2.289 2.846	2.282 2.867	2.182 2.930	1.287 2.444	−0.254 0.901	−0.516 0.584
200	2.317 2.798	2.312 2.814	2.234 2.883	1.409 2.482	−0.222 0.904	−0.493 0.585
250	2.332 2.752	2.329 2.764	2.264 2.822	1.493 2.459	−0.188 0.911	−0.477 0.572
300	2.338 2.713	2.335 2.727	2.279 2.781	1.563 2.439	−0.160 0.918	−0.468 0.565
400	2.342 2.651	2.341 2.660	2.302 2.706	1.648 2.430	−0.119 0.922	−0.445 0.559
500	2.345 2.607	2.342 2.613	2.313 2.658	1.723 2.410	−0.090 0.946	−0.462 0.559
700	2.342 2.550	2.341 2.559	2.316 2.592	1.816 2.404	−0.040 0.979	−0.461 0.559
1000	2.341 2.502	2.339 2.508	2.319 2.536	1.907 2.390	0.024 1.038	−0.455 0.587
2000	2.335 2.439	2.335 2.443	2.323 2.461	2.052 2.388	0.177 1.162	−0.493 0.587
3000	2.333 2.417	2.334 2.419	2.325 2.433	2.117 2.393	0.312 1.270	−0.513 0.643

Note Averages based on 10,000 trials. Each cell shows the 2.5% quantile of K_h estimates on the first line, and the 97.5% quantile on the second line

Table 2.24 95% quantiles of OLS estimates of K_h (The case $p = 0$)

Sample size	σ_v					
	0.05	0.1	0.25	0.5	1.0	2.0
50	2.697	2.693	2.650	2.044	0.786	0.556
80	2.821	2.828	2.813	2.214	0.802	0.524
100	2.836	2.837	2.845	2.272	0.807	0.517
120	2.829	2.840	2.855	2.315	0.796	0.499
150	2.798	2.815	2.851	2.314	0.791	0.492
200	2.760	2.769	2.810	2.353	0.797	0.484
250	2.714	2.725	2.763	2.343	0.804	0.475

(continued)

Table 2.24 (continued)

Sample size	σ_v					
	0.05	0.1	0.25	0.5	1.0	2.0
300	2.682	2.688	2.730	2.342	0.818	0.475
400	2.623	2.633	2.670	2.347	0.839	0.460
500	2.582	2.590	2.627	2.341	0.847	0.470
700	2.532	2.540	2.567	2.346	0.886	0.478
1000	2.488	2.492	2.518	2.345	0.943	0.494
2000	2.431	2.434	2.449	2.359	1.079	0.503
3000	2.411	2.412	2.424	2.369	1.187	0.536

Note Averages based on 10,000 trials. Each cell shows the 95% quantile of K_h estimates

Table 2.25 Skewness of OLS residuals (The case $p = 0$)

Sample size	σ_v					
	0.05	0.1	0.25	0.5	1.0	2.0
50	−1.527 (0.606)	−1.290 (0.590)	−0.568 (0.485)	−0.148 (0.364)	−0.027 (0.331)	−0.001 (0.324)
80	−1.650 (0.566)	−1.377 (0.530)	−0.612 (0.425)	−0.159 (0.302)	−0.024 (0.270)	−0.000 (0.262)
100	−1.684 (0.531)	−1.421 (0.512)	−0.633 (0.400)	−0.167 (0.273)	−0.025 (0.241)	−0.003 (0.236)
120	−1.712 (0.512)	−1.443 (0.488)	−0.643 (0.371)	−0.168 (0.251)	−0.024 (0.220)	−0.003 (0.219)
150	−1.741 (0.482)	−1.467 (0.456)	−0.649 (0.337)	−0.169 (0.231)	−0.027 (0.200)	−0.004 (0.195)
200	−1.772 (0.441)	−1.498 (0.412)	−0.661 (0.304)	−0.172 (0.200)	−0.029 (0.171)	−0.005 (0.171)
250	−1.790 (0.404)	−1.515 (0.385)	−0.671 (0.276)	−0.174 (0.181)	−0.028 (0.156)	−0.002 (0.152)
300	−1.813 (0.391)	−1.531 (0.362)	−0.676 (0.255)	−0.170 (0.165)	−0.027 (0.142)	−0.005 (0.140)
400	−1.820 (0.345)	−1.547 (0.320)	−0.687 (0.228)	−0.173 (0.144)	−0.029 (0.125)	−0.005 (0.122)
500	−1.834 (0.313)	−1.551 (0.287)	−0.686 (0.206)	−0.173 (0.130)	−0.029 (0.111)	−0.003 (0.110)
700	−1.845 (0.269)	−1.568 (0.259)	−0.690 (0.173)	−0.176 (0.110)	−0.027 (0.094)	−0.005 (0.093)
1000	−1.855 (0.231)	−1.571 (0.213)	−0.696 (0.149)	−0.178 (0.093)	−0.027 (0.077)	−0.004 (0.078)
2000	−1.869 (0.170)	−1.584 (0.155)	−0.701 (0.106)	−0.177 (0.065)	−0.029 (0.055)	−0.004 (0.055)
3000	−1.871 (0.138)	−1.588 (0.129)	−0.700 (0.088)	−0.178 (0.053)	−0.028 (0.046)	−0.003 (0.045)

Note Averages based on 10,000 trials. Each cell shows the mean of skewness estimates in the top row and their standard deviations in parentheses in the bottom row

Table 2.26 OLS estimates of K_h (Square normal-type distribution with $a = 0$): part I

σ_v	Sample size						
	50	100	150	200	500	1000	3000
0.00	2.705 (0.224)	3.095 (0.285)	3.229 (0.308)	3.280 (0.308)	3.246 (0.230)	3.158 (0.139)	3.062 (0.053)
0.01	2.704 (0.226)	3.100 (0.290)	3.227 (0.303)	3.277 (0.306)	3.247 (0.230)	3.161 (0.141)	3.062 (0.053)
0.05	2.707 (0.231)	3.095 (0.287)	3.230 (0.307)	3.276 (0.316)	3.256 (0.245)	3.160 (0.141)	3.062 (0.054)
0.10	2.703 (0.227)	3.098 (0.289)	3.229 (0.307)	3.277 (0.317)	3.248 (0.231)	3.159 (0.141)	3.062 (0.053)
0.20	2.702 (0.227)	3.091 (0.287)	3.232 (0.317)	3.278 (0.312)	3.259 (0.254)	3.162 (0.142)	3.061 (0.052)
0.30	2.698 (0.226)	3.096 (0.286)	3.232 (0.309)	3.277 (0.313)	3.252 (0.239)	3.161 (0.152)	3.062 (0.053)
0.40	2.694 (0.229)	3.096 (0.289)	3.225 (0.313)	3.277 (0.313)	3.249 (0.232)	3.160 (0.139)	3.063 (0.054)
0.50	2.688 (0.231)	3.092 (0.290)	3.223 (0.310)	3.274 (0.312)	3.251 (0.239)	3.164 (0.143)	3.063 (0.054)
0.60	2.675 (0.234)	3.083 (0.297)	3.220 (0.313)	3.275 (0.325)	3.254 (0.238)	3.162 (0.143)	3.064 (0.054)
0.70	2.666 (0.236)	3.074 (0.291)	3.216 (0.318)	3.269 (0.317)	3.254 (0.243)	3.166 (0.149)	3.064 (0.056)
0.80	2.652 (0.238)	3.064 (0.297)	3.209 (0.324)	3.267 (0.324)	3.258 (0.247)	3.167 (0.153)	3.065 (0.056)
0.90	2.632 (0.244)	3.048 (0.302)	3.193 (0.314)	3.250 (0.314)	3.250 (0.251)	3.165 (0.150)	3.066 (0.059)
1.00	2.614 (0.251)	3.026 (0.303)	3.179 (0.320)	3.247 (0.322)	3.252 (0.257)	3.164 (0.156)	3.066 (0.060)
1.10	2.586 (0.258)	3.005 (0.309)	3.158 (0.321)	3.220 (0.318)	3.238 (0.241)	3.165 (0.154)	3.066 (0.060)
1.20	2.554 (0.267)	2.980 (0.311)	3.133 (0.329)	3.204 (0.332)	3.231 (0.249)	3.160 (0.157)	3.065 (0.061)
1.30	2.518 (0.277)	2.941 (0.321)	3.111 (0.342)	3.186 (0.340)	3.222 (0.260)	3.152 (0.156)	3.062 (0.063)
1.40	2.473 (0.292)	2.906 (0.332)	3.074 (0.345)	3.150 (0.342)	3.198 (0.263)	3.146 (0.171)	3.059 (0.064)

Note Averages based on 10,000 trials. Standard deviations are shown in parentheses

Table 2.27 OLS estimates of K_h (Square normal-type distribution with $a = 0$): part II

σ_v	Sample size						
	50	100	150	200	500	1000	3000
1.50	2.423 (0.304)	2.854 (0.339)	3.027 (0.350)	3.104 (0.352)	3.174 (0.261)	3.132 (0.172)	3.055 (0.065)

(continued)

Table 2.27 (continued)

σ_v	Sample size						
	50	100	150	200	500	1000	3000
1.60	2.365 (0.319)	2.798 (0.356)	2.967 (0.358)	3.055 (0.354)	3.145 (0.271)	3.111 (0.176)	3.049 (0.071)
1.70	2.287 (0.337)	2.726 (0.363)	2.907 (0.374)	2.991 (0.366)	3.104 (0.272)	3.085 (0.175)	3.036 (0.071)
1.80	2.212 (0.357)	2.637 (0.374)	2.826 (0.385)	2.917 (0.372)	3.057 (0.288)	3.052 (0.179)	3.025 (0.076)
1.90	2.121 (0.378)	2.557 (0.398)	2.746 (0.400)	2.832 (0.375)	2.990 (0.281)	3.011 (0.180)	3.009 (0.079)
2.00	2.019 (0.398)	2.448 (0.413)	2.639 (0.408)	2.745 (0.398)	2.923 (0.299)	2.963 (0.192)	2.986 (0.084)
2.20	1.800 (0.432)	2.219 (0.443)	2.403 (0.422)	2.516 (0.406)	2.744 (0.298)	2.836 (0.206)	2.927 (0.096)
2.40	1.581 (0.462)	1.957 (0.462)	2.141 (0.438)	2.272 (0.422)	2.536 (0.315)	2.672 (0.215)	2.841 (0.107)
2.60	1.346 (0.476)	1.689 (0.467)	1.863 (0.449)	1.988 (0.426)	2.295 (0.328)	2.477 (0.224)	2.725 (0.120)
2.80	1.132 (0.471)	1.438 (0.469)	1.601 (0.449)	1.714 (0.432)	2.030 (0.325)	2.255 (0.238)	2.585 (0.136)
3.00	0.950 (0.467)	1.212 (0.462)	1.354 (0.443)	1.452 (0.415)	1.768 (0.317)	2.015 (0.243)	2.411 (0.150)
4.00	0.391 (0.389)	0.497 (0.377)	0.556 (0.353)	0.595 (0.337)	0.769 (0.293)	0.960 (0.265)	1.410 (0.224)
5.00	0.187 (0.349)	0.236 (0.318)	0.257 (0.309)	0.273 (0.298)	0.345 (0.272)	0.425 (0.264)	0.670 (0.269)
6.00	0.106 (0.337)	0.126 (0.304)	0.135 (0.283)	0.145 (0.278)	0.181 (0.266)	0.209 (0.264)	0.320 (0.282)
7.00	0.073 (0.328)	0.080 (0.300)	0.087 (0.281)	0.092 (0.277)	0.107 (0.262)	0.124 (0.265)	0.174 (0.290)
8.00	0.053 (0.321)	0.055 (0.296)	0.058 (0.283)	0.058 (0.270)	0.075 (0.258)	0.075 (0.266)	0.104 (0.296)

Note Averages based on 10,000 trials. Standard deviations are shown in parentheses

Table 2.28 2.5% and 97.5% quantiles of OLS estimates of K_h (Square normal-type distribution with $a = 0$): part I

σ_v	Sample size						
	50	100	150	200	500	1000	3000
0.00	2.311 3.192	2.667 3.803	2.797 4.034	2.868 4.062	2.958 3.825	2.976 3.489	2.977 3.178
0.01	2.308 3.189	2.664 3.806	2.808 4.007	2.867 4.061	2.959 3.815	2.977 3.505	2.976 3.176
0.05	2.308 3.209	2.663 3.811	2.802 4.005	2.853 4.100	2.964 3.886	2.974 3.490	2.977 3.181

(continued)

Table 2.28 (continued)

σ_v	Sample size						
	50	100	150	200	500	1000	3000
0.10	2.305 3.196	2.662 3.809	2.797 4.016	2.861 4.123	2.960 3.833	2.976 3.482	2.977 3.182
0.20	2.308 3.192	2.660 3.799	2.798 4.067	2.860 4.075	2.962 3.876	2.975 3.486	2.975 3.178
0.30	2.311 3.178	2.662 3.811	2.799 4.025	2.859 4.060	2.958 3.839	2.973 3.508	2.977 3.180
0.40	2.303 3.196	2.655 3.797	2.788 4.023	2.855 4.096	2.957 3.820	2.976 3.490	2.977 3.185
0.50	2.286 3.192	2.649 3.791	2.787 4.027	2.854 4.087	2.963 3.831	2.974 3.499	2.977 3.183
0.60	2.277 3.185	2.631 3.821	2.777 4.027	2.848 4.127	2.959 3.857	2.971 3.499	2.975 3.187
0.70	2.257 3.176	2.627 3.768	2.771 4.020	2.847 4.102	2.956 3.863	2.971 3.523	2.975 3.189
0.80	2.238 3.164	2.612 3.776	2.753 4.045	2.829 4.100	2.947 3.897	2.969 3.510	2.973 3.188
0.90	2.203 3.148	2.579 3.767	2.737 3.990	2.821 4.038	2.944 3.886	2.967 3.513	2.974 3.199
1.00	2.175 3.154	2.554 3.759	2.724 3.993	2.799 4.062	2.934 3.911	2.961 3.524	2.971 3.197
1.10	2.129 3.133	2.520 3.747	2.686 3.954	2.771 4.023	2.926 3.841	2.960 3.522	2.966 3.196
1.20	2.083 3.126	2.495 3.732	2.653 3.953	2.743 4.052	2.905 3.848	2.946 3.517	2.967 3.195
1.30	2.030 3.113	2.442 3.719	2.609 3.963	2.726 4.070	2.891 3.851	2.935 3.522	2.959 3.195
1.40	1.958 3.109	2.391 3.696	2.574 3.927	2.667 4.027	2.853 3.824	2.917 3.552	2.955 3.201

Note Averages based on 10,000 trials. Each cell shows the 2.5% quantile of K_h estimates on the first line, and the 97.5% quantile on the second line

Table 2.29 2.5% and 97.5% quantiles of OLS estimates of K_h (Square normal-type distribution with $a = 0$): part II

σ_v	Sample size						
	50	100	150	200	500	1000	3000
1.50	1.894 3.080	2.315 3.664	2.498 3.895	2.606 4.025	2.821 3.823	2.943 3.543	2.944 3.196
1.60	1.793 3.058	2.237 3.655	2.429 3.848	2.543 3.958	2.779 3.820	2.870 3.508	2.931 3.201
1.70	1.689 3.022	2.137 3.589	2.353 3.829	2.461 3.894	2.728 3.664	2.830 3.497	2.915 3.187

(continued)

Table 2.29 (continued)

σ_v	Sample size						
	50	100	150	200	500	1000	3000
1.80	1.575 2.973	2.035 3.534	2.249 3.761	2.363 3.857	2.660 3.788	2.788 3.462	2.896 3.192
1.90	1.451 2.941	1.921 3.503	2.145 3.719	2.271 3.754	2.592 3.664	2.703 3.425	2.870 3.178
2.00	1.320 2.890	1.781 3.433	2.022 3.647	2.156 3.730	2.502 3.606	2.682 3.400	2.838 3.165
2.20	1.056 2.744	1.518 3.269	1.757 3.457	1.902 3.492	2.303 3.456	2.524 3.289	2.755 3.129
2.40	0.785 2.617	1.217 3.070	1.457 3.202	1.626 3.307	2.067 3.255	2.335 3.141	2.647 3.064
2.60	0.541 2.448	0.932 2.778	1.169 2.937	1.328 3.007	1.802 3.030	2.107 2.964	2.506 2.973
2.80	0.323 2.205	0.685 2.543	0.900 2.658	1.046 2.744	1.521 2.767	1.856 2.760	2.334 2.859
3.00	0.167 2.032	0.471 2.286	0.654 2.414	0.802 2.455	1.247 2.477	1.587 2.527	2.125 2.720
4.00	−0.302 1.222	−0.167 1.335	−0.067 1.326	0.005 1.305	0.234 1.364	0.466 1.490	0.986 1.852
5.00	−0.470 0.905	−0.347 0.886	−0.332 0.891	−0.277 0.885	−0.167 0.889	−0.097 0.947	0.149 1.203
6.00	−0.547 0.786	−0.468 0.726	−0.415 0.703	−0.395 0.707	−0.333 0.716	−0.303 0.726	−0.225 0.875
7.00	−0.563 0.722	−0.496 0.685	−0.445 0.646	−0.448 0.641	−0.404 0.615	−0.394 0.646	−0.400 0.750
8.00	−0.590 0.689	−0.515 0.637	−0.485 0.618	−0.469 0.590	−0.430 0.586	−0.451 0.604	−0.477 0.687

Note Averages based on 10,000 trials. Each cell shows the 2.5% quantile of K_h estimates on the first line, and the 97.5% quantile on the second line

Table 2.30 95% quantiles of OLS estimates of K_h (Square normal-type distribution with $a = 0$)

σ_v	Sample size						
	50	100	150	200	500	1000	3000
0.00	3.104	3.650	3.821	3.864	3.649	3.390	3.152
0.01	3.110	3.659	3.808	3.850	3.648	3.391	3.150
0.05	3.125	3.652	3.819	3.878	3.680	3.396	3.153
0.10	3.110	3.662	3.821	3.876	3.661	3.396	3.155
0.20	3.111	3.642	3.846	3.865	3.677	3.390	3.151
0.30	3.104	3.636	3.839	3.868	3.669	3.400	3.154
0.40	3.108	3.645	3.827	3.871	3.655	3.390	3.153
0.50	3.107	3.644	3.812	3.872	3.662	3.402	3.156

(continued)

Table 2.30 (continued)

σ_v	Sample size						
	50	100	150	200	500	1000	3000
0.60	3.102	3.662	3.820	3.903	3.666	3.397	3.156
0.70	3.088	3.621	3.829	3.871	3.679	3.415	3.159
0.80	3.074	3.638	3.847	3.871	3.695	3.414	3.162
0.90	3.070	3.624	3.788	3.832	3.681	3.413	3.165
1.00	3.067	3.603	3.803	3.859	3.705	3.421	3.166
1.10	3.049	3.577	3.763	3.824	3.663	3.422	3.166
1.20	3.036	3.573	3.774	3.818	3.667	3.422	3.167
1.30	3.012	3.558	3.764	3.839	3.665	3.421	3.168
1.40	2.989	3.539	3.720	3.806	3.643	3.434	3.170
1.50	2.968	3.487	3.696	3.764	3.633	3.420	3.165
1.60	2.933	3.476	3.636	3.718	3.627	3.399	3.168
1.70	2.893	3.387	3.616	3.666	3.589	3.382	3.157
1.80	2.839	3.335	3.560	3.627	3.574	3.352	3.152
1.90	2.807	3.303	3.505	3.524	3.486	3.321	3.143
2.00	2.738	3.213	3.407	3.475	3.406	3.282	3.130
2.20	2.586	3.030	3.190	3.255	3.260	3.171	3.086
2.40	2.411	2.800	2.937	3.051	3.081	3.029	3.024
2.60	2.220	2.537	2.671	2.746	2.856	2.852	2.928
2.80	1.973	2.294	2.407	2.480	2.581	2.652	2.812
3.00	1.787	2.053	2.138	2.176	2.315	2.422	2.663
4.00	1.045	1.133	1.143	1.156	1.249	1.403	1.785
5.00	0.756	0.764	0.773	0.772	0.792	0.855	1.112
6.00	0.660	0.621	0.603	0.609	0.625	0.639	0.781
7.00	0.605	0.572	0.545	0.543	0.538	0.556	0.654
8.00	0.572	0.537	0.516	0.507	0.503	0.512	0.593

Note Averages based on 10,000 trials

Table 2.31 Log-log OLS estimates of $\log(K_h)$ (Square normal-type distribution with $a = 0$): part I

σ_v	Sample size						
	50	100	150	200	500	1000	3000
0.00	0.380 (0.033)	0.644 (0.022)	0.749 (0.018)	0.807 (0.017)	0.939 (0.013)	1.000 (0.011)	1.057 (0.008)
0.05	0.379 (0.034)	0.643 (0.022)	0.748 (0.018)	0.807 (0.017)	0.939 (0.013)	1.000 (0.011)	1.057 (0.008)
0.10	0.376 (0.034)	0.641 (0.022)	0.747 (0.018)	0.806 (0.017)	0.938 (0.013)	1.000 (0.011)	1.057 (0.008)

(continued)

Table 2.31 (continued)

σ_v	Sample size						
	50	100	150	200	500	1000	3000
0.20	0.365 (0.035)	0.634 (0.023)	0.743 (0.019)	0.803 (0.017)	0.937 (0.013)	1.000 (0.011)	1.056 (0.008)
0.30	0.350 (0.037)	0.622 (0.024)	0.736 (0.020)	0.799 (0.017)	0.936 (0.013)	0.999 (0.011)	1.056 (0.008)
0.40	0.334 (0.040)	0.604 (0.026)	0.725 (0.021)	0.791 (0.018)	0.933 (0.014)	0.998 (0.011)	1.056 (0.008)
0.50	0.323 (0.042)	0.584 (0.029)	0.710 (0.022)	0.780 (0.019)	0.929 (0.014)	0.996 (0.012)	1.055 (0.009)
0.60	0.320 (0.046)	0.562 (0.032)	0.691 (0.025)	0.766 (0.021)	0.925 (0.014)	0.993 (0.012)	1.054 (0.009)
0.70	0.325 (0.050)	0.543 (0.036)	0.670 (0.028)	0.749 (0.023)	0.919 (0.015)	0.990 (0.012)	1.053 (0.009)
0.80	0.336 (0.055)	0.531 (0.039)	0.649 (0.032)	0.729 (0.026)	0.911 (0.016)	0.987 (0.013)	1.052 (0.009)
0.90	0.351 (0.061)	0.527 (0.044)	0.634 (0.035)	0.709 (0.030)	0.902 (0.017)	0.982 (0.013)	1.050 (0.009)
1.00	0.370 (0.066)	0.533 (0.049)	0.625 (0.041)	0.693 (0.034)	0.890 (0.019)	0.977 (0.014)	1.048 (0.009)
1.10	0.388 (0.073)	0.544 (0.055)	0.623 (0.045)	0.683 (0.039)	0.876 (0.022)	0.971 (0.015)	1.046 (0.010)
1.20	0.408 (0.080)	0.560 (0.061)	0.631 (0.051)	0.681 (0.044)	0.860 (0.025)	0.963 (0.016)	1.044 (0.010)
1.30	0.425 (0.087)	0.581 (0.067)	0.644 (0.056)	0.686 (0.050)	0.844 (0.029)	0.954 (0.018)	1.041 (0.011)
1.40	0.442 (0.093)	0.603 (0.074)	0.664 (0.063)	0.700 (0.055)	0.831 (0.034)	0.942 (0.021)	1.038 (0.012)

Note Averages based on 10,000 trials. Standard deviations are shown in parentheses

Table 2.32 Log-log OLS estimates of $\log(K_h)$ (Square normal-type distribution with $a = 0$): part II

σ_v	Sample size						
	50	100	150	200	500	1000	3000
1.50	0.458 (0.099)	0.624 (0.080)	0.686 (0.070)	0.719 (0.061)	0.823 (0.039)	0.929 (0.024)	1.034 (0.013)
1.60	0.469 (0.108)	0.646 (0.086)	0.708 (0.076)	0.740 (0.067)	0.823 (0.044)	0.915 (0.028)	1.030 (0.014)
1.70	0.482 (0.114)	0.667 (0.095)	0.733 (0.083)	0.764 (0.073)	0.831 (0.050)	0.904 (0.033)	1.024 (0.016)
1.80	0.492 (0.121)	0.684 (0.101)	0.755 (0.089)	0.790 (0.081)	0.846 (0.055)	0.897 (0.039)	1.017 (0.018)

(continued)

Table 2.32 (continued)

σ_v	Sample size						
	50	100	150	200	500	1000	3000
1.90	0.503 (0.130)	0.702 (0.108)	0.778 (0.095)	0.815 (0.087)	0.865 (0.061)	0.897 (0.044)	1.007 (0.021)
2.00	0.511 (0.134)	0.719 (0.114)	0.797 (0.103)	0.838 (0.094)	0.890 (0.069)	0.904 (0.049)	0.997 (0.024)
2.20	0.522 (0.148)	0.746 (0.128)	0.834 (0.115)	0.883 (0.106)	0.948 (0.081)	0.941 (0.061)	0.976 (0.033)
2.40	0.533 (0.159)	0.768 (0.138)	0.868 (0.127)	0.923 (0.120)	1.006 (0.093)	0.996 (0.074)	0.968 (0.043)
2.60	0.540 (0.168)	0.786 (0.150)	0.894 (0.140)	0.953 (0.130)	1.059 (0.105)	1.058 (0.086)	0.988 (0.054)
2.80	0.549 (0.177)	0.800 (0.160)	0.914 (0.149)	0.982 (0.142)	1.110 (0.116)	1.122 (0.097)	1.032 (0.066)
3.00	0.552 (0.186)	0.812 (0.167)	0.933 (0.160)	1.004 (0.152)	1.150 (0.128)	1.179 (0.108)	1.097 (0.077)
4.00	0.567 (0.209)	0.854 (0.198)	0.990 (0.192)	1.070 (0.189)	1.283 (0.172)	1.378 (0.157)	1.427 (0.128)
5.00	0.585 (0.220)	0.871 (0.213)	1.014 (0.210)	1.105 (0.204)	1.345 (0.191)	1.480 (0.183)	1.610 (0.163)
6.00	0.584 (0.226)	0.885 (0.220)	1.027 (0.218)	1.126 (0.215)	1.379 (0.208)	1.526 (0.199)	1.703 (0.183)
7.00	0.590 (0.228)	0.888 (0.226)	1.039 (0.222)	1.134 (0.223)	1.397 (0.213)	1.558 (0.206)	1.756 (0.196)
8.00	0.594 (0.232)	0.893 (0.225)	1.046 (0.225)	1.142 (0.222)	1.408 (0.215)	1.575 (0.211)	1.784 (0.204)

Note Averages based on 10,000 trials. Standard deviations are shown in parentheses

Table 2.33 2.5% and 97.5% quantiles of log-log OLS estimates of $\log(K_h)$ (Square normal-type distribution with $a = 0$): part I

σ_v	Sample size						
	50	100	150	200	500	1000	3000
0.00	0.311 0.443	0.600 0.686	0.713 0.784	0.775 0.839	0.913 0.965	0.979 1.022	1.041 1.073
0.01	0.312 0.444	0.601 0.685	0.713 0.784	0.775 0.840	0.913 0.965	0.979 1.023	1.041 1.073
0.05	0.310 0.442	0.599 0.685	0.713 0.784	0.775 0.840	0.913 0.965	0.979 1.023	1.041 1.073
0.10	0.306 0.441	0.598 0.683	0.711 0.783	0.774 0.839	0.913 0.965	0.978 1.022	1.041 1.073
0.20	0.294 0.432	0.589 0.678	0.706 0.779	0.769 0.836	0.911 0.963	0.978 1.022	1.040 1.073
0.30	0.272 0.421	0.574 0.668	0.696 0.774	0.764 0.833	0.909 0.961	0.977 1.022	1.040 1.072

(continued)

Table 2.33 (continued)

σ_v	Sample size						
	50	100	150	200	500	1000	3000
0.40	0.253 0.409	0.551 0.653	0.684 0.765	0.755 0.826	0.906 0.959	0.975 1.020	1.040 1.072
0.50	0.238 0.403	0.524 0.638	0.666 0.753	0.743 0.817	0.902 0.957	0.973 1.018	1.038 1.071
0.60	0.226 0.407	0.497 0.622	0.641 0.738	0.726 0.807	0.897 0.953	0.970 1.016	1.037 1.071
0.70	0.224 0.422	0.470 0.611	0.614 0.722	0.703 0.793	0.889 0.948	0.967 1.014	1.036 1.070
0.80	0.224 0.441	0.452 0.606	0.585 0.711	0.675 0.779	0.880 0.943	0.962 1.012	1.034 1.069
0.90	0.233 0.469	0.439 0.613	0.563 0.702	0.648 0.766	0.868 0.935	0.957 1.008	1.033 1.069
1.00	0.239 0.499	0.435 0.626	0.542 0.701	0.625 0.759	0.852 0.927	0.950 1.004	1.029 1.067
1.10	0.243 0.529	0.435 0.652	0.531 0.710	0.604 0.757	0.833 0.917	0.942 1.000	1.027 1.066
1.20	0.251 0.562	0.437 0.679	0.527 0.728	0.595 0.766	0.809 0.908	0.931 0.996	1.024 1.065
1.30	0.254 0.593	0.450 0.710	0.533 0.753	0.588 0.783	0.786 0.900	0.916 0.989	1.020 1.063
1.40	0.261 0.627	0.454 0.747	0.539 0.785	0.591 0.807	0.764 0.895	0.900 0.981	1.016 1.061

Note Averages based on 10,000 trials. Each cell shows the 2.5% quantile of $\log(K_h)$ estimates on the first line, and the 97.5% quantile on the second line

Table 2.34 2.5% and 97.5% quantiles of log-log OLS estimates of $\log(K_h)$ (Square normal-type distribution with $a = 0$): part II

σ_v	Sample size						
	50	100	150	200	500	1000	3000
1.50	0.268 0.654	0.466 0.778	0.547 0.822	0.599 0.838	0.746 0.897	0.880 0.976	1.009 1.059
1.60	0.253 0.680	0.476 0.814	0.560 0.857	0.607 0.870	0.735 0.909	0.859 0.969	1.002 1.058
1.70	0.262 0.707	0.480 0.852	0.574 0.895	0.620 0.910	0.731 0.926	0.837 0.967	0.993 1.055
1.80	0.260 0.732	0.490 0.884	0.580 0.930	0.632 0.950	0.735 0.953	0.819 0.971	0.981 1.052
1.90	0.250 0.761	0.490 0.916	0.593 0.967	0.645 0.984	0.744 0.985	0.811 0.983	0.966 1.048
2.00	0.249 0.789	0.499 0.945	0.606 0.999	0.655 1.015	0.748 1.017	0.799 0.995	0.952 1.044

(continued)

Table 2.34 (continued)

σ_v	Sample size						
	50	100	150	200	500	1000	3000
2.20	0.251 0.848	0.510 1.005	0.629 1.060	0.676 1.080	0.764 1.076	0.779 1.015	0.919 1.036
2.40	0.250 0.907	0.519 1.064	0.647 1.117	0.693 1.141	0.779 1.135	0.766 1.035	0.895 1.026
2.60	0.250 0.967	0.524 1.121	0.661 1.172	0.709 1.201	0.794 1.195	0.754 1.054	0.869 1.017
2.80	0.250 1.026	0.529 1.177	0.674 1.227	0.724 1.260	0.809 1.255	0.742 1.074	0.842 1.009
3.00	0.251 1.085	0.532 1.231	0.685 1.281	0.737 1.318	0.822 1.314	0.729 1.093	0.814 1.000
4.00	0.248 1.329	0.544 1.461	0.725 1.505	0.783 1.533	0.883 1.536	0.662 1.201	0.648 0.905
5.00	0.247 1.451	0.547 1.589	0.737 1.631	0.797 1.655	0.907 1.657	0.657 1.232	0.582 0.822
6.00	0.244 1.534	0.547 1.674	0.746 1.715	0.807 1.737	0.924 1.737	0.661 1.270	0.539 0.776
7.00	0.240 1.594	0.546 1.729	0.753 1.770	0.814 1.790	0.936 1.788	0.669 1.305	0.513 0.746
8.00	0.236 1.643	0.543 1.771	0.758 1.811	0.819 1.830	0.945 1.827	0.677 1.338	0.496 0.728

Note Averages based on 10,000 trials. Each cell shows the 2.5% quantile of $\log(K_h)$ estimates on the first line, and the 97.5% quantile on the second line

Table 2.35 95% quantiles of log-log OLS estimates of $\log(K_h)$ (Square normal-type distribution with $a = 0$)

σ_v	Sample size						
	50	100	150	200	500	1000	3000
0.00	0.433	0.679	0.778	0.834	0.960	1.019	1.070
0.01	0.433	0.678	0.779	0.835	0.960	1.019	1.070
0.05	0.433	0.678	0.778	0.834	0.961	1.019	1.070
0.10	0.430	0.676	0.777	0.834	0.960	1.018	1.070
0.20	0.422	0.671	0.773	0.831	0.959	1.018	1.070
0.30	0.410	0.660	0.768	0.827	0.957	1.018	1.070
0.40	0.397	0.646	0.758	0.820	0.955	1.016	1.069
0.50	0.390	0.630	0.746	0.811	0.953	1.015	1.069
0.60	0.393	0.613	0.731	0.800	0.948	1.013	1.068
0.70	0.407	0.600	0.714	0.786	0.943	1.010	1.067
0.80	0.424	0.594	0.700	0.771	0.937	1.008	1.066
0.90	0.451	0.599	0.690	0.757	0.930	1.004	1.066
1.00	0.479	0.612	0.690	0.748	0.921	1.000	1.064

(continued)

Table 2.35 (continued)

σ_v	Sample size						
	50	100	150	200	500	1000	3000
1.10	0.506	0.633	0.696	0.746	0.911	0.995	1.063
1.20	0.539	0.658	0.712	0.753	0.901	0.990	1.061
1.30	0.566	0.690	0.737	0.768	0.892	0.983	1.059
1.40	0.596	0.722	0.766	0.789	0.886	0.975	1.058
1.50	0.622	0.754	0.801	0.820	0.886	0.968	1.055
1.60	0.645	0.788	0.834	0.851	0.896	0.961	1.053
1.70	0.669	0.824	0.869	0.885	0.912	0.957	1.050
1.80	0.689	0.850	0.901	0.921	0.936	0.959	1.047
1.90	0.717	0.881	0.938	0.958	0.966	0.969	1.042
2.00	0.729	0.906	0.966	0.995	1.003	0.985	1.037
2.20	0.763	0.958	1.026	1.056	1.080	1.041	1.029
2.40	0.792	0.994	1.079	1.117	1.157	1.116	1.038
2.60	0.818	1.033	1.125	1.169	1.229	1.198	1.076
2.80	0.842	1.065	1.157	1.218	1.301	1.283	1.140
3.00	0.856	1.089	1.194	1.253	1.362	1.359	1.222
4.00	0.909	1.186	1.309	1.386	1.567	1.638	1.639
5.00	0.947	1.228	1.361	1.444	1.658	1.788	1.881
6.00	0.957	1.250	1.391	1.482	1.724	1.859	2.005
7.00	0.968	1.268	1.406	1.505	1.749	1.901	2.078
8.00	0.981	1.266	1.419	1.519	1.770	1.930	2.120

Note Averages based on 10,000 trials

References

Doornik JA, Hansen H (2008) An omnibus test for univariate and multivariate normality. Oxf Bull Econ Stat 70:927–939

Elteto T, Molnar S (1999) On the distribution of round-trip delays in TCP/IP networks. In: Proceedings 24th Conference on Local Computer Networks. LCN'99, pp 172–181. IEEE

Greene WH (1990) A gamma-distributed stochastic frontier model. J Econ 46(1–2):141–163

Lee L-f (1983) On maximum likelihood estimation of stochastic frontier production models. J Econ 23(2):269–274

Oikawa K (2016) A microfoundation for stochastic frontier analysis. Econ Lett 139:15–17

Rahman M, Gokhale DV (1996) On estimation of parameters of the exponential power family of distributions. Commun Stat-Simul Comput 25(2):291–299

Schmidt P, Lin T-F (1984) Simple tests of alternative specifications in stochastic frontier models. J Econ 24(3):349–361

Shenton LR, Bowman KO (1977) A bivariate model for the distribution of $\sqrt{b1}$ and b2. J Am Stat Assoc 72(357):206–211

Stevenson RE (1980) Likelihood functions for generalized stochastic frontier estimation. J Econ 13(1):57–66

Teigen, LD (1995) Weather and yield, 1950-94: relationships, distributions, and data. Report No 9527, Economic Research Service, Commercial Agriculture Division

Torii A (2001) Efficiency in Japanese industries. NTT Publishing, Tokyo (in Japanese)
Tsionas MG (2017) Microfoundations for stochastic frontiers. Eur J Oper Res 258(3):1165–1170
Tsionas MG (2023) Bayesian learning in performance. Is there any? Eur J Oper Res 311(1):263–282
Wang WS, Amsler C, Schmidt P (2011) Goodness of fit tests in stochastic frontier models. J Prod Anal 35:95–118
Yu Q, Du B, Sun Q (2006) Earnings management at rights issues thresholds—evidence from China. J Bank Financ 30(12):3453–3468

Chapter 3
Dynamic Model Explaining the Asymmetric Distribution of Deviations from the Production Frontier

In this chapter, we present a stochastic process model to trace the mechanism of inefficiency generation for testing the existence of X-inefficiency. By setting up a stochastic process model, we demonstrate that technical inefficiency, which has traditionally tended to be viewed as a static phenomenon, can be understood as arising from the dynamic mechanism described in the stochastic process model. Before the relationship between the concepts of technical inefficiency and X-inefficiency is discussed in detail in Chapter 4, the mechanism of technical inefficiency generation is investigated here in this chapter. The technical inefficiency considered in this chapter is defined as a downward deviation from the production frontier, following Farrell's definition. If technical inefficiency, defined as a deviation from the frontier, exhibits an asymmetric distribution, it can be observed through SFA. However, if it does not form an asymmetric distribution, it cannot be detected by SFA. When such a distinction is crucial in the discussion in this chapter, the terms "observable technical inefficiency" and "unobservable technical inefficiency" or similar expressions are explicitly stated in the text.

Technical inefficiency and X-inefficiency have been viewed in a static manner. One method of estimating technical inefficiency is the distribution-free estimates proposed in Berger (1993). This method typically assumes that the productivity of individual samples is stable over time. Here, "stable" refers to a setting in which the technical inefficiency level for each sample is exogenously given to the system as a fixed value and does not change over time. Schmidt and Sickles (1984), who were the first to estimate the level of technical inefficiency using panel data, assumed that the level of technical inefficiency is unique to each sample and does not vary over time. This assumption was relaxed in Cornwell, Schmidt and Sickles (1990), who allowed for the possibility that the technical inefficiency level varies slowly over time. In both cases, however, they were based on the idea that both the technical inefficiency level and its changes are given as fixed values. By assuming that the observed technical inefficiency represents X-inefficiency, researchers have been able to avoid considering the mechanism of technical inefficiency generation. Instead, it

A. Torii, *Production Efficiency with the Stochastic Management Model*,
https://doi.org/10.1007/978-981-95-3501-9_3

has been treated as exogenously given to the statistical model system, while *a priori* assuming a distribution type for technical inefficiency that facilitates estimation in most studies.[1]

This chapter introduces two dynamic models: a putty-clay-type vintage inefficiency model and a model describing managerial inefficiency. By formulating a stochastic process model, we show that a specific distributional form of technical inefficiency corresponds to a model of technical inefficiency. This correspondence is not one-to-one. However, by testing hypotheses regarding the distributional form of technical inefficiency and its shape parameters, it is possible to test hypotheses about the mechanism by which inefficiency arises. In the process of setting up the two models, we will show that the managerial inefficiency model presented here can also be described as basically the same mechanism as the vintage-type model. This implies that by analyzing the vintage-type model, we can not only analyze the inefficiency due to the obsolescence of invested facilities, but also analyze a wide range of inefficiency generation mechanisms to some extent.

3.1 Vintage Inefficiency Model

A few studies have captured the mechanism of the occurrence of technical inefficiency in a dynamic model. Among studies that have carefully attempted to estimate the production function of specific industries, some have used the vintage model approach for the mechanism of technological inefficiency. A representative example is the study by Førsund and Hjalmarsson (1987), which is based on the putty-clay approach. They constructed a model with an explicit vintage structure, assuming that the productivity of each establishment reflects the technology in place at the time when it was set up. It is assumed that newly constructed machinery and equipment will exhibit a much higher productivity; therefore, it is inevitable that all technology embodied in facilities or equipment will become obsolete compared with the frontier technology at the current point in time. In a vintage model that incorporates

---

[1] Besides Cornwell, Schmidt and Sickles (1990), other studies that estimate the time variation of technical inefficiency by assuming a specific time function include Kumbhakar (1990) and Battese and Coelli (1992). Furthermore, Lee and Schmidt (1993) consider a model in which firm-specific individual effects vary over time. In Greene (2004, 2005a, b), panel data models are generalized into the true fixed effect model and true random effect model, which incorporate time-invariant individual effects, such as a firm's location and business environment, as well as time-varying individual effects, which are considered to reflect technical inefficiency. Furthermore, in Colombi et al. (2014), Kumbhakar et al. (2014), and Tsionas and Kumbhakar (2014), a more generalized panel data model is presented, in which time-invariant individual effects are separated into components representing firm heterogeneity and long-term persistent technical inefficiency, while time-varying individual effects are decomposed into a random component and a component representing transient technical inefficiency, which fluctuates over a short period. For more details on this generalized panel data stochastic production frontier model, see Kumbhakar and Lai (2022). These models are formulated with consideration of the generation mechanism of inefficiency, as they take into account the differences in the time-varying characteristics of firm heterogeneity and inefficiency.

such technological progress, the level of technical inefficiency changes constantly after construction. In the following sections, we construct a vintage model of the putty-clay type, which is an extension of Førsund and Hjalmarsson's (1987) model.

Caves and Barton (1990) addressed the occurrence of technical inefficiency from a similar perspective. They examined whether an oligopolistic market structure slows down facility turnover owing to a lack of competitive pressure, thereby leading to the continued adoption of obsolete technology and a decline in productive capacity. In fact, a considerable number of researchers expressed concern that the stagnation of the U.S. manufacturing industry in the 1980s was due to such a decline in productive capacity caused by the oligopolistic market structure. Clearly, this line of inquiry reflects the perspective that the structure of technical inefficiency within an industry is to be understood in a dynamic way.

3.1.1 Determination of Facility Renewal Timing Using Vintage Inefficiency Model

Suppose that the frontier production function in an industry can be expressed as $y = f(k)\exp(\alpha t)$, where $y = Y/L, k = K/L$, Y: output, K: capital, L: labor, and α: technology growth rate. This implies that the production technology in this industry advances at a constant rate each year in a Hicks-neutral manner. The frontier production function represents the maximum output achievable using the most efficient technology available at time t. We assume that the wage rate and interest rate remain constant. Under this assumption, the optimal capital-labor ratio is also constant at k^*, and all establishments construct facilities in line with this ratio each year. The constructed production technology remains fixed until the establishment next renews its facilities, and the establishment must operate under the same technology and level of productivity during that period. If the facility is renewed in a given year, the facility will be upgraded to the latest technology and efficiency standards available at that time, and its peak productivity will be sustained until the next renewal. This is the putty-clay vintage model. Unless an establishment continuously renews its facilities every year to incorporate the latest technology, it can only achieve relatively low productivity compared to the technological frontier. In this sense, it is inefficient relative to the frontier production technology. The industry consists of N establishments, and the output of the jth establishment is $L_j f(k^*)\exp\left(\alpha t_j\right)$. Then, the total output of the industry is $\sum_j L_j f(k^*)\exp\left(\alpha t_j\right)$. Here, t_j is the construction year of the jth establishment, and labor productivity is $f(k^*)\exp\left(\alpha t_j\right)$. Thus, the efficiency of the jth establishment with respect to the frontier technology at time τ is:

$$\frac{f(k^*)\exp\left(\alpha t_j\right)}{f(k^*)\exp(\alpha\tau)} = \exp\left(\alpha\left(t_j - \tau\right)\right).$$

Here, the production function is assumed to be expressed in logarithmic form as:

$$\log y = \log f(k) + \alpha t.$$

Using the same logarithmic representation, the efficiency of the jth site with respect to the frontier technology at time τ is $\alpha(t_j - \tau) < 0$, with the frontier technology set to 0. For simplicity of notation, we call this situation "inefficiency is $\alpha\left(\tau - t_j\right) > 0$." The inefficiency of a facility is 0 at the time of construction; it increases at a rate of α per unit time and reaches αt when time t has passed since its construction. Thus, the degree of inefficiency of each establishment increases at a constant rate.

If the degree of inefficiency is x at time τ, investing in upgradation saves a cost stream of $C(\exp(x) - 1)$ per unit of output compared to making no such investment. C is the unit cost level of the frontier technology at time τ. Let C_0 be the unit cost level in the frontier technology at time 0, then $C = C_0 \exp(-\alpha\tau)$. The discounted present value, calculated as the time integral of the cost savings stream $C(\exp(x) - 1) = C_0 \exp(-\alpha\tau)(\exp(x) - 1)$, is $C_0 \exp(-\alpha\tau)(\exp(x) - 1)/r$, where r is the discount rate. Assuming that a facility is renewed through rational decision-making, then the company renews a facility when the discounted present value of cost savings exceeds the cost of facility renewal. For example, suppose that the cost of upgrading a production facility with a supply capacity Q is expressed as $(F_0 + QK_0)\exp(-\alpha\tau)$, where F_0 and K_0 are constants. This cost consists of a fixed amount, regardless of the scale, and that depends on the scale. It is assumed that the cost of facility renewal also decreases with time, owing to technological progress similar to that of frontier technologies. Therefore, the timing of the facility renewal is optimal when the following condition is satisfied:

$$C_0 \frac{\exp(-\alpha\tau)(\exp(x) - 1)}{r} \times Q = (F_0 + QK_0)\exp(-\alpha\tau),$$

or equivalently, when the level of efficiency, x, satisfies:

$$\left(\frac{C_0(\exp(x) - 1)}{r} - K_0\right) Q = F_0.$$

Thus, if the choice is rational, the firm renews its facilities at uniform intervals as described in:

$$\frac{1}{\alpha}\log\left(\frac{r}{C_0}\left(\frac{F_0}{Q} + K_0\right) + 1\right). \tag{3.1}$$

As the simplest example, consider a case in which there are N establishments of equal size in an industry, each operated by a different firm. If the total market demand is fixed at D, and each establishment supplies D/N to the market, then the optimal interval for each establishment to renew its facilities is given by Equation (3.1) with $Q = D/N$. This implies that, as long as $F_0 > 0$, the facility renewal interval is an increasing function of the number of firms N. A longer interval between facility renewals leads to a higher average degree of inefficiency relative to frontier technology, and consequently, a higher observed level of technical inefficiency. Thus, as long as there is a fixed portion of the cost associated with facility renewals, the level of technical inefficiency depends on the market structure. Specifically, the more competitive the market structure, the higher the technical inefficiency level.

However, this explanation has omitted several points for simplicity. While it mentions the market structure, it fails to account for competitive interdependence. It assumes that the entity responsible for facility renewal decisions is the establishment and does not account for companies that operate multiple establishments. Furthermore, the analysis does not account for social welfare optimization. For further analysis of some of these points, see the Appendix to this chapter. Using a model, a more elaborate discussion of the facility renewal decisions of firms with multiple establishments and competitive interdependence is presented. The model demonstrates how differences in market structure determine observed technical inefficiencies.[2]

3.1.2 Mechanism of Technical Inefficiency Generation (Without Considering Adjustment Costs)

As indicated in Sect. 3.1.1, the optimal facility replacement period for each establishment is given as a function of replacement cost, discount rate, total supply, and rate of technological progress. Among these determinants, the discount rate and the rate of technological progress can be considered common across all establishments. In the last part of the previous subsection, a very simple case was shown in which supply and renewal costs are also assumed to be the same for each establishment; however, in general, they will differ from establishment to establishment. Depending on supply and facility renewal costs, the optimal facility renewal period generally varies.

Let z_j be the facility renewal period for the jth establishment, then this establishment periodically renews its facility when the level of inefficiency reaches αz_j. At the time of that facility renewal, the inefficiency becomes 0, and it increases at the rate of α per unit time. Thus, if all establishments have the same facility renewal period Z, and the initial timing of renewal for each establishment is uniformly distributed, then the inefficiency level of a randomly chosen establishment at a given point in time can be treated as a random variable. In that case, the probability density function $\psi(x)$ follows a uniform distribution:

$$\psi(x) = \begin{cases} \dfrac{1}{\alpha Z} & \text{for } 0 \le x \le \alpha Z, \\ 0 & \text{otherwise.} \end{cases}$$

[2] Other related aspects are discussed in Torii (2001).

Similarly, if the distribution density of the facility renewal period across establishments is given by $\phi(z)dz$, then under the assumption that the initial timing of facility renewal is uniformly distributed, the inefficiency level of a randomly selected establishment at a given point in time follows the probability density function:

$$\psi(x) = \int_{x/\alpha}^{\infty} \frac{\phi(z)}{\alpha z} dz. \tag{3.2}$$

Using the method of estimating the frontier production function, technical inefficiency should be observed according to this probability density function, $\psi(x)$. For example, when the optimal facility renewal period for each establishment is uniformly distributed as represented by:

$$\phi(z) = \begin{cases} \dfrac{1}{a-b} & \text{for } b \le z \le a, \\ 0 & \text{otherwise,} \end{cases},$$

the level of inefficiency distributes with a skewed distribution:

$$\psi(x) = \begin{cases} \dfrac{1}{\alpha(a-b)} \log\left(\dfrac{a}{b}\right) & \text{for } 0 \le x < b, \\ \dfrac{1}{\alpha(a-b)} \log\left(\dfrac{a}{x}\right) & \text{for } b \le x < a, \\ 0 & \text{for } a < x. \end{cases}$$

Conversely, when the distribution of technical inefficiency is observed as a density function, $\psi(x)$, the relation which is given by differentiating Equation (3.2) provides the density function of the facility renewal period,

$$\phi(w) = -\alpha^2 w \psi'(\alpha w). \tag{3.3}$$

3.1.3 *Mechanism of Technical Inefficiency Generation (Considering Adjustment Costs)*

To construct a vintage model that aligns with the neoclassical interpretation of technical inefficiency, a more general formulation is required. In the neoclassical framework, optimal behavior does not imply that all economic agents always attain the optimal state. Rather, agents determine how closely they approach optimal behavior by weighing the costs associated with optimization. For example, accurately identifying the optimal timing for facility renewal and carrying it out precisely on schedule would incur costs for each establishment. Therefore, each establishment must consider the trade-off between the cost of making precise renewal decisions and the benefit of achieving a more optimal replacement schedule. In what follows, we attempt to describe a setting in which each establishment engages in such cost-conscious optimization behavior.

First, consider the distribution of facility renewal periods when no managerial effort is made and each establishment randomly selects its renewal interval. Let this distribution be denoted by the probability density function $\xi(z)$. Suppose further that managerial effort allows establishments to adjust the initially selected renewal period z toward a more optimal value, and that this adjustment is described by a transformation function $\zeta(w - z \mid z)$. Here, z represents the unadjusted renewal period, w is the adjusted renewal period, and $\zeta(w - z \mid z)$ denotes the probability density that, given z, the renewal period is adjusted by $w - z$ to become w. If all establishments share the same optimal renewal period w_0, and if managerial effort perfectly corrects the initial choice to this optimum, then the transformation function becomes $\zeta(w - z \mid z) = \delta(w_0 - z)$, where $\delta(\cdot)$ is the Dirac delta function. Even when the optimal renewal period differs across establishments, if there exists a one-to-one correspondence between w and z, the transformation function still reduces to a form expressed using the delta function. This implies that establishments making the same initial random choice without managerial effort undergo identical adjustments. In general, however, the transformation function need not take the form of a delta function. This is because the cost of identifying and implementing the optimal renewal period likely differs across establishments. Consequently, the extent to which the initial period is adjusted toward the optimal value will vary depending on the specific conditions of each establishment.

The transformation function $\zeta(w - z \mid z)$ must satisfy the following condition:

$$\int_0^\infty \zeta(w - z \mid z)\, dw = 1.$$

Beyond this, there are few *a priori* restrictions on the functional forms of $\xi(z)$ and $\zeta(w - z \mid z)$, so quite general specifications can be considered applicable. Through this adjustment process, the probability density of the facility renewal period is transformed from $\xi(z)$ to:

$$\phi(w) = \int_0^\infty \zeta(w - z \mid z)\, \xi(z)\, dz.$$

Accordingly, the probability density function for the level of inefficiency becomes:

$$\psi(x) = \int_{x/\alpha}^\infty \frac{\phi(w)}{\alpha w}\, dw = \int_{x/\alpha}^\infty \frac{1}{\alpha w} \left(\int_0^\infty \zeta(w - z \mid z)\, \xi(z)\, dz \right) dw. \tag{3.4}$$

3.1.4 The Level of Inefficiency and Renewal of Facility

Consider the distribution of the level of inefficiency u:

$$\psi(u) = C\exp\left(-\frac{u^{1+p}}{K}\right), \quad \text{for } u \geq 0, \tag{3.5}$$

which generalizes the half-normal and exponential distributions, where p, C, and K are constants. The half-normal and exponential distributions are among the most frequently assumed forms in the literature on the estimation of technical inefficiency. Distribution (3.5) becomes the half-normal distribution when $p = 1$, and the exponential distribution when $p = 0$. Assuming (3.5) as the probability density function of inefficiency in the vintage model is equivalent, according to Equation (3.3), to assuming the following form for the density function $\phi(w)$ of the adjusted facility renewal timing w:

$$\phi(w) = -\alpha^2 w\psi'(\alpha w) = C' w^{1+p}\exp\left(-\frac{(\alpha w)^{1+p}}{K}\right), \quad \text{for } w \geq 0, \tag{3.6}$$

where C' is a constant.

In the vintage model, the parameter p in the probability density function (3.5) indicates how the likelihood of an establishment renewing its facility depends on the power of its inefficiency level. For example, a half-normal distribution ($p = 1$) arises when the probability of renewal increases in proportion to the inefficiency level, whereas an exponential distribution ($p = 0$) corresponds to a situation where the same probability remains constant regardless of inefficiency. In this way, the exponential and half-normal distributions reflect different relationships between the incentive for facility renewal investment and the level of inefficiency. Each can be interpreted as arising from a different dynamic mechanism governing the determination of market structure.

Here, we state the proposition.

Proposition 3 *Assuming that the density function of facility renewal timing is given by Equation (3.6), the parameter p indicates the degree to which the probability that an establishment renews its facility is proportional to a power of its inefficiency level.*

Proof We derive the probability that an establishment with a given inefficiency level x, selected at random, renews its facilities within a time interval Δt from an arbitrary point in time. First, since the inefficiency level is already at x, the facility renewal interval cannot be less than x/α. If the facility renewal interval of a randomly selected establishment is w, then its inefficiency level is uniformly distributed over the interval $[0, \alpha w]$. Therefore, the probability that the inefficiency level lies in the range $[x, x + \Delta x]$ is given by $\Delta x/(\alpha w)$. This is the conditional probability of the inefficiency level falling within $[x, x + \Delta x]$, given that the facility renewal interval is w. Applying Bayes' theorem, the probability density that the facility renewal interval is w, given that the inefficiency level lies in $[x, x + \Delta x]$, is:

$$\frac{\Delta x/(\alpha w)\cdot\phi(w)}{\int_{x/\alpha}^{\infty}\frac{\Delta x}{\alpha w'}\cdot\phi\left(w'\right)dw'}=\frac{\phi(w)/w}{\int_{x/\alpha}^{\infty}\frac{\phi\left(w'\right)}{w'}dw'}$$

$$=\frac{C'w^{p}\exp\left(-\frac{(\alpha w)^{1+p}}{K}\right)}{\frac{C'}{1+p}\cdot\exp\left(-\frac{x^{1+p}}{K}\right)}.$$

Given that the inefficiency level is x, the renewal will occur within Δt only if the renewal interval falls within the range $[x/\alpha, x/\alpha+\Delta t]$. The probability of this event is:

$$\frac{\left(\frac{x}{\alpha}\right)^{p}\exp\left(-\frac{x^{1+p}}{K}\right)}{\frac{1}{1+p}\cdot\exp\left(-\frac{x^{1+p}}{K}\right)}\Delta t=(1+p)\left(\frac{x}{\alpha}\right)^{p}\Delta t.$$

□

Thus, when we observe the renewal behavior of establishments, it appears that the probability of renewal is proportional to the p-th power of the inefficiency level x.

3.1.5 Probabilistic Process Model of Facility Renewal

In Sect. 3.1.4, we explained that the parameter p in the probability density function (3.5) reflects the tendency that the probability of an establishment renewing its facilities is proportional to a power of its inefficiency level. In fact, the converse also holds. That is, if we assume that facility renewal occurs stochastically depending on the level of inefficiency, then the probability density function of inefficiency also takes the form of (3.5), as shown in Proposition 4.

Proposition 4 *Assume that an establishment with inefficiency level x at a given point in time renews its facility within a time interval Δt with probability $\kappa x^{p}\Delta t$, where κ and p are constants. Then, the probability density function of the inefficiency level is given by:*

$$\rho(x;p)=\frac{(1+p)^{\frac{p}{1+p}}\left(\frac{\kappa}{\alpha}\right)^{\frac{1}{1+p}}}{\Gamma(\frac{1}{1+p})}\exp\left(-\frac{\kappa}{(p+1)\alpha}x^{1+p}\right).\tag{3.7}$$

This density function has the same functional form as distribution (3.5). It corresponds to the exponential power-type distribution (2.1) introduced in Chapter 2, with the parameter $\kappa/\alpha=\theta$. If $p=1$, the facility is renewed in proportion to the establishment's level of inefficiency. If $p = 0$, the facility is renewed at a constant rate, regardless of inefficiency. Specifically, since we are selecting establishments at random from a population with a given distribution (3.6) of facility renewal intervals, the actual timing of facility renewal is probabilistic.

Proof Let $\rho(x, t)$ be the probability density function representing the likelihood that a given establishment has inefficiency level x at time t. Under the facility renewal behavior described above, the probability that the establishment does not renew its facility within the next Δt units of time is $1 - \kappa x^p \Delta t$. In that case, the inefficiency increases by $\alpha \Delta t$ due to technological obsolescence. This evolution of the probability density can be expressed as:

$$\rho\left(x + \alpha \Delta t,\ t + \Delta t\right) = \rho\left(x, t\right)\left(1 - \kappa x^p \Delta t\right).$$

Expanding this equation and ignoring terms of order $(\Delta t)^2$ and higher, we obtain:

$$\alpha \frac{\partial}{\partial x} \rho\left(x, t\right) + \frac{\partial}{\partial t} \rho\left(x, t\right) = -\rho\left(x, t\right) \kappa x^p.$$

Let $\rho(x)$ denote the asymptotic distribution of $\rho(x, t)$ as $t \to \infty$. This distribution is defined on the domain $0 < x < \infty$. Because $\frac{\partial \rho(x)}{\partial t} = 0$,

$$\frac{\partial}{\partial x} \rho\left(x\right) = -\frac{\kappa x^p}{\alpha} \rho\left(x\right).$$

This differential equation has the solution:

$$\rho\left(x\right) = C_1 \exp\left(-\frac{\kappa}{\left(1 + p\right)\alpha} x^{1+p}\right),$$

where C_1 is a constant.

So far, we have considered only the domain $0 < x$ for $\rho(x)$, excluding the case $x = 0$. Establishments whose inefficiency lies in the range $0 \leq x < \alpha \Delta t$ will move to the region $x \geq \alpha \Delta t$ after a time interval Δt, unless they renew their facilities during that period. The establishments that enter this region are those that have upgraded their facilities within the Δt time span and thus embody the latest frontier technology. The total number of establishments that have renewed their facilities within this time interval across all regions is

$$\int_0^\infty \rho\left(x\right) \kappa x^p \Delta t\, dx = \int_0^\infty C_1 \exp\left(-\frac{\kappa}{\left(1 + p\right)\alpha} x^{1+p}\right) \kappa x^p \Delta t\, dx = C_1 \alpha \Delta t.$$

These establishments fall in the region $[0, \alpha \Delta t)$, and therefore the probability density is $C_1 \alpha \Delta t / (\alpha \Delta t) = C_1$. This value matches $\rho(0)$, the value of the probability density function defined for $0 < x$. Accordingly, the density function can be extended to the domain $0 \leq x$ and defined in the same manner. Since $\rho(x)$ is a probability density function, we require:

$$\int_0^\infty \rho(x)\,dx = \int_0^\infty C_1 \exp\left(-\frac{\kappa}{(1+p)\alpha}x^{1+p}\right)dx$$
$$= C_1 \cdot \frac{\Gamma\left(\frac{1}{1+p}\right)}{(1+p)^{\frac{p}{1+p}}\left(\frac{\kappa}{\alpha}\right)^{\frac{1}{1+p}}} = 1.$$

This condition determines the value of the constant. □

3.1.6 *Symmetric Distribution of Inefficiency and the Rationality of Decision*

Consider the density function in the simplest case where the optimum renewal timings are the same for all establishments, as there is no specific cost factor for each enterprise, and where each enterprise makes rational decisions. This case corresponds to the limit $p \to \infty$ in the stochastic renewal process model described in Sect. 3.1.5. Let W be the optimal facility renewal interval given by Equation (3.1) derived in Sect. 3.1.1. Then, $\varphi(w) = \delta(W - w)$, since all rational establishments will choose W as the facility renewal period as a result of adjustment. Note that the corresponding transformation function is $\zeta(w - z \mid z) = \delta(W - z)$. Therefore, the probability density function indicating the level of inefficiency has a uniform distribution:

$$\psi(x) = \int_x^\infty \frac{\delta(W - w)}{w}\,dw = \begin{cases} \frac{1}{W} & \text{for } x < W, \\ 0 & \text{otherwise.} \end{cases} \tag{3.8}$$

This distribution corresponds to the case $p \to \infty$ in Equation (3.7). As $p \to \infty$, the renewal probability $\kappa x^p \Delta t$ in Equation (3.7) becomes concentrated at $x = 1$, effectively fixing the timing of facility renewal at that point. Although this formulation assumes that the timing of facility renewal is fixed at $x = 1$, this restriction can be easily generalized by replacing the renewal probability with $\kappa\,(x/a)^p\,\Delta t$, allowing for an arbitrary renewal threshold a.

This implies that the stochastic renewal model described above also includes rational renewal behavior as the limiting case $p \to \infty$ and that the resulting inefficiency distribution is uniform. Although this uniform distribution (3.8) is not centered at $x = 0$, it is symmetric and therefore does not produce asymmetry in the productivity distribution. Even when p is not infinite, a larger value of p indicates a stronger tendency for facility renewal to occur at more obsolete establishments, implying that the renewal process is conducted more efficiently. However, the degree of efficiency is not determined solely by the value of p. Rather, it is determined jointly by the parameter κ, which governs the general tendency to invest in facility renewal, and

p, which characterizes the responsiveness of the renewal probability to the level of inefficiency.

The observation that no asymmetric distribution of inefficiency is observed when establishments rationally invest in facility renewal under a homogeneous cost structure and follow the same optimal renewal interval offers an important implication. When examining the dynamic process of productivity growth among establishments within an industry, a slight technological lag relative to the frontier does not necessarily imply the presence of inefficiency. A persistent problem in identifying inefficiency arises from the fact that observed technical inefficiency often includes inefficiencies that result from such rational decision-making. However, as shown here, inefficiencies arising from rational decisions do not necessarily follow an asymmetric distribution. If such rationally induced inefficiencies are not asymmetrically distributed, then methods that assume an asymmetric distribution to identify technical inefficiency will fail to capture this component. In other words, such methods allow us to avoid the problem of mistakenly attributing inefficiencies that cannot reasonably be considered X-inefficiencies to technical inefficiency.

However, this observation does not apply in cases where the industry is experiencing rapid growth and there is a distortion in the distribution of establishment vintages. In this context, vintages refer to the number of years since construction or renewal investment. Suppose that, as a result of rational decision-making, each establishment undertakes renewal investment every T years. Further assume that, in each period, a proportion a of new establishments, relative to the number of establishments undertaking renewal, enters the market. In this case, the total number of establishments either engaging in renewal or entering the market increases annually at a rate of $100a/T$ percent. Therefore, if the number of establishments with vintage V, meaning that V years have passed since construction or last renewal, becomes continuously distributed due to a long history of renewal investment, then the density distribution of vintage V is given by:

$$\frac{ae^a}{T\left(e^a-1\right)}e^{-V/T},\quad \text{for } 0 \le V \le T,$$

which corresponds to a truncated exponential distribution. Thus, assuming that the rate of technological progress at the frontier is α, the distribution of inefficiency is also expressed as

$$\frac{ae^a}{\alpha T\left(e^a-1\right)}e^{-\frac{x}{\alpha T}},\quad \text{for } 0 \le x \le \alpha T,$$

which is a truncated exponential distribution. The second and third moments of this distribution are given by

$$T^2\left(\frac{1}{a^2}-\frac{e^a}{\left(e^a-1\right)^2}\right),\quad T^3\left(\frac{2}{a^3}-\frac{e^a\left(e^a+1\right)}{\left(e^a-1\right)^3}\right),$$

both of which are strictly positive. When the method of moments is employed to estimate the level of technical inefficiency, the estimation is based on these moment values.

3.1.7 Power-Law Proportional Rational Facility Renewal Decision

In the previous subsection, we demonstrated that in the simplest case of the vintage model, where all establishments have the same rational facility renewal period and the timing of facility renewal is uniformly distributed, the level of technical inefficiency is uniformly distributed, resulting in no asymmetric deviation term. Since the facility renewal period is determined by factors such as each establishment's individual demand structure, the cost structure of facility renewal, and the discount rate, it generally varies even if all establishments make rational decisions, exhibiting dispersion over a certain range. In this subsection, we show that there exists a case where the probability of rational facility renewal decision-making is approximately proportional to a power of an establishment's level of technical inefficiency. Consequently, the distribution of technical inefficiency can be approximated by an exponential power-type distribution.

We consider a model that follows the setting in Sect. 3.1.1. However, whereas Sect. 3.1.1 did not take into account the competitive pressure from potential new entrants, we now assume the presence of such competitive pressure. The level of inefficiency of establishment j relative to the frontier at time τ is expressed as

$$\alpha(\tau - t_j) + v_j^0 + v_{jt}^1.$$

Here, t_j represents the most recent facility renewal time of establishment j. The term v_j^0 captures a persistent individual effect due to establishment-specific heterogeneity, which is assumed to follow a normal distribution, $N(0, \sigma_0^2)$. Furthermore, v_{jt}^1 represents short-term fluctuations for establishment j at time t. These stochastic components correspond to the time-invariant individual effects and the random component in the *generalized panel data model* proposed by Colombi et al. (2014), Kumbhakar et al. (2014), and Tsionas and Kumbhakar (2014).

Each establishment is exposed to competitive pressure from potential new entrants. If its level of inefficiency exceeds E, it is forced to exit the industry and is replaced by a new entrant. However, this exit can be avoided by renewing the facility. Updating the facility at the point when inefficiency reaches E, thereby embodying the latest technology, has the same effect on the distribution of technical inefficiency as the case in which the incumbent exits and is immediately replaced by a new entrant equipped with the latest technology. Here, we assume that $E \geq 0$. The case $E > 0$ implies that incumbent establishments have an advantage over potential entrants. This advantage arises from the operational know-how gained through learning effects accumulated by incumbent firms that have continued their business activities within the industry. The fact that new entrants require a certain amount of time to acquire such know-how contributes to this advantage.

We consider the rational decision-making regarding facility renewal under such competitive pressure. First, among the factors determining the level of inefficiency, we assume that the term v^1_{jt}, which represents short-term fluctuations, does not directly influence entry and exit decisions.[3] Next, we replace $\alpha(\tau - t_j)$ with u_{jt}. This inefficiency term takes the value $u_{jt} = 0$ immediately after facility renewal and increases by α per unit time. When the inefficiency level u_{jt} of an establishment is given as u^*, the decision to renew the facility at that moment implies that the establishment has chosen u^*/α as the facility renewal interval.

Facility renewal entails associated costs. Rational decision-making is based on both the cost of renewal and its effect on productivity. In the model presented in Sect. 3.1.1, in order to examine its relationship with market structure, we assumed that the cost incurred during renewal depends on the facility's capacity. In this discussion, however, we focus on decisions concerning the interval between renewals, and therefore assume that both the facility capacity and the scale of investment for renewal are fixed. Furthermore, we assume that the renewal cost does not arise at the moment of renewal but is instead incurred as a constant overhead cost per unit of time over the operational period of the renewed facility. Additionally, we specify that this time-based renewal cost increases as the renewal interval shortens, and is set at a level inversely proportional to the length of the renewal period, C/u^*, where C is a constant. This assumption corresponds to fixing the cost per renewal and allocating it as a time-based cost that is inversely proportional to the renewal interval.

In this way, in addition to the inefficiency level $u_{jt} + v^0_j$ identified above, there is a facility renewal cost incurred per unit of time. In practice, both represent increases in cost relative to the unit production cost associated with frontier-level technology. Therefore, we interpret the renewal cost as having the effect of increasing the inefficiency level by an amount equivalent to the per-unit-time renewal cost, and we analyze the renewal decision by considering the total increase in cost. When an establishment chooses a renewal interval of u^*/α, its inefficiency level immediately after renewal is given by $u_{jt} + v^0_j + C/u^* = v^0_j + C/u^*$. This level then increases at a rate of α per unit of time. Just before the next renewal, the inefficiency reaches its maximum at $u^* + v^0_j + C/u^*$. When this maximum inefficiency level reaches the threshold E, the facility is either renewed or replaced by a new entrant. Given the assumption that $v^0_j \sim N(0, \sigma_0^2)$, the inefficiency level at the time of facility renewal follows a probability distribution of $N(u^* + C/u^*, \sigma_0^2)$.

[3] Whether it affects entry and exit decisions depends on how long the short-term period is defined. However, since considering this term does not change the fundamental working of the model, we focus on a simplified case.

The probability that this inefficiency level exceeds E is given by:

$$P\left(u^* + \frac{C}{u^*} + v_j^0 > E \,\middle|\, u^*\right) = 1 - \Phi\left(\frac{E - u^* - C/u^*}{\sigma_0}\right),$$

where $\Phi(\cdot)$ denotes the CDF of the standard normal distribution.

The limit of the probability per unit time that the establishment undergoes facility renewal, given that it has not made a renewal decision until the inefficiency level reaches this threshold, i.e., the hazard rate with respect to the facility renewal period, is:

$$\begin{aligned}
&\lim_{\Delta\tau\to 0} \frac{P\left(t_j + \frac{u^*}{\alpha} \le T < t_j + \frac{u^*}{\alpha} + \Delta\tau \,\middle|\, T \ge t_j + \frac{u^*}{\alpha}\right)}{\Delta\tau} \\
&= \lim_{\Delta\tau\to 0} \frac{\phi\left(\frac{E - u^* - C/u^*}{\sigma_0}\right)\left(-\Delta v_j^0\right)}{\Delta\tau} \cdot \frac{1}{\Phi\left(\frac{E - u^* - C/u^*}{\sigma_0}\right)} \\
&= \lim_{\Delta\tau\to 0} \frac{\left(1 - \frac{C}{(u^*)^2}\right)\Delta u_{jt}}{\Delta\tau} \cdot \frac{\phi\left(\frac{E - u^* - C/u^*}{\sigma_0}\right)}{\Phi\left(\frac{E - u^* - C/u^*}{\sigma_0}\right)} \\
&= \alpha\left(1 - \frac{C}{(u^*)^2}\right) \cdot \frac{\phi\left(\frac{E - u^* - C/u^*}{\sigma_0}\right)}{\Phi\left(\frac{E - u^* - C/u^*}{\sigma_0}\right)}.
\end{aligned}$$

Here, $\phi(\cdot)$ denotes the Probability Density Function (PDF) of the standard normal distribution. The random variable T represents the time at which the establishment undergoes facility renewal. The terms Δv_j^0 and Δu_{jt} represent the variations in the variables v_j^0 and u_{jt}, respectively, corresponding to the time interval $[t_j + u^*/\alpha, t_j + u^*/\alpha + \Delta\tau]$.

When considering this hazard rate as a function of the variable u^* given the parameters (E, C, α, σ_0), it is very well approximated by a power function of u^*. Figure 3.1 illustrates the hazard function under the assumption that $(C, \alpha, \sigma_0) = (0.2, 1, 1)$, for $E = 2.5, 3, 3.5, 4$, along with the power functions $b_0 u^{a_0}$ that are tangent to each hazard function at $u = 1.5, 1.75, 2, 2.25$, respectively. The bold solid curves represent the hazard functions, while the thin solid curves depict the power functions that approximate each hazard function. In the main region, the hazard functions and their approximating curves are so closely matched that they are nearly indistinguishable. When u^* is in the range $0 \le u^* \le \sqrt{C}$, the hazard rate is zero. This reflects the reasoning that no establishments will decide to renew facilities in

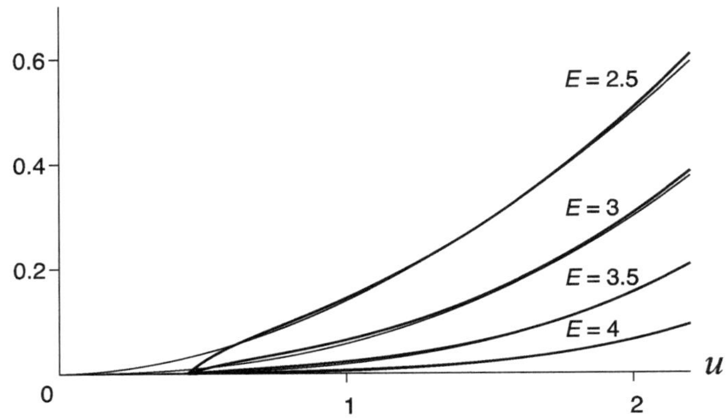

Fig. 3.1 Hazard functions and their approximating curves

this region because the cost of renewal per unit time is extremely high when u^* is very small, making it more cost-effective to delay renewal and choose a higher u^*.

From this, it is confirmed that given an inefficiency level u^*, the probability that an establishment, which has not yet undergone facility renewal, decides to renew its facility is well approximated by a power function of the inefficiency level. Consequently, the observed distribution of technical inefficiency is also expected to be well approximated by an exponential power-type distribution.

3.2 A Management Inefficiency Model

In this section, we present another dynamic model that has a different mechanism for the generation of inefficiency than the vintage model. Suppose that the production process of a certain good is indexed continuously over the interval [0, 1] on the real line. It is assumed that, within a small time interval Δt, inefficiency arises at some point in this process with probability $\eta \Delta t$. In other words, inefficiencies occur within the interval [0, 1] according to a Poisson process. These inefficiencies are assumed to be caused by factors pointed out in the theory of X-inefficiency, discussed in Chapter 4, such as opportunistic behavior, free-riding behavior that leads to a prisoner's dilemma, or inertial behavior that is unresponsive to environmental change. The occurrence of inefficiency at each point in the process reduces the productivity of the overall manufacturing system represented by the interval [0, 1]. If a total of M inefficiencies arises within this interval, the production cost increases by $100Ma$ percent compared with the case in which no inefficiencies occur. Furthermore, due to observational problems such as noise and uncertainty, managers are assumed to be unable to determine whether a decline in productivity is due to the emergence of inefficiency within the process or due to environmental factors.

Suppose that management has a policy of conducting a review of each process at some point in time to address the problem of inefficiency. Two policies are considered when setting the timing of this productivity review. The first policy ensures that managers check and improve all processes at regular intervals and implement controls to ensure that inefficiencies are eliminated. The second policy is such that managers do not take remedial action unless inefficiencies have actually been confirmed through random checks. Managers randomly select certain processes at regular intervals and examine whether inefficiencies exist. If no inefficiencies are found, nothing is done. Contrarily, if inefficiencies are found, all processes are checked and control is strengthened to ensure that inefficiencies do not remain. In either case, after the inefficiencies are eliminated by tightened controls, they are assumed to occur again through the same mechanism.

In the case of the former policy, the inefficiency structure is the same as that in the vintage inefficiency model in the previous section. Without regular managerial checks, the expected productivity of this manufacturing process would decline at a rate of $100a\eta$ percent per unit time, and inefficiency would return to zero after a regular performance check.[4,5] The only differences between this model and the vintage inefficiency model are whether relative productivity shifts due to technological progress or declines due to X-inefficiency, and whether productivity changes at a deterministically constant rate or declines stochastically. The problems of deciding when to renew a facility and when to perform control share the same structure. When the interval between managerial checks is T, the average inefficiency is $Ta\eta/2$. Therefore, if the unit cost of production at inefficiency 0 is C_1, then at output Q the average additional cost caused by inefficiency is $QC_1Ta\eta/2$ on average over time.

---

[4] Assume that the initial point, at which there are no inefficiencies at all, is defined as 0. The probability that M inefficiencies occur after t periods is given by

$$\frac{(\eta t)^M \exp(-\eta t)}{M!}.$$

Since $E(M) = \eta t$, the cost increases by $at\eta$ due to inefficiency.

[5] The stochastic process of the inefficiency level caused by inefficiencies generated through a Poisson process can be approximated by the following stochastic process, in which the degree of inefficiency increases at a constant rate. Suppose that at some time t, M inefficiencies are present. Within a time interval Δt, with probability $\eta\Delta t$, the number of inefficient processes increases by 1, from M to $M+1$. With the remaining probability $1-\eta\Delta t$, the number of inefficient processes remains at M. This process is described below using the probability density function $\rho(x,t)$, introduced later:

$$\rho(M+1, t+\Delta t) = \rho(M,t)\eta\Delta t + \rho(M+1,t)(1-\eta\Delta t).$$

The second term on the right-hand side describes the case where $M+1$ inefficiencies had already occurred but did not change within Δt. If Δt is sufficiently small, we can expand this equation and ignore terms of order $(\Delta t)^2$ and higher to obtain:

$$\rho_t(M+1,t) = -\eta\left(\rho(M+1,t) - \rho(M,t)\right).$$

Clearly, this equation represents a probability density function wave moving with velocity η. Note that the subscript denotes partial differentiation with respect to the variable.

Furthermore, assuming the cost of the management check is $F_1 + K_1 Q$, consisting of a fixed portion F_1 and a quantity dependent portion $K_1 Q$, as in the previous model, the time average of the management cost is $(F_1 + K_1 Q)/T$. The optimal interval T, that minimizes the sum of both costs is

$$T = \sqrt{\frac{2}{a\eta C_1}\left(\frac{F_1}{Q} + K_1\right)}.$$

The only difference from the vintage inefficiency model is that it does not consider the discount factor because the unit time is supposed to be much shorter than that for the capital investment problem.

Next, consider the case in which management adopts the second control method, that is, directly inspecting the state of one process at a time at random with a constant probability. This inspection is assumed to be conducted at a rate corresponding to the interval of measure $\delta \Delta t$ per Δt unit time. As in the vintage inefficiency model, we define the inefficiency state x as the state in which the production cost per unit increases by $C_1 x$. In the inefficiency state x, inefficiency occurs in x/a of all processes. Therefore, when a process within the region of measure $\delta \Delta t$ is randomly inspected, the probability of detecting inefficiency is given by $1 - (1 - \delta \Delta t)^{x/a}$.

The efficiency at each time point is a random variable. Let $\rho(x, t)$ denote the probability density function of the level of inefficiency being x at time t. Within a small time interval Δt, with probability $1 - (1 - \delta \Delta t)^{x/a}$, all processes are inspected because a random examination detects an inefficient process, and x resets to 0 as described above. With the remaining probability $(1 - \delta \Delta t)^{x/a}$, inefficiency is overlooked. Under the condition that inefficiency is overlooked, with probability $\eta \Delta t$ within the same Δt interval, the number of inefficient processes increases by one, raising the inefficiency level from x to $x + a$. With probability $1 - \eta \Delta t$, the inefficiency level remains at x. Therefore, the probability density function satisfies the following equation:

$$\begin{aligned} \rho(x + a, t + \Delta t) = {} & \rho(x, t)\,(1 - \delta \Delta t)^{\frac{x}{a}}\, \eta \Delta t \\ & + \rho(x + a, t)\,(1 - \delta \Delta t)^{\frac{x}{a}+1}\,(1 - \eta \Delta t). \end{aligned} \tag{3.9}$$

The second term on the right-hand side represents the case where inefficiency had already occurred in $M + 1 = (x/a + 1)$ processes, but the inefficiency did not change within Δt.

We consider the distribution of x as a stationary (equilibrium) distribution of the stochastic process indicated by Equation (3.9). Since the state space of x is assumed to be discrete, it is assumed that a is sufficiently small to approximate the stationary distribution in (3.9) as a continuous distribution. This requires further assumptions regarding the following parameters:

$$\text{as}\, a \to 0,\ a\eta \to H, \text{ and } \delta/a \to G,$$

where, H and G are constants. According to the first assumption, the smaller the impact of inefficiency at each point in the process, the higher the probability that inefficiency will occur there. However, the overall rate at which the efficiency level of the entire process declines per unit of time remains unchanged. By contrast, the second assumption posits that the number of processes that can be inspected, δ, depends on the rate at which inefficiencies occur, a. This reflects the idea that the more pronounced the inefficiency in a process, the easier it is to detect and examine.

By Taylor expansion of (3.9) with respect to a and Δt, assuming that a and Δt are sufficiently small, we obtain

$$\begin{aligned}
&\rho(x,t) + \rho_x(x,t)a + \rho_t(x,t)\Delta t + \rho_{xt}(x,t)a\Delta t + o(a^2) + o(\Delta t^2)\\
&\quad = \rho(x,t)\,(1-\delta\Delta t)^{x/a}\,\eta\Delta t\\
&\quad + \left(\rho(x,t) + \rho_x(x,t)\,a + o\left(a^2\right)\right)(1-\delta\Delta t)^{x/a}\,(1-\delta\Delta t)(1-\eta\Delta t),
\end{aligned}$$

where subscripts indicate partial derivatives. From this equation,

$$\begin{aligned}
&\rho_x(x,t)a/\Delta t + \rho_t(x,t) + \rho_{xt}(x,t)a + o(a^2)/\Delta t + o(\Delta t)\\
&\quad = \rho(x,t)((1-\delta\Delta t)^{x/a} - 1)/\Delta t - \rho(x,t)\,(1-\delta\Delta t)^{x/a}\,\delta(1-\eta\Delta t)\\
&\quad + \rho_x(x,t)\,(1-\delta\Delta t)^{x/a}\,(1-\delta\Delta t)(1-\eta\Delta t)a/\Delta t\\
&\quad + o(a^2)/\Delta t\,(1-\delta\Delta t)^{x/a}\,(1-\delta\Delta t)(1-\eta\Delta t)
\end{aligned}$$

is given. Here, denoting $b = a/\Delta t$, taking the limit of $\Delta t \to 0$ and $a \to 0$, we obtain

$$\begin{aligned}
\rho_x(x,t)\,b + \rho_t(x,t) &= -Gx\rho(x,t) - \rho(x,t)\cdot 1\cdot 0\cdot\left(1-\frac{H}{b}\right)\\
&\quad + \rho_x(x,t)\cdot 1\cdot 1\cdot\left(1-\frac{H}{b}\right)\cdot b.
\end{aligned}$$

Then,

$$\rho_t(x,t) = -Gx\rho(x,t) - H\rho_x(x,t)\,.$$

Note that,

$$\begin{aligned}
\lim_{(\Delta t,a)\to(0,0)} (1-\delta\Delta t)^{x/a} &= \lim_{(\Delta t,a)\to(0,0)} (1-\delta\Delta t)^{-\frac{1}{\delta\Delta t}\left(-a\frac{\delta}{a}\right)\frac{\Delta t}{a}x}\\
&= \left(e^{-0\cdot G}\right)^{x/b} = 1,
\end{aligned}$$

and

$$\lim_{(\Delta t,a)\to(0,0)} \frac{(1-\delta\Delta t)^{\frac{x}{a}} - 1}{\Delta t} = \lim_{(\Delta t,a)\to(0,0)} \frac{-\dfrac{\delta x}{a}\,(1-\delta\Delta t)^{\frac{x}{a}-1}}{1} = -Gx.$$

Here, we consider the asymptotic distribution $\rho(x) = \lim_{t\to\infty} \rho(x,t)$ defined in $0 < x < \infty$. Then, $\rho(x)$ satisfies a differential equation:

$$\rho_x(x) = -\frac{Gx}{H} \cdot \rho(x)$$

whose solution is

$$\rho(x) = R \cdot \exp\left(-\frac{G}{2H}x^2\right), \tag{3.10}$$

where R is a constant. Note that this stationary distribution does not depend on b, which is assumed on the conversion $\Delta t \to 0,\ a \to 0$. As $\rho(x)$ is a probabilistic density function

$$\int_0^\infty \rho(x)\,dx = \int_0^\infty R\exp\left(-\frac{G}{2H}x^2\right) = Ra\sqrt{\frac{\pi H}{2G}} = 1.$$

This leads to the value of R, and the stationary probabilistic density function is

$$\rho(x) = \sqrt{\frac{\pi H}{2G}} \exp\left(-\frac{G}{2H}x^2\right).$$

Thus, under the assumptions set in this section, the inefficiency is half-normally distributed, as indicated by the above function. The management inefficiency model is a hypothetical model that explains half-normally distributed technical inefficiency.

The average efficiency is

$$E(x) = \sqrt{\frac{2H}{\pi G}}. \tag{3.11}$$

G is the parameter that represents the effort level of managerial inspection per unit time. Unit production cost is represented as $C_1(1 + C_2/\sqrt{G})$, where $C_2 = a\sqrt{2H/\pi}$. The management efforts to conduct more frequent audits reduce production costs, although an administrative cost is involved in implementing this management effort. Assuming that this management cost is expressed as $C_m(G, Q)$, a function of production Q and audit effort G, then the managers choose G that minimizes the total cost $QC_1(1 + C_2/\sqrt{G}) + C_m(G, Q)$, whose first-order condition is

$$-\frac{QC_1C_2}{2G^{\frac{3}{2}}} + \frac{\partial}{\partial G}C_m(G, Q) = 0.$$

3.3 Conclusion

In this chapter, we construct stochastic process models where the degree of inefficiency of each establishment fluctuates probabilistically, providing an explanation for the distribution assumed for technical inefficiency. These models demonstrate that distributions commonly assumed in SFA, such as the half-normal distribution, can be understood as stationary distributions resulting from stochastic processes. Adjustments to parameters such as demand structure, cost structure, and discount rate allow for the explanation of a diverse set of stationary distributions. Furthermore, constructing various stochastic process models allows us to describe different distributions of technical inefficiency as stationary distributions. In doing so, we can examine how the characteristics of the mechanism generating technical inefficiency are reflected in the statistical properties of these distributions.

What is common to the two fundamental models presented—the vintage model and the management control model—is that the productivity of each establishment declines at a certain rate unless management efforts such as facility renewal or management checks are undertaken, and that productivity undergoes probabilistic upward jumps as a result of such efforts. As long as some dynamic process satisfies these properties, it is expected to exhibit a similar asymmetric stationary distribution.

In these models, each economic agent is assumed to behave rationally, as in standard microeconomic models. This means that when each economic agent acts rationally and efficiently, in the sense of maximizing profit, we observe the inefficiency term, which is identified as technical inefficiency in SFA. This result plays an important role in the discussion in Chapter 4, which examines the relationship between the observed inefficiency term and X-inefficiency.

Appendix: Vintage-type Technical Inefficiency and Market Structure

In this appendix, a model is developed as an extension of the vintage inefficiency model presented in Sect. 3.1.1. While the original model simplifies competitive interdependencies and other factors for intuitive explanation, it is extended here to consider the relationship between market structure and the level of technical inefficiency, assuming that each firm operates only a single establishment and does not manage multiple establishments. For the analysis of technical inefficiency in markets composed of large oligopolistic firms with multiple establishments, please refer to Torii (1992, Section 2.3.1, Model Analysis B).

As in Sect. 3.1, we assume that the average and marginal production cost at a plant built at time τ is constant regardless of production quantity and remains $C_0 \exp(-\alpha\tau)$ until the next renewal investment, where $C_0(> 0)$ and $\alpha(> 0)$ are constants. The renewal investment cost is $(F_0 + q K_0) \exp(-\alpha\tau)$ when building a plant with supply capacity $q(\geq 0)$. The market inverse demand function is $P = P_1 - b\,Q$, and the individual inverse demand curve, which represents the demand for firm j, is $P = P_0 - b\,q_j$, where $P(>0), q_j(\geq 0), Q = \sum_j q_j$, are the price, the supply by firm j, and the total market supply, and $P_0(>0)$, and $P_1(>0)$ are constants. The quantity supplied by each establishment is given by the Cournot-Nash equilibrium. Each establishment is managed by a single firm, and there is no distinction between establishments and firms.

The absolute timing of capital renewal for each establishment is determined by the historical process of the last renewal investment. Many equilibria depend on the historical process; therefore, we consider an equilibrium in which each establishment invests in upgrading its facilities at equal intervals, and at a point in time, the vintages of each establishment are uniformly distributed. For the proof of the existence of such an equilibrium, see Førsund and Hjalmarsson (1987, p.46, Theorem 2.1). This model may be considered to be based on a special form of the Førsund and Hjalmarsson model as the basis for its setting.

Assume a time unit Δt, and any time is expressed as a multiple of this time unit. The common interval for facility renewal is assumed to be $N\Delta t$. The unit cost of each establishment at time $M\Delta t$ $(M > N)$ is $C_0 \exp(-\alpha j \Delta t)$ $(j = M - N, \cdots, M - 2, M - 1)$, under the assumption that the vintages of establishments are uniformly distributed. The most efficient establishment is the one that renewed its facilities Δt unit time ago $(j = M - 1)$, while the least efficient establishment is the one that renewed its facilities $N\Delta t$ unit time ago $(j = M - N)$. If an establishment with cost level $C_0 \exp(-\alpha(M - N)\Delta t)$ invests in renewal at this time, it can realize cost level $C_0 \exp(-\alpha M \Delta t)$.

Consider the decision of renewal investment for this establishment. Here, to analyze the relationship between market structure and the level of technical inefficiency, the number of establishments N is set as a variable. The assumption that the vintages of establishments are uniformly distributed implies that the renewal interval for each establishment is $N\Delta t$, which means that optimizing the facility renewal for each establishment involves determining the value of Δt.

If the establishment with the highest cost level, the j-th establishment $(j = M - N)$, does not renew its facility and operates at the current cost level, the outputs of each establishment are determined by the Cournot-Nash equilibrium, and the solution of the system of equations:

$$P_1 - b\sum_{h\neq j} q_h - 2bq_j = C_0 \exp\left(-\alpha\left(M - j - 1\right)\Delta t\right),$$
$$(j = 0, 1, \cdots, N - 1).$$

We sum the N equations:

$$\sum_h q_h = \frac{NP_1 - C_1 N_1}{b(N+1)}.$$

where $C_1 \equiv C_0 \exp(-\alpha(M-N)\Delta t)$ and $N_1 \equiv \{1-\exp(-\alpha N \Delta t)\}/\{1-\exp(-\alpha \Delta t)\}$. Then, the price level is given as

$$P = \frac{P_1 + C_1 N_1}{N+1}.$$

The present value of cash flow of jth $(j = M - N)$ enterprise is

$$\frac{1}{br}\left\{\frac{P_1 + C_1 N_1}{N+1} - C_1\right\}^2.$$

Here, each establishment is assumed to be unable to fully anticipate technological progress, and it is assumed to decide on its facility renewal under the assumption that the current prices and cost levels of other establishments will remain unchanged in the future. In the same manner, if the establishment renews its facility at the time, the present value of the cash flow is

$$\frac{1}{br}\left\{\frac{P_1 + C_1 N_1 \exp(-\alpha \Delta t)}{N+1} - C_1 \exp(-\alpha N \Delta t)\right\}^2.$$

If the difference of these cash flows,

$$\frac{2(P_1 - C_1)\, C_1 N^2 \alpha \Delta t}{br\,(N+1)^2}$$

exceeds the investment cost for facility renewal, the establishment decides to renew. Here, the difference is approximated when $\alpha \ll 1$, that is, with approximations, $\exp(-\alpha \Delta t) \simeq 1 - \alpha \Delta t$, and $N_1 \simeq N - N(N-1)\alpha \Delta t / 2$.

The supply q^*, representing the quantity supplied when the enterprise renews its facility, is approximated as

$$q^* = \frac{P_1 - C_1}{b(N+1)} + \frac{C_1 N \alpha \Delta t}{2b}.$$

The investment cost associated with this renewal is given by $F_0 + q^* K_0$. The condition that this investment cost equals the difference between the discounted present value of cash flows allows us to determine Δt, which gives the optimal interval of renewal investment as follows:

$$N \Delta t = \frac{2r(N+1)}{\alpha C_1} \cdot \frac{(b(N+1)F_0 + (P_1 - C_1)K_0)}{4(P_1 - C_1)N - rK_0(N+1)^2}.$$

If the renewal investment cost does not depend on the quantity ($K_0 = 0$), the optimal interval is

$$N \Delta t = \frac{br(N+1)^2 F_0}{2\alpha C_1 N (P_1 - C_1)}.$$

As long as C_1 (the cost level of the firms at the time of renewal) is given, it is an increasing function of the number of firms N in the market. This is because the rent per firm decreases as N increases, requiring renewal investment opportunities for greater cost reductions to make investment worthwhile when renewal investment involves a fixed cost. As the facility renewal interval increases, the magnitude of the average technical inefficiency increases. Thus, the greater the number of competing establishments in a market, the greater the technical inefficiency.

If no fixed cost is involved in renewal investment ($F_0 = 0$), the optimal interval of facility renewal is

$$N\Delta t = \frac{2r\,(N+1)}{\alpha C_1} \cdot \frac{(P_1 - C_1)\,K_0}{4\,(P_1 - C_1)\,N - rK_0\,(N+1)^2},$$

that is a function of N. Differentiating this by N gives,

$$\frac{\partial}{\partial N} N\Delta t = \frac{2r\,(P_1 - C_1)\,K_0}{\alpha C_1} \cdot \frac{-4\,(P_1 - C_1) + rK_0\,(N+1)^2}{\left\{4\,(P_1 - C_1)\,N - rK_0\,(N+1)^2\right\}^2},$$

which takes a positive value for a sufficiently large value of N. This indicates that, even if renewal investment costs are proportional to supply quantity, the size of the rents per unit of supply quantity decreases as competition drives prices lower, thereby influencing the facility renewal interval in the same way as in cases where fixed costs are present. This implies that, in this case, the greater the number of competing establishments in the market, the greater the technical inefficiency.

References

Battese GE, Coelli TJ (1992) Frontier production functions, technical efficiency and panel data: with application to paddy farmers in India. J Prod Anal 3:153–169

Berger AN (1993) "Distribution-free" estimates of efficiency in the US banking industry and tests of the standard distributional assumptions. J Prod Anal 4(3):261–292

Colombi R, Kumbhakar SC, Martini G, Vittadini G (2014) Closed-skew normality in stochastic frontiers with individual effects and long/short-run efficiency. J Prod Anal 42(2):123–136

Cornwell C, Schmidt P, Sickles RC (1990) Production frontiers with cross-sectional and time-series variation in efficiency levels. J Econometrics 46(1-2):185–200

Førsund FR, Hjalmarsson L (1987) Analyses of industrial structure: a putty-clay approach. Almqvist & Wiksell International

Greene W (2004) Distinguishing between heterogeneity and inefficiency: stochastic frontier analysis of the World Health Organization's panel data on national health care systems. Health Econ 13(10):959–980

Greene W (2005a) Fixed and random effects in stochastic frontier models. J Prod Anal 23:7–32

Greene W (2005b) Reconsidering heterogeneity in panel data estimators of the stochastic frontier model. J Econometrics 126(2):269–303

Kumbhakar SC (1990) Production frontiers, panel data, and time-varying technical inefficiency. J Econometrics 46(1–2):201–211

Kumbhakar SC, Lai H-P (2022) Recent advances in the panel stochastic frontier models: heterogeneity, endogeneity and dependence. Int J Empirical Econ 1(01):1–38

Kumbhakar SC, Lien G, Hardaker JB (2014) Technical efficiency in competing panel data models: a study of Norwegian grain farming. J Prod Anal 41:321–337

Lee YH, Schmidt P (1993) A production frontier model with flexible temporal variation in technical efficiency. In: The measurement of productive efficiency: techniques and applications, pp 237, 255

Schmidt P, Sickles RC (1984) Production frontiers and panel data. J Bus Econ Stat 2(4):367–374

Torii A (1992) Technical efficiency in Japanese industries. In: Industrial efficiency in six nations, pp 31–120

Torii A (2001) Efficiency in Japanese industries. NTT Publishing, Tokyo (in Japanese)

Tsionas EG, Kumbhakar SC (2014) Firm heterogeneity, persistent and transient technical inefficiency: a generalized true random-effects model. J Appl Econ 29(1):110–132

Chapter 4
Technical Inefficiency and X-inefficiency

Debates over X-inefficiency have been active since Leibenstein (1966). However, those debates did not address the measurement of X-inefficiency.[1] Most discussions on X-inefficiency dealt with the problem of inefficiencies arising in the internal organization of firms. Although X-inefficiency concerns firm behavior, it was by no means a concept based on empirical analysis, but rather one derived from theoretical analysis. Indeed, many studies have observed the dispersion of productivity among firms, and many of these studies have clearly stated that they aimed to measure X-inefficiency. Leibenstein himself noted that the starting point of the debate on X-inefficiency was the observation that productivity varied across firms and not all firms were efficient. However, what has actually been measured in these empirical studies is not X-inefficiency itself, but rather technical inefficiency estimated econometrically as deviations from the frontier production function. If it can be demonstrated that the observed technical inefficiency is in fact nothing other than X-inefficiency, then X-inefficiency may be regarded as a concept whose existence can be empirically confirmed. Unfortunately, there has been little discussion as to whether the observation of technical inefficiency can really be taken as evidence for the existence of X-inefficiency.

This chapter examines the proposition of whether the empirical observation of technical inefficiency can be regarded as proof of the existence of X-inefficiency. It begins by explaining that such econometric observations are neither a sufficient nor a necessary condition for the existence of X-inefficiency. Tests for technical inefficiency alone cannot demonstrate the existence of X-inefficiency. The next question, then, is what kind of econometric evidence would be required to establish the existence of X-inefficiency. While the existence test for technical inefficiency is not sufficient to test for X-inefficiency, this does not imply that technical inefficiency is unrelated to it. Even if merely confirming the existence of technical inefficiency is not enough, one can still ask whether some statistical property of the observed inef-

[1] See Frantz (1988).

A. Torii, *Production Efficiency with the Stochastic Management Model*,
https://doi.org/10.1007/978-981-95-3501-9_4

ficiency provides evidence of X-inefficiency. For example, one might ask whether certain characteristics of the econometrically estimated dispersion in productivity, interpreted as technical inefficiency, are consistent with theoretical arguments for X-inefficiency, or whether testing statistical properties of the estimators of technical inefficiency can help identify whether the observed inefficiency is in fact generated by X-inefficiency.

This study shows the difficulty of asserting the existence of X-inefficiency on the basis of some statistical fact as long as we use the conventional definition of X-inefficiency. There has been a long-standing debate between researchers on X-inefficiency and neoclassical microeconomists, but with the conventional definition the discussion cannot go beyond the question "what is rational behavior?" Next, we discuss the following question: If the conventional definition of X-inefficiency is not sufficient to demonstrate its existence, then what feature of X-inefficiency can be taken as an econometrically refutable concept instead? In this chapter, we consider various characteristics of X-inefficiency and examine which of them can be tested using econometric analysis. Redefining X-inefficiency with these characteristics may contribute to the goal of empirically verifying its existence, so each possible candidate characteristic is considered in turn.

In conclusion to this examination, this study proposes to consider X-inefficiency as "inefficiency that is not controlled in any way by managerial efforts." The following chapters show that, by defining X-inefficiency in terms of the absence of control, it becomes possible to devise a method for empirically testing its existence. Furthermore, an empirical test of the existence of X-inefficiency is attempted using actual input–output data for the Japanese manufacturing industry.

The remainder of this chapter is organized as follows. In Section 4.1, we provide standard descriptions and definitions of X-inefficiency and technical inefficiency. Section 4.2 examines the relationship between the two concepts and explains that testing for the existence of technical inefficiency alone does not prove the existence of X-inefficiency. Section 4.3 argues that X-inefficiency cannot be observed as a statistical fact as long as it is defined in terms of causes, and Section 4.4 examines several candidates for a refutable definition of X-inefficiency that could replace the cause-based definition. Finally, Section 4.5 concludes by proposing the redefinition of X-inefficiency in terms of the absence of control for the purpose of empirical verification.

Before beginning the discussion, it should be noted that, to avoid confusion caused by terminology, in this chapter we refer to X-inefficiency as the inefficiency inherent in business organizations that Leibenstein sought to explain, and to technical inefficiency as the dispersion of productivity observed through econometric methods. Since the central theme of this chapter is how X-inefficiency can be defined, we use this terminology for the discussion without providing an explicit definition at this stage. In the final section of this chapter, we propose a statistically refutable concept of X-inefficiency.

Leibenstein himself used the term "technical efficiency" to refer not to the quantitative concept defined above, but rather to a concept specific to traditional microeconomics. He compared technical efficiency with X-efficiency and emphasized that it was a completely different concept. According to Leibenstein, technical inefficiency is "the seeming deviation from the maximum possible output resulting from the profit-maximizing or cost-minimizing behavior of firms." For example, as illustrated in the vintage model, under technological progress, a factory cannot achieve maximum output with the technology available in a given period unless it immediately embodies the new technology in its production equipment as soon as it is discovered. However, continually replacing factories or production equipment in every period to pursue the latest efficient technology is clearly "inefficient" unless the cost of replacement is zero. A rational plant chooses to renew its production equipment at appropriate intervals. As a result, production equipment will continue to be used even if it is somewhat obsolete compared with equipment embodying the latest technology. In Leibenstein's wording, this situation is "technically inefficient" but not "X-inefficient." Thus, even though technical inefficiency is often used by empirical economists as a synonym for "X-(in)efficiency," it should be noted that it is also sometimes used in the limited sense of "seemingly inefficient" outcomes resulting from the optimizing behavior of economic agents. [2]

4.1 Leibenstein's X-inefficiency and the Technical Inefficiency in Econometrics

This section introduces Leibenstein's X-inefficiency and the econometric concept of technical inefficiency. In later sections, the relationship between the two is analyzed.

4.1.1 Leibenstein's X-inefficiency

First, we review the arguments presented by Leibenstein as a theory of X-inefficiency. His arguments are wide-ranging and have been presented in many of his books. Presenting all of them is beyond my ability; therefore, please allow me to give a very limited summary of only those parts that are necessary for the following discussion: X-inefficiencies are usually thought of as problems in the internal organization of the firm, as typified by the theory of X-inefficiency developed in the book by Leibenstein (1987), *Inside the Firm, The Inefficiencies of Hierarchy*. To summarize, the factors that cause inefficiencies in internal organizations can be illustrated as follows:

> Consider an organization that produces some identifiable and measurable product or service. A proper subset of its members (even a single individual) may refrain from taking the actions necessary to maximize the output of the organization as a whole, acting instead in the interest of that subset.

[2] What further complicates the wording is that, in discussions on X-inefficiency, there are cases where the observed results of technical inefficiency reported by econometricians are interpreted as evidence demonstrating X-inefficiency.

Leibenstein (1976) defined X-inefficiency in the same way. The causes of X-inefficiency highlighted in Leibenstein's book are the prisoner's dilemma, existence of inert areas, and superego.

Prisoner's Dilemma

A typical explanation of the prisoner's dilemma in game theory refers to a state of Nash equilibrium with dominant strategies, assuming a rational choice of agents. When the equilibrium does not maximize the sum of the joint profits, the state is considered to be in a prisoner's dilemma. However, since the rationality of economic agents is questioned in the theory of X-inefficiency, such an equilibrium is not necessarily considered a prisoner's dilemma by Leibenstein. The prisoner's dilemma described by Leibenstein (1976, p.185) occurs in a situation where there is no dominant strategy for either agent, nor is there any cell that constitutes a Nash equilibrium. In this prisoner's dilemma, each agent adopts the strategy that yields the greatest profit for themselves among all possible payoffs. That is, the situation is described as one where each agent attempts to "free ride" on the strategy that would be most beneficial for them, assuming the other agent adopts the strategy that is most favorable for their counterpart.[3]

In the prisoner's dilemma described by Franz (1988), the players in the game are the firm's managers and employees, respectively. The employee's strategy represents the level of effort, while the management's strategy represents the working conditions. In the prisoner's dilemma, the manager expects an employee who is loyal to the interests of the firm (a hardworking employee under poor working conditions) to remain diligent and productive despite unfavorable conditions, while the employee determines their behavior under the assumption that the manager prioritizes the employee's interests (a lazy employee under comfortable working conditions). Management betrays the expectations of workers, and workers, in turn, attempt to maximize their own benefits by betraying the expectations of management. As a result, poor working conditions lead to low productivity.

Furthermore, the combination of strategies, where the employee exerts a moderate level of effort and the management provides moderate working conditions, is also described as an alternative situation to the prisoner's dilemma, referred to as the Peer Group Standard. The payoffs may be adopted as a "convention" because the state is a "fair" situation that is not highly inefficient; that is, the payoff brings about "a fair day's work for a fair day's pay." The state of peer standard is similar to that of the prisoner's dilemma, where productivity is below the maximum level; thus, in the sense of failing to reach the maximum level of productivity, both situations are inefficient.

---

[3] In the explanation on Leibenstein (1976, p.146) of the same book, the state of the prisoner's dilemma is a Nash equilibrium. It is shown as an example where the outcome of individual optimization does not lead to joint profits.

Inert Area

Inertial behavior arises in the effort-level decisions of economic agents who continuously engage in tasks that require sustained effort. The level of effort at each moment determines the economic performance at that point in time. It is assumed that, for each point in time, there exists a level of effort that maximizes the flow of economic output. However, since adjusting the level of effort involves a cost, agents will not make such adjustments if the expected improvement in performance is not greater than the adjustment cost, even when they are aware that the current performance is below the maximum. In this situation, the agent is considered to be in a state of inertia.

Although not explicitly stated, both the economic outcomes and adjustment costs are assumed to represent aggregated present values. As long as the agent remains within the inert area, the agent has no incentive to change the effort level and continues to perform the assigned task at the same level of effort. The agent adjusts the effort level only when environmental changes or shifts in performance push the current effort level out of the inert area. Consequently, the economic outcomes achieved before the adjustment remain below the maximum attainable level. In this sense, inefficiency exists.

Thus, Leibenstein explains the existence of the inert area as a result of individual utility maximization that accounts for adjustment costs. He also suggests that inert behavior may arise because individuals are unable to perceive small differences in their own utility levels. Moreover, a group inert area is also considered. While the inert area is fundamentally a concept defined at the individual level, the presence of individual inert areas inevitably affects the economic performance of the group. Changes in an individual's effort level naturally influence the behavior of other connected individuals. When such changes affect the performances of others, they may require corresponding adjustments in the effort levels of those affected. These interdependencies necessitate negotiations, which in turn raise adjustment costs. Therefore, the individual inert area is likely to be larger than in the case of an isolated individual. As a result, if we regard the vector composed of each individual's effort levels as representing collective behavior, we can identify an inert area at the group level. This group inert area is expected to expand as the size of the group increases. This phenomenon is referred to as the group inert area. [4]

Superego

The superego, along with the id, is one of the fundamental concepts in Freudian psychoanalysis. Both are used to explain "selective rationality." The superego represents

[4] This explanation is based on Leibenstein (1976, Chapter 7). Leibenstein explains the existence of the inert area as the result of individual utility maximization with adjustment costs. In contrast, Franz (1988) does not rely on rational behavior to explain it. According to his view, the group inert area is defined as the level of individual effort that is socially accepted within the group, and, therefore, the individual inert area tends to shrink as the group becomes larger.

a disposition that aspires toward higher standards. It refers to an attitude marked by a sense of duty, responsibility, and a persistent commitment to achieving specific standards in a given role or task. In contrast, the id is the source of impulses, exemplified by the notion of a "spree"; it seeks ease and avoids rigid decision-making. It is commonly understood that the superego and the id are in constant conflict within the same individual. Both contribute to the formation of individual utility; however, it is important to emphasize that they are not substitutes. That is, preferences over combinations of (level of superego satisfaction, level of id satisfaction) are not necessarily ordered, and the axiom of completeness is not assumed to hold.

Both the superego and the id are influenced by "pressure" and various forms of "rationality of action." Pressure refers to the internal and external forces that demand a change in behavior. Rationality in this context refers to the characteristics required to be an economic agent. It includes awareness of constraints and objective functions (constraint concern and purposiveness), calculatedness, realism in assessing the context, independence of judgment, and similar traits. The superego is assumed to be an increasing function of pressure and rationality of action, while the id is a decreasing function of the same variables. That is, in terms of the combination of pressure and rationality, both the superego and the id are considered to satisfy the conditions of completeness and transitivity. The superego is regarded as being more satisfied when an individual acts more rationally under greater pressure. Conversely, the id is more satisfied when pressure is low and there is little demand for rigor in decision-making.

In a typical negotiation framework, individual preferences can be represented by iso-utility curves, which indicate combinations of outcomes that yield the same level of satisfaction. Similarly, in the context of the superego and the id, an iso-superego curve represents combinations of pressure and behavioral rationality that result in the same level of superego satisfaction, while an iso-id curve represents those that yield the same level of id satisfaction. The iso-superego curve is convex, reflecting increasing marginal costs of rational behavior under pressure, whereas the iso-id curve is concave, reflecting diminishing marginal returns to id satisfaction. An individual's behavior is determined by the combination of pressure and rationality that maximizes the id satisfaction subject to a given level of superego satisfaction. These optimal combinations trace out a conceptual "contract curve." When a particular task requires a specific level of superego satisfaction, the corresponding point on this contract curve determines the individual's behavior. The chosen level of rationality influences productivity, and since this level varies with the superego requirement, it may lead to observable inefficiencies.

When an individual obtains a job within an organization, a certain level of superego is required, corresponding to the expectations associated with that role. The point on the contract curve that satisfies this required level of superego indicates the behavior that the individual will exhibit within the organization. The level of behavioral rationality chosen at this point determines the resulting productivity. Consequently, productivity may vary depending on the level of superego required. In this sense, inefficiency arises.

4.1.2 Definition of Technical Inefficiency

As long as production facilities are perfectly divisible, economic agents engaged in profit-maximizing behavior will always operate on the production frontier. However, the converse does not necessarily hold: even if production activities occur on the production frontier, they may still be inefficient. Such inefficiency arises from incorrect choices regarding production scale or technology, and is distinct from technical inefficiency, which refers to failing to operate on the production frontier. Farrell (1957) defined technical inefficiency in this way, explicitly distinguishing it from inefficiencies stemming from decision-making errors. According to Farrell, inefficiency can be classified into three types: technical inefficiency, allocative price inefficiency, and scale inefficiency.

The relationship between the input vector $\boldsymbol{x}$ and output y is expressed as $y = f(\boldsymbol{x}) - u$, where $f(\boldsymbol{x})$ is the frontier production function representing the maximum attainable output for a given input $\boldsymbol{x}$. Let $(\boldsymbol{x}_0, y_0)$ denote the observed input vector and output. Then, technical inefficiency is present if $u > 0$; that is, when $y_0 < f(\boldsymbol{x}_0)$. Let w_h and w_g denote the prices of the hth and gth input factors, and let p denote the output price. Allocative inefficiency with respect to input factors arises when $f_h(\boldsymbol{x}_0)/f_g(\boldsymbol{x}_0) \neq w_h/w_g$. Similarly, scale inefficiency is defined as the case where $p \neq c_y(y_0, \boldsymbol{w})$, with $c(y, \boldsymbol{w}) = \min_x\{\boldsymbol{w} \cdot \boldsymbol{x} \mid f(\boldsymbol{x}) \geq y,\ \boldsymbol{x} \geq 0\}$. Here, $\boldsymbol{w}$ denotes the vector of input prices, and the subscripts of the function denote partial derivatives.

Following Farrell (1957), the relationship between technical inefficiency and input allocative inefficiency can be illustrated as in Fig. 4.1, where the production function is homogeneous of degree one and there are two input goods. In the figure, the horizontal and vertical axes, x_1 and x_2, represent the amounts of input goods 1 and 2 used per unit of output, respectively. Suppose the production frontier is given by the curve UU'. Owing to the homogeneity of degree one, this frontier is represented by the equation $1 = f(x_1/y, x_2/y)$. If the price ratio of the two inputs is indicated by the slope of line PP', the cost-minimizing (and therefore fully efficient) input combination is located at point C. If the observed production activity occurs at point A, then the production is both technically inefficient and allocatively inefficient with respect to input prices.

First, the same output can be achieved by combining the inputs represented by point B without changing the input ratio indicated by the slope of OA. At point A, additional costs corresponding to the distance AB are incurred due to input waste and other factors. This additional cost reflects the magnitude of technical inefficiency. By producing at point B instead of point A, the unit cost of output can be reduced by the ratio OB/OA. Second, even if technical inefficiency is eliminated and production takes place on the frontier at point B, further cost reduction is possible by adopting a different technology that changes the input ratio from the slope of OB to that of OC, thereby shifting production to point C. At point B, the suboptimal input ratio results in additional costs corresponding to the distance BD, which reflect the magnitude of input allocative inefficiency. Producing at point C instead of point B reduces the unit cost further by the ratio OD/OB. The ratios OB/OA and OD/OB

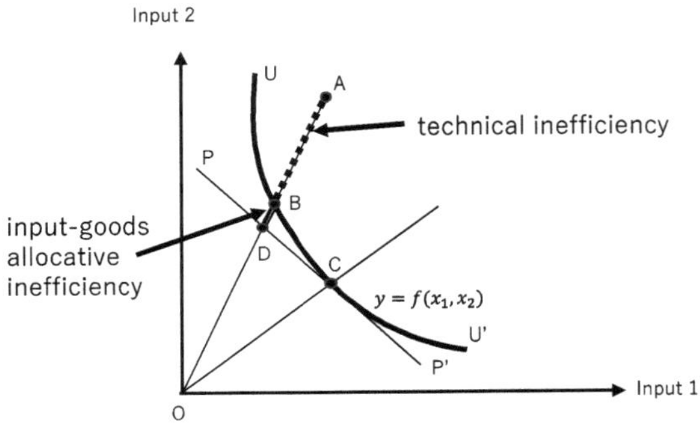

Fig. 4.1 Technical inefficiency and input-good allocative inefficiency

serve as measures of technical and allocative inefficiency, respectively. Their product, OD/OA, represents total efficiency.

Technical inefficiency is defined as a situation in which the output falls short of the maximum attainable level given a certain physical input. This is distinct from the failure to achieve maximum output under a given monetary input. When the output is submaximal under a budget constraint, the cause may lie in technical inefficiency or the use of a suboptimal technology. In particular, if the output attains the maximum level feasible under the chosen technology, but the inefficiency arises from an inappropriate choice of input combination (i.e., an inappropriate technology), then the inefficiency is not technical but rather allocative with respect to input goods.

4.1.3 Stochastic Production Frontier Model

Assuming technical inefficiency, the relationship between the input vector $\boldsymbol{x}_j$ and the output y_j is expressed as

$$y_j = f_i(\boldsymbol{x}_j; \boldsymbol{\beta}_i) - u_j,$$

where $f_i(\cdot)$ denotes the production function for industry i, $\boldsymbol{\beta}_i$ is the corresponding parameter vector, and u_j represents the deviation from the production frontier due to technical inefficiency. The subscript j refers to the jth establishment in industry i. For variables indexed by j, the industry subscript i is omitted for simplicity.

It has long been recognized that directly estimating this input–output relationship raises concerns about the robustness of the estimator. Statistical errors and misspecification of the production frontier are, to some extent, unavoidable in empirical analysis. The noise arising from these issues affects both the estimated production frontier and the parameter estimates for the distribution of u, which represents the level of technical inefficiency. In particular, the estimates are highly sensitive to outliers generated by factors with a positive skew. For example, consider a sample observation that shows significantly higher productivity than others. Because deviations from the frontier are permitted only in the negative direction, the production frontier must be determined so as to include this observation as a technically efficient case; that is, the frontier is effectively pulled upward to accommodate it. If the production frontier is characterized by only one parameter, that single observation can determine the entire frontier. Even when multiple parameters are involved, the frontier may be determined by as few observations as there are parameters. This problem stems from the strict adherence to the economic definition of the frontier, in which each observation is modeled as the sum of a deterministic frontier and a one-sided deviation due to inefficiency. As a result, there is no allowance for a positive error term. This issue is thus inherently tied to the economic interpretation of the production frontier. From a statistical standpoint, however, the problem may be mitigated through appropriate outlier-removal algorithms. One such approach is proposed by Timmer (1971), in which outliers are iteratively excluded as long as the estimated parameters continue to vary substantially. Nevertheless, arbitrariness is inevitable while selecting an algorithm.

Thus, allowing for error terms beyond those representing technical inefficiency in the estimation of the production frontier is a natural extension. Aigner, Lovell and Schmidt (1977) and Meeusen and van Den Broeck (1977) defined the stochastic frontier by acknowledging not only statistical noise but also disturbances from uncontrollable factors such as equipment malfunction and weather, which may cause variation in the production frontier itself. The key distinction between such uncontrollable disturbances and the residual term representing technical inefficiency lies in the directionality of their variation. While deviations due to inefficiency occur only in the negative direction, disturbances arising from uncontrollable factors are assumed to be symmetric around zero. Accordingly, the production frontier is formulated as introduced in Chapter 1:

$$y_j = f_i\left(\boldsymbol{x}_j; \boldsymbol{\beta}_i\right) + v_j - u_j, \tag{1.1}$$

where v_j denotes a normally distributed random error. Once the distribution of u_j is specified, the Maximum Likelihood Estimator (MLE) for that distribution parameter can be estimated. It should be emphasized that in equation (1.1), the stochastic production frontier corresponds to the term $f_i(\boldsymbol{x}_j; \boldsymbol{\beta}_i) + v_j$, which introduces randomness into the frontier itself. This distinguishes it conceptually from the deterministic production function $f_i(\boldsymbol{x}_j; \boldsymbol{\beta}_i)$. For clarity, we refer to $f_i(\boldsymbol{x}_j; \boldsymbol{\beta}_i)$ as the production function, and to $f_i(\boldsymbol{x}_j; \boldsymbol{\beta}_i) + v_j$ as the stochastic frontier.

Defining the production frontier in this manner avoids the problems associated with deterministic estimation methods. If a deterministic frontier is assumed, the estimated production function is highly dependent on outliers unless an appropriate outlier elimination algorithm is incorporated. In contrast, assuming a stochastic production frontier allows a substantial portion of the outlier effect to be absorbed into the symmetric error term v_j. This reduces the instability in estimating the production function $f(\boldsymbol{x}_j; \boldsymbol{\beta})$ that would otherwise be caused by unusually high productivity observations.[5]

This approach to handling outliers is both a strength and a limitation of stochastic models. In estimating the stochastic frontier, it is necessary to make an *a priori* assumption about the distribution of technical inefficiency in order to separate the asymmetric component u_j from the symmetric component v_j. Common assumptions include the half-normal, exponential, truncated normal, and gamma distributions. However, the choice of distribution type is not grounded in any specific economic theory. In stochastic models, observations that do not conform to the assumed distribution of technical inefficiency tend to be absorbed into the noise term v_j, as previously described. As a result, when the distribution of technical inefficiency is chosen without theoretical justification, the estimated parameters of v_j may vary depending on that choice. Moreover, the estimated parameters for the distribution of technical inefficiency are also affected.

The deviation term that is assumed to follow an asymmetric distribution is attributed solely to technical inefficiency. However, the sources of the symmetric error term may include not only aggregation errors but also factors that are not subject to control, such as weather conditions. It is important to note that when such uncontrollable factors are treated as noise in the stochastic frontier model, as in the present framework, the model is subject to a fundamental issue pointed out by Førsund, Lovell and Schmidt (1980). Specifically, adopting a stochastic production frontier model and treating all symmetric error components as noise leads to the unintended consequence that beneficial effects, such as favorable weather conditions, are also absorbed into the noise term. In the original deterministic frontier model, given by $y = f(\boldsymbol{x}) - u$, the maximum output represents the literal maximum possible output, achieved when all favorable conditions are simultaneously realized. In contrast, the maximum output in the stochastic frontier model reflects an average level that

---

[5] In a stochastic production frontier model, the deviation from the production function is expressed as $v_j - u_j$. The parameters governing the distributions of u_j and v_j are jointly estimated along with the production function itself. For example, under Maximum Likelihood (ML) estimation, the shape of the production function and the distributions of u_j and v_j are chosen to maximize the likelihood function. Observations that significantly deviate from the distribution assumed for technical inefficiency, which is typically skewed in the negative direction, such as establishments exhibiting exceptionally high productivity, tend to be accommodated by increasing the estimated variance of the noise term v_j. In this way, the stochastic frontier model systematically treats such outliers as noise. Thus, an effective mechanism for dealing with outliers is inherently built into the estimation process.

Consider the case where the production function and distribution parameters are determined by MOLS, which will be introduced in Section 5.3. If there is an establishment that exhibits significantly higher productivity compared with other establishments, the presence of this outlier will shift the third-order moment in a positive direction. Consequently, estimation of the parameters using the method of moments will lead to a lower estimate of σ_u, which corresponds to the technical inefficiency term. This is because the third-order moment takes a negative value when technical inefficiency is present. In general, the second-order moment is an increasing function of both σ_u and σ_v. Therefore, if the second-order moment of the observed OLS residuals is fixed, an increase in one of these estimates results in a decrease in the other. As a result, the estimate of σ_v, which represents the noise term, becomes larger.

varies with changing external conditions. Thus, the meaning of the expression "maximum possible" in the definition of the production frontier must be reconsidered in the context of the stochastic framework.

Another limitation is that it is not possible to determine the extent to which each establishment is (in)efficient. The deviation of each sample from the production function is always expressed in the form $v_j - u_j$, and thus the inefficiency component u_j for each sample cannot be separately identified. In other words, since the production frontier is represented by the stochastically varying component $f(\boldsymbol{x}_j; \boldsymbol{\beta}) + v_j$, it is not meaningful to measure how far an individual observation is from the frontier. What is estimated are merely the parameters that characterize the shape of the distribution, and no information is provided that allows the separation of u_j and v_j at the individual sample level. Nevertheless, based on the estimated distribution, we can compute the mean and variance of u_j, allowing us to evaluate the average level of technical inefficiency across the entire industry as a whole. Therefore, this limitation does not pose a problem when the objective is to assess inefficiency at the industry level.

4.2 Relation Between X-inefficiency and Technical Inefficiency

This section examines the relationship between the theoretical concept of X-inefficiency and the empirical concept of technical inefficiency. It considers the implications of the empirical observation that technical inefficiency is widespread across many industries for the theory of X-inefficiency.

At the beginning of Section 4.1, Leibenstein's definition of X-inefficiency is introduced as the conflict between an organization's profit-maximizing behavior and the optimizing behavior of its individual members or groups of members. A review of the three arguments presented in Section 4.1 as theories of X-inefficiency reveals that Leibenstein's definition is consistent with all of them. The prisoner's dilemma clearly exemplifies such inefficiency. The existence of an inertial area can also be interpreted as an inefficiency arising from a misalignment between the optimal domain for organizational members and the organization's profit, considering that adjustment costs are borne by individual members and are not counted as the organization's production costs. Furthermore, in the theory of the superego, the rationality referred to as one of its components is evidently defined from the standpoint of the organization. As a result of individuals pursuing their own optimal behavior, a level of rationality may be selected that is not necessarily optimal for the organization.

If Leibenstein's definition is adopted as the definition of X-inefficiency, it entails defining X-inefficiency in terms of the underlying causes of inefficiency. Many standard formulations of X-inefficiency follow this approach by characterizing it based on its causes. As a starting point for the discussion, we begin by examining this cause-based definition of X-inefficiency as a first step toward exploring the relationship between X-inefficiency and technical inefficiency.

4.2.1 *Existence of Technical Inefficiency That Is Not X-inefficiency*

We begin by explaining that not all observed technical inefficiencies necessarily arise from X-inefficiency. To this end, this subsection demonstrates that technical inefficiency can be identified by an econometric model even in the absence of internal inefficiencies within firms, such as those described in Subsection 4.1.1.

Consider the inefficiency that arises in firms' decisions to renew capital equipment. This issue is examined in detail in the vintage inefficiency model discussed in Chapter 3. Assuming a putty-clay type model, capital renewal enables a firm to acquire the most advanced technology available at the time of investment, thereby attaining the maximum level of efficiency. Productivity remains unchanged thereafter until the next capital renewal. If the production frontier is continuously shifting outward due to technological progress, then unless firms constantly renew their equipment to incorporate the latest technologies, their productivity will remain relatively lower than that of the frontier. In other words, firms are almost always inefficient relative to the latest production frontier, except immediately after capital renewal. However, continually updating capital equipment to embody the latest technology at all times would require unbounded investment, which is not a rational managerial choice. Rational managers determine the optimal timing for capital renewal by weighing the costs of investment against the productivity gains from newer technologies. In the model presented in Subsection 3.1.7, managers operating under competitive pressure choose capital renewal timing accordingly. As a result, the hazard rate representing the probability of capital renewal is zero in the region where u^* is extremely small. The same model also shows that commonly assumed distributions of technical inefficiency—such as the half-normal and exponential—can be derived as outcomes of such capital renewal behavior.

Thus, even if equipment renewal is optimally chosen, the achieved productivity deviates from the frontier technology, meaning that technical inefficiency is observed as a deviation from the frontier function. However, this observed technical inefficiency is clearly unrelated to internal organizational issues of the firm and does not imply "waste." Therefore, it cannot be considered X-inefficiency. In the absence of externalities, the firm's optimality and efficiency coincide with social optimality and efficiency. Hence, it does not represent social inefficiency either. Førsund and Hjalmarsson (1987) supported this proposition, stating that "a dispersed structure that appears statically inefficient may be only one aspect of an optimal dynamic outcome" (p. 69). In this way, the mere existence of dispersed productivity is not sufficient evidence for the existence of inefficiency. The technical inefficiency observed in the vintage inefficiency model may be merely apparent inefficiency.

In addition to the putty-clay type vintage model, another model is introduced that allows technical inefficiency to be observed in SFA. This model, presented below, is referred to as the "misspecification inefficiency model." Suppose that the frontier production function in an industry is given by $y = f(k, z)$, where $y = Y/L$, $k = K/L$, Y denotes output, K denotes capital, and L denotes labor. The variable z is one of the production factors, but it is assumed to be unobservable. Given constant wage and interest rates, the optimal capital–labor ratio is fixed at k^*, and all establishments construct their facilities based on this ratio. However, since the value of z varies across establishments, productivity also differs. It is assumed that the realized values of z at each establishment do not deviate significantly from the mean and are symmetrically distributed around z_0. In Subsection 1.5.2 of Chapter 1, we introduced a case where an important production factor, managerial effort, was unobservable, but we considered it to be a controllable factor. Here, by contrast, the variable z is assumed to represent an exogenous factor, such as location or natural environment, that affects productivity but lies beyond managerial control.

If we denote the deviations as Δz, then $z = z_0 + \Delta z$, Taylor expansion of the production function $y = f(k^*, z)$ around z_0 with respect to z yields,

$$y = f\left(k^*, z_0\right) + f_z(k^*, z_0)\Delta z + f_{zz}\left(k^*, z_0\right)(\Delta z)^2 + o((\Delta z)^3). \tag{4.1}$$

When the unobserved production factor z has a symmetric distribution around its mean value z_0, a deviation from the production frontier $f(k^*, z_0)$ is observed. Since Δz is assumed to be symmetrically distributed, the deviations shown in the second term are also symmetrically distributed. In contrast, the deviations shown in the third term are asymmetrically distributed. This is because, under typical symmetric distributions, the distribution of $(\Delta z)^2$ is asymmetric and takes only positive values, while the coefficient f_{zz} is negative by assumption due to the concavity of the production frontier. Equation (4.1) has the same structure as the stochastic production frontier model. Therefore, if the actual input–output relationship follows Equation (4.1), estimating the input–output relationship using the stochastic production frontier model (1.1) is appropriate. In this case, the third-order moment of the regression residuals is expected to be negative when using a stochastic production frontier model, such as Ordinary Least Squares (OLS). Thus, if the input–output relationship follows Equation (4.1), the presence of technical inefficiency is confirmed when the regression model (4.1) is estimated in SFA using the observed input–output data.

Thus, the inefficiency caused by the misspecification inefficiency model is statistically observed as technical inefficiency in SFA. However, this inefficiency is not technical inefficiency in nature but rather a form of allocative inefficiency in input use. The observed technical inefficiency arises because the econometric model mistakenly attributes allocative inefficiency to technical inefficiency due to a misspecified production function that omits an important production factor. Therefore, technical inefficiency arising through this mechanism cannot be regarded as X-inefficiency. It should be emphasized that this model does not assert that all observed technical inefficiency is attributable to such misspecification. Rather, it should be understood that some portion of the observed technical inefficiency may reflect misspecification-induced allocative inefficiency arising from estimation issues. Whether the observed technical inefficiency actually includes such components is a separate issue and must be addressed through empirical investigation. This issue will be examined in greater detail in Chapter 5, Subsection 5.1.1.

In this subsection, we have shown that technical inefficiency can be observed in econometric models even when it does not stem from internal organizational inefficiencies as described by Leibenstein. Specifically, we examined two such cases: inefficiency arising from the vintage inefficiency model and inefficiency resulting from the misspecification of the production function. These examples demonstrate that not all observed technical inefficiency originates from X-inefficiency.

4.2.2 X-inefficiency Not Observed as Technical Inefficiency

As discussed in Subsection 4.2.1, not all observed technical inefficiencies are X-inefficiencies. Conversely, if X-inefficiencies exist, are they necessarily observed as technical inefficiencies? This subsection explains that even if X-inefficiency exists, it may not necessarily be observed as technical inefficiency in an econometric model.

If X-inefficiency is defined based on its causes, then in order to determine whether a given cause of inefficiency constitutes X-inefficiency, we must consider how that cause can be observed. As long as we attempt to observe technical inefficiency through SFA, we require a theoretical framework that explains how the observed asymmetrical distribution arises as technical inefficiency.

To enable the observation of causes, one should begin by examining whether the assumed distribution can be rationalized as the asymptotic distribution of a dynamic stochastic process. By considering a stochastic process, we can analyze the mechanism that generates the observed distribution. If no dynamic stochastic process is assumed, inefficiency must be treated as a fixed value at a specific point in time. In that case, the justification for assuming a particular distribution for these fixed values must rely on empirical observations, such as instances where a specific distributional form is known to occur, as with innate characteristics in biological organisms.

Alternatively, one may assume that inefficiency is generated by a specific mechanism but becomes fixed after a certain point in time. One possible form of such a mechanism is that the characteristics of establishments are generated randomly, but the probability of their survival varies depending on the values of these characteristics at a given time. Establishments with favored characteristics are more likely to survive. However, even in this case, some form of probabilistic selection mechanism must be assumed. In models based on microeconomics, if survival is determined deterministically as a result of competition, discontinuity between survival and exit becomes unavoidable. Consequently, it would be inconsistent with such a framework to assume a typical smooth probability distribution for either a symmetric disturbance term or an asymmetric technical inefficiency term.

The econometric conditions for being observed as technical inefficiency depend on the observation method used. However, regardless of the method used, technical inefficiency will not be observed if there is no productivity dispersion among the observed samples, even after adjusting for other conditions. When the stochastic production frontier model (1.1) is employed, the model is estimated by assuming that the observed productivity is the sum of the frontier-level productivity, a random disturbance term, and an inefficiency term. Using econometric methods such as maximum likelihood estimation, the observed productivity dispersion is decomposed into a part $f_i(\boldsymbol{x}_j; \boldsymbol{\beta}_i)$ that can be explained by differences in factor combinations, a symmetric error term v_j, and an asymmetric deviation term u_j owing to technical inefficiency. Assuming this standard stochastic production frontier model, the dispersion in productivity is not sufficient to observe technical inefficiencies. Another requirement is that the third-order moments of the regression residuals must be negative when OLS is used to estimate the production function, as discussed in the wrong skewness problem.[6]

Thus, for technical inefficiency to be observed, especially under a stochastic production frontier model, the productivity data must exhibit certain statistical properties. However, the theory of X-inefficiency merely states that productivity is lower when X-inefficiency is present than when it is absent, without indicating that any specific statistical characteristics should be observed. Therefore, even if X-inefficiency causes dispersion in productivity, there is no guarantee that such dispersion will be captured as technical inefficiency.

We observe technical inefficiency through the asymmetric distribution of productivity when using SFA. In general, for the distribution of productivity to become asymmetric as a result of some dynamic mechanism and to be interpreted as technical inefficiency, three conditions must be satisfied: first, there must be a persistent tendency to deviate from the frontier; second, the deviating productivity must have a stochastic tendency to return to the frontier; and third, ergodicity is required. [7] The third condition, ergodicity, is necessary because it allows inefficiency-generating mechanisms within a single establishment to be inferred from cross-sectional observations of productivity across many establishments. [8]

In general, the three conditions above are necessary for productivity to include a component represented by an asymmetric distribution in its probability distribution, as a result of repeated variation described by a stochastic process model. This component distorts the overall distribution of productivity, so that technical inefficiency

---

[6] Several methods have been proposed to enable estimation even when the third-order moment of the residuals is positive in the context of the wrong skewness problem, as discussed by Hafner, Manner and Simar (2018), among others. These models extend the assumed distribution of technical inefficiency to accommodate the skewness of either sign.

[7] In Chapter 3, a vintage model of equipment renewal and a managerial inefficiency model are constructed to illustrate how the distribution of inefficiency asymptotically converges to an asymmetric form. See Chapter 3 for details.

[8] In the vintage model in Chapter 3, the first tendency corresponds to the tendency of existing facilities to become obsolete and to deviate from the expanding frontier, while the second corresponds to the role of investment in equipment renewal in catching up with frontier production technology. In the managerial inefficiency model, the first tendency reflects the decline in productivity caused by inefficiencies within the internal organization, while the second corresponds to the process of eliminating inefficiencies through managerial review.

can be observed through such distortion. If any of the three conditions is lacking, technical inefficiency that forms a stationary distribution will not be observed. If the first tendency is not satisfied, no deviation from the frontier occurs. If the second tendency is not satisfied, observed productivity will converge to its minimum level, as all samples will eventually settle at the lowest attainable productivity. [9] In other words, productivity stabilizes at a low level across all samples, and technical inefficiency cannot generally be observed in the form of an asymmetric distribution. Thus, even when their causes fall squarely within the category of X-inefficiency, such as opportunistic behavior, not all X-inefficiencies can be observed as technical inefficiency. For example, if all establishments exhibit the same degree of X-inefficiency, no variance in productivity can be observed. This situation is entirely plausible when the free economic activities of establishments are constrained by government regulations. [10]

The proposition that not all X-inefficiencies can be observed as technical inefficiency holds for the technical inefficiency observed in the stochastic production frontier model. It also applies when the frontier production function does not assume a specific functional form or a particular distribution of technical inefficiency. This is the case with Data Envelopment Analysis (DEA), where the conditions for observing technical inefficiency are less stringent than in stochastic frontier models. Technical inefficiency is identified when the observed productivity falls short of the productivity defined by the envelopment surface. Therefore, if productivity is lowered due to X-inefficiency, it is highly likely to be detected as technical inefficiency when DEA is used. For this reason, many studies assume that deviations from the frontier observed through DEA serve as proxies for the presence of X-inefficiency.[11]

However, first, as in the case of assuming a stochastic production frontier model, if external conditions such as government regulations are the source of X-inefficiency and all establishments exhibit X-inefficiency to the same extent, then productivity dispersion will not arise, and technical inefficiency will not be observed even when using DEA. Second, even if deviations from the frontier are observed in DEA, they may not necessarily be interpreted as technical inefficiency. Since DEA tends to capture dispersion caused by various factors, identifying the sources of inefficiency becomes crucial. Not all deviations are necessarily attributed to inefficiency.

Let us consider a situation in which the level of inefficiency is identified as being correlated with the organizational characteristics of establishments. In such a case, the expected relationship predicted by the theory is considered to be identified, and this is interpreted as supporting the hypothesis of the existence of X-inefficiency (Zelenyuk and Zheka, 2006).

As an example, consider the following scenario. In a certain industry, as explained in Subsection 4.1.1, the productivity of each establishment is determined along a

---

[9] For example, in the managerial inefficiency model in Chapter 3, if the checking mechanism based on managerial effort is not functioning, the system reaches a steady state when all processes become inefficient.

[10] For example, in the regional banking market in Japan during the last decades of the 20th century, frequent herding behavior under strong government regulation has been reported. See Nakagawa (2008); Nakagawa, Oiwa and Takeda (2012) and Hirakata, Kido and Thum (2017).

[11] For example, see Zelenyuk and Zheka (2006).

contract curve resulting from the relative balance between the average employee's "superego" and "id." The equilibrium within the establishment is assumed to be influenced by market competition pressure, which determines the position selected along the contract curve. Furthermore, suppose that in the initial state, all establishments have similar levels of "superego." Consequently, there is little variation in productivity across establishments. However, different establishments may respond differently to market competition pressure: when competitive pressure increases, some establishments experience a significant rise in the "superego" level of employees, leading to higher productivity, whereas others are relatively insensitive to such pressure.

Now, suppose that a change in market structure increases competitive pressure. Establishments that respond strongly to such pressure improve their productivity significantly, thereby pushing the frontier upward. As a result, the gap between these frontier establishments and those with relatively smaller productivity gains widens, leading to an observed increase in technical inefficiency through DEA. Since this increase in inefficiency is accompanied by an increase in competition, the observed negative correlation contradicts the hypothesis of X-inefficiency. However, such a tendency does not necessarily hold in all cases. In general, the relationship depends on how productivity changes are distributed across establishments in response to market conditions. Conversely, if competitive pressure declines, establishments that are more sensitive to such pressure may experience a sharp fall in productivity. Consequently, an increase in technical inefficiency is again observed. In this case, the observed negative correlation between competition and inefficiency supports the X-inefficiency hypothesis.

The following presents another example in which the relationship between technical inefficiency, as measured by DEA, and market competition is not straightforward. Suppose that a change in market structure reduces competitive pressure, causing an overall increase in X-inefficiency and a general decline in productivity across establishments. If establishments closer to the frontier are relatively immune to such declines, then the dispersion in productivity increases, and DEA detects a rise in technical inefficiency. This outcome would appear to support the X-inefficiency hypothesis, as competition and inefficiency are negatively correlated. However, the opposite scenario is also possible. If establishments near the frontier are more vulnerable to structural changes in the market and experience larger declines in productivity, the overall dispersion in productivity may decrease. In such cases, the level of observed technical inefficiency may actually fall. For example, under unstable market conditions, some slack in the production process may be necessary to maintain stable performance. Establishments on the frontier, being highly optimized, often lack such slack. As a result, they may suffer greater productivity losses when conditions change. Thus, a general decline in productivity due to X-inefficiency does not necessarily lead to an increase in technical inefficiency as measured by DEA. Since the estimated frontier in DEA is more susceptible to market conditions than that in SFA, as these examples illustrate, it is rather easy to conceive of situations where the observed correlation between the average level of technical inefficiency and market conditions becomes unstable.

The discussion above shows that even if X-inefficiency exists, it is not necessarily observed as technical inefficiency. Combined with the discussion in Subsection 4.2.1, this implies that there can be technical inefficiencies that are not X-inefficiencies, and X-inefficiencies that are not observed as technical inefficiencies. Thus, insofar as X-inefficiency is defined by its cause, the observation of technical inefficiency is neither a sufficient nor a necessary condition for the existence of X-inefficiency. Contrary to common optimism, the existence of technical inefficiency does not constitute proof of the existence of X-inefficiency.

4.3 "Irrational" Behavior and the Neoclassical Critique of X-inefficiency

As clarified in the analysis in the previous section, defining X-inefficiency by its cause does not allow us to establish any specific relationship between X-inefficiency and econometrically observed technical inefficiency. This section further argues that, insofar as X-inefficiency is defined in terms of irrational behavior, it cannot be observed as a statistical phenomenon.

4.3.1 Relativity of Rationality

Researchers who acknowledge the existence of X-inefficiency often argue that its existence is supported by empirical findings, such as the widespread observation of technical inefficiency in empirical studies.[12] Despite this, there has been a long-standing debate over whether X-inefficiency truly exists. Since the theories of X-inefficiency are highly diverse, the debate necessarily takes on many forms. With this in mind, and at the risk of oversimplification, one might say that the core of the debate centers around the question of whether irrational behavior can actually exist. More precisely, the issue is whether differences in the performance of economic agents can be attributed to irrational behavior on the part of agents with relatively low performance.

In this context, irrationality refers to a counter-concept to the rational agent assumed in traditional microeconomics. When it is argued that real-world economic agents do not always act in accordance with the rational behavior postulated by traditional microeconomic theory, the behaviors excluded from such rational conduct are referred to here as irrational. For instance, the behaviors described in Section 4.1, such as those explained by the prisoner's dilemma, inertia areas, and the superego, are not necessarily considered irrational in the conventional sense of microeconomic analysis. However, when it is claimed that X-inefficiency exists, these behaviors are regarded as not being accounted for by traditional microeconomics. In this sense,

[12] For example, see various articles in Weiermair and Perlman (1990).

these behaviors are treated as irrational in the present discussion. In other words, when X-inefficiency is defined in terms of its causes, the behaviors included in the set of causal factors are interpreted here as irrational behaviors. This usage enables us to consider a broad range of behaviors claimed to cause X-inefficiency.

Researchers who regard X-inefficiency as a phenomenon commonly observed in corporate behavior argue that the essence of the X-inefficiency framework is to expand and generalize the traditional neoclassical view, which interprets economic behavior as the result of rational and optimizing decisions, by incorporating non-rational elements into the decision-making of economic agents.[13] In contrast, neoclassical microeconomics, which questions the existence of X-inefficiency, can assume that there are costs to making rational decisions. Under this assumption, economic agents are said to optimize the degree to which they act rationally by weighing the trade-off between the efficiency gains from rational behavior and the costs required to make accurate decisions. According to this view, the irrationality claimed by the theory of X-inefficiency can be fully subsumed within the neoclassical framework or interpreted as part of optimizing behavior. In this sense, irrational behavior, as defined above, is deemed not to exist. Therefore, many researchers argue that even if inefficiency is observed, the concept of X-inefficiency does not constitute an extension of neoclassical economics. Many researchers do not acknowledge the existence of X-inefficiency at all. Some even go so far as to claim that all economic behavior is super-rational and that any observable outcome is the result of some form of optimization.

To examine this issue, we revisit the example discussed in detail in the managerial inefficiency model presented in Chapter 3. In this model, internal efficiency within a firm continues to decline, and management makes efforts to increase productivity. Assume that the manufacturing process of a product is divided into a series of stages, and that inefficiencies may occur stochastically at any point in the process. These inefficiencies are assumed to arise from factors identified in the theory of X-inefficiency, such as opportunistic behavior, free-riding that can lead to a prisoner's dilemma, and inertia that is unresponsive to changes in the environment. Such inefficiencies increase production costs. However, due to uncertainty and other issues, management cannot determine whether inefficiencies exist merely by observing increases in production costs. If inefficiencies are discovered, management can strengthen oversight across all stages to eliminate them; however, inefficiencies are likely to recur through the same mechanism. Setting the criteria for conducting audits determines the probability distribution of productivity dispersion caused by inefficiencies.[14] Management efforts to increase audit frequency reduce inefficiencies and lower production costs. However, implementing such efforts entails administrative costs. When management seeks to reduce administrative costs, the expected value of production costs rises due to inefficiencies. Thus, management determines the optimal audit criteria by weigh-

---

[13] See Franz (1988) and various articles in Weiermair and Perlman (1990).

[14] Under suitable assumptions, this productivity distribution becomes asymmetric, and technical inefficiency is observed. See Chapter 3 for details.

ing the savings in production costs against the increase in administrative costs. The resulting level of technical inefficiency reflects this decision-making process.

In this model, deviations from the frontier are assumed to be caused by X-inefficiency. That is, inefficiencies observed as high production costs are, by definition, X-inefficiencies in terms of their cause. Furthermore, management selects the optimal level of auditing by weighing the trade-off between administrative costs and the benefit of reduced production costs. This optimal behavior on the part of management is nothing other than behavior that optimally controls the level of inefficiency. At this point, management acts rationally in the sense that the level of efficiency is chosen so as to minimize the combined total of administrative and production costs. In this sense, inefficiency does not arise.

In this example, it is possible to explain how the level of X-inefficiency, which is the result of so-called "irrational" behavior, is determined through rational decision-making. Even the "theory" of X-inefficiency is often formulated within a framework of some form of optimizing behavior. For instance, the prisoner's dilemma discussed in Section 4.1 is explained using the idea of a subjective equilibrium, though it does not employ the concept of a Nash equilibrium. The explanation of inertia-based behavior also characterizes individual choice as optimization under adjustment costs. The superego argument is even more explicitly presented as a result of optimizing behavior. The assumption of "rational behavior" is a powerful analytical tool for describing economic actions. Indeed, it is not difficult to imagine that explaining behavior in a way that does not rely on some objective function representing rationality would be an extremely challenging task. If "irrational behavior" must ultimately be explained in rational terms, then it becomes all the more straightforward to reinterpret these "theories" within a neoclassical framework.

A typical neoclassical approach to explaining the behavior of inefficient economic agents, aside from the idea of the "cost of rational behavior" mentioned above, is to incorporate leisure, which arises from sloth or slacking off, into the utility function of the economic agent.[15] Among rational behaviors, those that maximize components measurable in monetary terms are the most observable and easiest to formalize. Leisure is frequently used to represent the non-monetary component of the utility function. Introducing leisure makes it possible to interpret actions that cannot be observed as the maximization of monetary economic variables as, nevertheless, resulting from some form of optimizing behavior. In this case, the behavior of workers whose utility functions include leisure may not be desirable for firms that aim to maximize output. In this sense, allocative inefficiency may arise in resource allocation. From this perspective, neoclassical microeconomics criticizes the concept of X-inefficiency by interpreting it as a form of allocative inefficiency that is simply difficult to observe.

Thus, even when one attempts to define and explain irrational behavior by identifying its causes, any discussion of how its level is determined ultimately requires consideration of some form of maximization or optimization. In order to examine why the level of X-inefficiency takes the value that is observed (i.e., how the level

[15] This factor can also be considered a cost in a broad sense.

of X-inefficiency is determined), some assumption of rational behavior inevitably becomes necessary at some stage in the analysis. Therefore, the problem can be reformulated, at least at some level, as one of rational decision-making within the framework of neoclassical microeconomics. This dilemma is referred to here as the "relativity of rationality."

Stigler (1976) argues that inefficiencies that occur under uncertainty are not X-inefficiencies. He argues as follows:

> higher costs do not involve waste; ex-post waste arises because ex-ante plans were developed in the presence of uncertainty. This type of waste is unavoidable but controllable. (Stigler, 1976)

He attempts to dismiss the argument of X-inefficiency on the grounds that, while inefficiency cannot be avoided under uncertainty, it can nonetheless be controlled. Here, controllability does not refer to eliminating X-inefficiency by, for example, reducing market concentration or applying competitive mechanisms. Rather, it refers to the idea that rational economic agents can optimize the ex-post level of inefficiency through some form of internal check mechanism. As long as the level of X-inefficiency is controllable in this sense, the criticism stemming from the relativity of rationality cannot be avoided. [16]

4.3.2 *Observation of X-inefficiency*

The theories of X-inefficiency introduced in Section 4.1 are all intended to explain the occurrence of X-inefficiency. Their purpose is to explain the behavior of economic agents using the framework of X-inefficiency theory. By clarifying the reasons why X-inefficiency arises, these theories seek to account for economic behaviors that cannot be explained by neoclassical microeconomics. However, analyzing the causes of inefficiency does not help advance the discussion on the observability of X-inefficiency. This subsection explains why this is the case. It should be emphasized that our concern here lies solely with the observability problem of X-inefficiency, not with reconsidering the theoretical proposition of its existence.

Consider a set of neoclassical theories on the behavior of economic agents. This set includes elements such as the maximization principle and utility theory. Let this set be denoted by C. Let $N(C)$ denote the set of behaviors of economic agents that can be explained by the set C. Next, let I denote the set of behavioral theories, including those described in the theory of X-inefficiency. Naturally, I includes concepts such as the prisoner's dilemma,[17] inertia areas, and the "superego" and the "id." Let $N(I)$ be the set of economic behaviors that can be explained by I. The discussion of X-efficiency expands the scope to include irrational behavior, while also encompassing

[16] Note that Førsund, Lovell and Schmidt (1980), a representative survey of technical efficiency estimation, rejects the neoclassical criticism of X-inefficiency on the grounds that it lacks refutability.

[17] This prisoner's dilemma is not the standard one used in game theory, but rather a special form introduced in Section 4.1 to explain X-inefficiency.

neoclassical rational behavior as a limiting case. Therefore, one could argue that the X-efficiency framework I, as a set of behavioral theories, strictly contains the neoclassical analytical tool C (i.e., $I \supset C$).[18] Here, the relation $A \supset B$ is defined as:

$$\forall b \in B \rightarrow b \in A, \quad \text{and} \quad \exists a \in A \text{ such that } a \notin B.$$

If the inclusion relations among sets of behavioral theories are preserved in the inclusion relations among the sets of explainable actions, then $N(I) \supset N(C)$ holds. If this proposition $N(I) \supset N(C)$ is provable (i.e., if it can be shown that $N(C)$ is a strict subset of $N(I)$), then it is evident that the X-inefficiency argument constitutes an extension of neoclassical microeconomic theory. This proof is established by demonstrating the existence of an element x such that $x \in N(I)$ and $x \notin N(C)$. In other words, it suffices to identify an event or behavior that cannot occur under neoclassical behavioral theory but can be explained by the theory of X-inefficiency. Once such an existence is demonstrated, the remaining issue becomes whether this behavior can be identified econometrically. Thus, the observation problem of X-inefficiency is explicitly formulated.

However, the set C refers to a set of theories of economic behavior, not to a set of economic behaviors themselves. Since C consists of theoretical constructs, it is inherently extensible. For example, by incorporating leisure as an element of economic behavior, the set of explainable actions is simultaneously expanded. This property complicates our task. Even if the theory of X-inefficiency enables an expansion of neoclassical theory, the set $N(C)$ itself has the property of being easily extendable. Therefore, it is difficult to determine whether the expansion through X-inefficiency theory genuinely leads to a broader set of explainable economic behaviors. Consequently, there remains a strong possibility that $N(I) = N(C)$, and this possibility cannot be easily ruled out. As long as the set of economic behaviors under consideration remains the same, meaning that both neoclassical and X-inefficiency theories explain the same behaviors, it is meaningless to assign distinct statistical properties to such behaviors. Unless one identifies behavior that is truly distinct between the two theoretical frameworks, it is not possible to meaningfully address the observation problem.

Here, the claim that $N(C)$ itself is easily expanded suggests that specifying the set X of behavioral theories does not uniquely determine $N(X)$; in other words, $N(X)$ is not well-defined. This implies that the fundamental assumptions break down. Therefore, it is not possible to evaluate the superiority or inferiority of one set of behavioral theories over another based solely on inclusion relations. Put differently, analyzing only the causes of X-inefficiencies does not make it possible to discuss their observability.

[18] It is also possible to argue that all behavioral theories related to X-inefficiency fall within the scope of neoclassical action theories. However, as with the discussion of rationality, this leads to the issue of relativity, and we do not pursue that line of argument here.

4.4 Refutable Definition of X-inefficiency as an Alternative to Cause

As discussed above, the observation of technical inefficiency is neither a necessary nor a sufficient condition for the existence of X-inefficiency. Therefore, technical inefficiency cannot be used as a substitute for the observation of X-inefficiency. More generally, as long as X-inefficiency is defined as the result of irrational behavior—that is, in terms of its cause—it is difficult to argue that any statistically observable phenomenon serves as definitive proof of the existence of X-inefficiency. Given this property, the argument for X-inefficiency is difficult to reconcile with the analytical framework of neoclassical microeconomics.

Is it possible to define X-inefficiency using a criterion other than its cause? Defining X-inefficiency by its cause presents the problems discussed thus far and poses difficulties in statistical verification. At the same time, such a definition has allowed for a clear determination of whether a given inefficiency qualifies as X-inefficiency. In this section, we examine possible alternative definitions of X-inefficiency that do not rely on its cause. Such an alternative definition would provide a clear criterion for determining whether an inefficiency is X-inefficient, and this criterion is expected to be statistically refutable. If there exists a property of X-inefficiency that can be tested through econometric analysis, then redefining X-inefficiency in terms of that property could contribute to the empirical verification of its existence. This section explores that possibility.

The definition we seek is an operational definition of X-inefficiency, one that allows for statistical testing. Moreover, whenever X-inefficiency is observed under this new definition, the observed inefficiency must necessarily include inefficiencies arising from the causes introduced in Section 4.1. In other words, if X-inefficiency is statistically identified under the new definition, that identification must also serve as evidence for the existence of inefficiencies caused by those behavioral factors. This is because the aim is to identify phenomena that cannot be explained within the neoclassical framework but can be explained within the framework of X-efficiency. Otherwise, no matter how much technical inefficiency is observed through econometric methods, it would not be possible to refute the criticisms raised by neoclassical theory.

Note that what we seek in this section is a definition of X-inefficiency specifically intended for econometric analysis. This definition is not necessarily meant to replace the existing theories of X-inefficiency, nor are we attempting to establish a new theory of X-inefficiency here.

4.4.1 Definition as Residual Inefficiency After Rational Decision-Making

As discussed in Section 4.2, some instances of observed technical inefficiency appear inefficient in terms of deviation from the production frontier but are not inefficient from the perspective of maximizing social surplus. This raises the question of whether it would be useful to define X-inefficiency as the portion of technical inefficiency that excludes such apparent inefficiencies. For example, using a vintage model, one can theoretically estimate the degree of inefficiency that inevitably arises from rational decisions regarding the frequency of capital investment needed to catch up with frontier technologies. Such inefficiency is merely apparent: although technical inefficiency is observed, the capital investment level is optimized over the long run, and thus, social surplus is not reduced. In this definition, inefficiencies resulting from rational decision-making are not classified as X-inefficiencies. Accordingly, by deducting from the observed technical inefficiency the portion attributable to rational decisions, the residual can be defined as the new X-inefficiency. If the vintage model is appropriately constructed, inefficiency under this definition becomes observable. That is, if one can estimate the time variation in demand functions and the rate of technological progress within the vintage model, then the magnitude of technical inefficiency arising from rational behavior can also be estimated. This allows for both the level of apparent inefficiency and the overall technical inefficiency to be identified, thereby making it possible to observe the remaining portion empirically.

However, in order to make X-inefficiency quantitatively observable under this definition, one must accept the trade-off that certain inefficiencies that are not observed as technical inefficiency but are considered X-inefficiency based on their cause are excluded from the outset. For example, if X-inefficiency arises uniformly across all providers due to government regulations or other institutional factors, then it does not manifest as technical inefficiency and, consequently, cannot be observed as X-inefficiency under this definition.

Furthermore, since a decline in social surplus can also generally arise due to allocative inefficiency, it is difficult to distinguish inefficiency observed as a residual from inefficiency that should be classified as allocative. For example, in a monopolistic market, the incentive for capital renewal is reduced according to the same logic as the theory that R&D investment declines under monopoly. [19] As a result, the rate of capital renewal becomes slower than the second-best rate under monopoly supply, leading to inefficiency. Even in this case, the monopolist is optimizing the rate of capital renewal from the perspective of its own profit maximization, so X-inefficiency does not exist. The inefficiency that arises here is an allocative inefficiency caused by the reduced incentive for capital investment under monopoly. The portion of inefficiency resulting from rational decision-making can be estimated based on the given supply quantity and the rate of technological progress. Since only a part of the inefficiency caused by the slowed rate of capital renewal is estimated as inefficiency

[19] This effect is analyzed in detail in Section 2.3.1 in Torii (1992).

resulting from rational decision-making, some portion of the technical inefficiency induced by allocative inefficiency remains unaccounted for. Although this residual inefficiency is in fact an additional inefficiency caused by monopoly-induced allocative inefficiency, it is nevertheless observed as X-inefficiency under this definition.

In general, it is difficult to estimate the portion of allocative inefficiency caused by a monopoly that manifests as technical inefficiency. As long as this portion cannot be estimated, even if the observed technical inefficiency exceeds the level theoretically predicted as a result of rational decision-making, the excess may simply be attributable to reduced investment incentives under monopoly. This does not constitute evidence for the existence of X-inefficiency as defined by its cause. In such cases, the monopolist merely adjusts the level of capital renewal investment to a privately optimal level. This does not imply that the capital investment is made at an irrational level.

4.4.2 Avoidable Inefficiency That Still Occurs

As examined in Section 4.3.1, the inefficiency in the managerial inefficiency model is classified as X-inefficiency in terms of its cause, but it is an inefficiency that can be controlled to an optimal level. The fact that it can be controlled invites criticism from the perspective of neoclassical microeconomics and raises the issue of the relativity of rationality. Here, conversely, can we define X-inefficiency as an inefficiency that could be avoided if sufficient managerial effort were made, even at the expense of disregarding costs? If X-inefficiency is literally interpreted as "waste," then the wasteful portion should, in principle, be eliminable through managerial effort. X-inefficiency could thus be defined as inefficiency that remains despite being avoidable.

This definition requires, as a criterion for determining whether inefficiency is X-inefficiency, an assessment of whether the inefficiency could have been reduced. In this respect, it resembles the definition based on cause, as it requires similar judgment. However, by defining X-inefficiency as the variable portion of inefficiency, it may become observable. As Hatch (1990) argues, one of the characteristics of X-inefficiency is that production costs are not fixed but vary depending on the economic environment.[20]

When X-inefficiency is defined in terms of its variable component, we must still explain why the observed inefficiency can be judged as reducible. And in order to justify its reducibility, we inevitably have to trace it back to the cause of the inefficiency. As a result, the issue of the relativity of rationality becomes unavoidable. Even if this definition enables X-inefficiency to be observed, the fact of its measurement alone will not convince researchers adhering to the neoclassical framework of its existence.

---

[20] It is often noted that, in this respect, the theory of X-inefficiency shares much in common with the contestability argument.

However, this problem can be avoided if it is possible to demonstrate the reducibility of inefficiency without reference to its cause. This may be achieved by examining whether the level of technical inefficiency identified through statistical methods varies over time or across cross-sectional units. If statistical analysis reveals that part of the observed technical inefficiency fluctuates, that portion may be defined as X-inefficiency. This approach is potentially implementable using methods of decomposing time-varying inefficiency as proposed by Colombi, Kumbhakar, Martini and Vittadini (2014), Kumbhakar, Lien and Hardaker (2014), Tsionas and Kumbhakar (2014), and Kumbhakar and Lai (2022).

Nonetheless, for the purposes of the present argument, several problems remain. First, the extent to which variable inefficiency actually varies is likely to depend on the cost of reducing inefficiency. When the cost is high, little variation will be observed, and only a portion of variable inefficiency will manifest as observable variation. Still, this method may suffice to demonstrate that there exists a component of inefficiency that does vary in practice. Second, as illustrated in the vintage model, the level of inefficiency resulting from rational decision-making is itself likely to vary with changes in market structure or the competitive environment. Thus, even if time-varying inefficiency is econometrically identified, it may include inefficiency that arises rationally under changing conditions. In such cases, it would be difficult to isolate only the reducible inefficiency. Once inefficiency arising from rational decision-making is mixed into the econometrically identified time-varying inefficiency, the relativity of rationality problem reemerges, and criticisms from the neoclassical perspective cannot be avoided. This definition appears to be close to the definition based on cause.

4.4.3 Correlation with Market Structure

DEA, one of the methods for estimating technical inefficiency, has been widely applied, particularly in industries subject to government regulation. A comparison of these studies reveals that, in many cases, the measured level of inefficiency depends on the degree of protection from competitive pressures, such as entry barriers. Numerous examples show that industries more insulated from competition, and thus more monopolistic, tend to exhibit higher levels of inefficiency. This observation is consistent with the theory of X-inefficiency.

Caves and Barton (1990) and Caves and Associates (1992) analyzed the relationship between the level of technical inefficiency, as measured by parametric estimation, and market structure. Their detailed analyses reveal that correlations with market structure, such as market concentration and entry barriers, are consistently observed across countries. In particular, a study of the Japanese manufacturing industry shows that the level of technical inefficiency is significantly correlated with uniquely Japanese characteristics, such as the subcontracting system and strong government regulation and protection. These findings suggest that the observed technical inefficiency may in fact be X-inefficiency, insofar as it is systematically associated with structural factors that hinder competitive pressure.

Based on this observation, X-inefficiency can be defined as the portion of technical inefficiency that is correlated with market structure. This definition serves to further specify the avoidability-based definition discussed in the previous subsection. Because the level of X-inefficiency is determined by the competitive structure of the market, production costs should not be viewed as absolute values determined from an engineering perspective, but rather as variable figures dependent on market structure.

However, even in cases where technical inefficiency arises from causes other than X-inefficiency, it is possible that the level of inefficiency is systematically related to market structure. Consider, for example, the vintage inefficiency model. The more market demand is divided among a larger number of establishments, the greater the fixed cost of equipment renewal per establishment becomes. As a result, the optimal interval for equipment renewal increases. That is, the optimal renewal interval is an increasing function of the number of firms.[21] As the renewal interval increases, the average deviation from frontier technology also increases, which in turn enlarges the observed technical inefficiency. Therefore, the level of technical inefficiency becomes an increasing function of the number of firms, a market structure variable, and thus, it is negatively correlated with market concentration. This negative correlation is expected to hold particularly when the number of establishments constituting the market is relatively large. This is because, when individual establishments are small relative to market size, the fixed portion of the capital investment for equipment renewal becomes a burden, giving rise to the observed correlation. The technical inefficiency that arises in this case clearly does not constitute X-inefficiency, as it results from firms' rational decisions regarding their equipment renewal intervals. Nonetheless, it is correlated with market structure.

Conversely, when an industry is oligopolistic, the level of technical inefficiency is positively correlated with market concentration, which is the opposite of the case where the number of firms is large.[22] This correlation arises, as already explained, because the incentive for cost-reducing investment diminishes as the market becomes more monopolistic. Even in monopolistic markets, firms or establishments determine their equipment renewal intervals based on decisions that are optimal for maximizing their own profits. As a result of such optimizing behavior, a positive correlation emerges between market concentration and technical inefficiency. Therefore, the inefficiency observed in this case is not X-inefficiency. While it is inefficient in the sense that social surplus is not maximized, the inefficiency arises solely because the investment level that is optimal for individual firms differs from the level that would maximize social surplus. Thus, the technical inefficiency correlated with market concentration is an allocative inefficiency, not X-inefficiency.

---

[21] The optimal renewal interval given in Equation (3.1) in Chapter 3 determines the level of observed technical inefficiency. This interval is an increasing function of the number of firms N.

[22] This proposition is discussed in detail in Torii (1992).

In conclusion, technical inefficiencies that are not X-inefficiencies may also be correlated with market structure. Therefore, merely showing that technical inefficiency is observed and correlated with market structure is not sufficient to assert that the observed inefficiency is X-inefficiency.

Next, we consider the relationship between the level of inefficiency and market structure in the managerial inefficiency model introduced in Subsection 4.3.1. If management increases its effort by conducting audits more frequently, the probability of detecting inefficient processes rises, thereby improving productivity. Now, if total managerial costs are proportional to total production costs (excluding managerial costs), then the optimal level of managerial control does not depend on the scale of output. Consequently, the resulting level of technical inefficiency is also independent of output volume. In this case, the state of market structure, i.e., how market demand is allocated among multiple firms, has no effect on the magnitude of the observed technical inefficiency. [23] However, if total managerial costs are not proportional to total production costs, then the level of technical inefficiency will depend on market structure variables such as each firm's output and the number of firms. [24] Although it is generally not possible to determine *a priori* how such correlations manifest under standard constraints, it is clear that the level of technical inefficiency is, in some form, determined by market structure.

Thus, in this model where inefficiency is controlled through managerial effort, technical inefficiencies that are regarded as X-inefficiencies based on their cause may or may not depend on market structure. In the vintage inefficiency model, we observed that the level of technical inefficiency, which cannot be regarded as X-inefficiency based on its cause, does depend on market structure. Therefore, even if the existence of technical inefficiency is empirically confirmed and its level is found to be correlated with market structure, this alone still does not constitute sufficient evidence for the existence of X-inefficiency.

4.5 Defining X-inefficiency as Uncontrolled Inefficiency

What has been clarified so far is that the relationship between X-inefficiency and econometrically observed technical inefficiency cannot be definitively established,

---

[23] If managerial effort is increased in the form of a rise in parameter G, representing the frequency of managerial inspections within a given period, then the equilibrium deviation due to inefficiency will be inversely proportional to $\sqrt{G}$, thereby increasing productivity. The first-order condition for the optimal choice that minimizes the sum of production and managerial costs is given by Equation (3.11) in Chapter 3. If $C_m(G, Q)$ is linear in output Q, so that $C_m(G, Q) = Q \cdot c_m(G)$, then the optimal level of managerial control G^* is independent of Q and is determined as the solution to the equation

$$\frac{C_1 C_2}{2(G^*)^{3/2}} = c'_m(G^*).$$

[24] That is, whether technical inefficiency increases or decreases with higher market concentration depends on the functional form of C_m.

and that merely confirming the existence of technical inefficiency does not provide a sufficient basis for determining the existence of X-inefficiency. More generally, as long as X-inefficiency is defined in terms of its cause, it is difficult to argue that any statistically observed phenomenon constitutes definitive evidence for the existence of X-inefficiency. On the other hand, many observable alternative definitions are inappropriate, as they cannot effectively exclude technical inefficiencies that arise as a result of rational decision-making. If, due to the difficulty of excluding such rationally arising inefficiencies, X-inefficiency is defined so broadly as to include technical inefficiencies that can be controlled by incurring managerial costs, then the problem of the relativity of rationality becomes unavoidable. As long as this problem of the relativity of rationality remains, it is ultimately impossible to verify whether inefficiencies unexplained by neoclassical microeconomics truly exist.

This suggests that, conversely, to verify the existence of inefficiency that cannot be explained by neoclassical microeconomics, it is necessary to adopt a definition that does not raise the problem of the relativity of rationality. This problem arises when optimal decisions are made at some level and the degree of technical inefficiency is thereby controlled. Therefore, to avoid this problem, we are compelled to consider defining X-inefficiency as

> inefficiency that could be controlled by incurring some managerial cost but is, in reality, left uncontrolled,

or, in other words, as inefficiency characterized by an absence of control despite its controllability.

As this definition does not refer to the cause of inefficiency, it acknowledges, as in the previous discussion, that the source of X-inefficiency arises from issues within the firm's internal organization. However, it is not limited to this; therefore, it may also encompass some inefficiencies caused by allocative inefficiencies. That said, not all observed inefficiencies are regarded as X-inefficiencies: only those inefficiencies whose existence is neither recognized nor controlled—that is, those marked by an *absence of control*—are considered X-inefficiencies. Inefficiencies whose existence is recognized and that are optimally controlled according to some criterion are no longer regarded as "X"-inefficiencies.

For example, if we focus on the causes, the allocative inefficiency introduced in the misspecification inefficiency model in Subsection 4.2.1 is not considered X-inefficiency. However, if there is a resource that is one of the production factors but is not observed, and its input is not controlled, then it meets the present definition and is included in X-inefficiency. Under this definition, however, the inefficiencies in the managerial inefficiency model introduced in Subsection 4.3.1 are not considered X-inefficiencies. Inefficiencies that stochastically arise within a firm's internal organization are, based on their causes, classified as X-inefficiencies under the conventional definition. However, as long as the level of such inefficiency is optimally controlled by the firm's management, that inefficiency is not considered X-inefficiency under this definition based on the absence of control, even if it appears as technical inefficiency. Additionally, for inefficiencies observed in the vintage model, if the equipment renewal interval is optimally determined, the observed technical inefficiency is likewise not included in X-inefficiency under this definition. In other words, all inefficiencies that give rise to the problem of the relativity of rationality are excluded from X-inefficiency, regardless of their causes, because they are optimized at some stage. This definition, based on the absence of control, provides a clear conceptual basis for defining X-inefficiency in this manner.[25]

However, saying that inefficiency is not controlled does not mean that its level is constant and unchanging. As argued in the theory of X-inefficiency, the level of inefficiency is variable in the sense that it is influenced by the competitive structure of the market. When competitive pressure in the market is strong, the equilibrium level of superego among organizational members rises, and the proportion of members inclined to behave rationally is expected to increase. As a result, overall productivity is likely to be higher compared to when members are insulated from competitive pressure. Conversely, when competitive pressure is weak, the proportion of members whose opportunistic behavior is left unaddressed tends to increase, leading to lower overall productivity. The fluctuations in the level of inefficiency that arise in response to changes in the external environment are different from the fluctuations that result from choices made with consideration of the cost of rational behavior.[26]

If management can influence how organizational members subjectively perceive competitive pressure in the economic environment—such as by ensuring the disclosure of information or by providing incentives to encourage learning—by incurring a cost, and if management is able to adjust the level of superego of the members to

[25] This definition is based on the presence or absence of control by management. However, there may be cases where control exists but is not exercised at an optimal level. In such cases, to avoid falling back into the problem of the relativity of rationality, this definition does not classify them as X-inefficiency. As long as inefficiency is subject to some form of control, even if not at the optimal level for the firm or establishment, it is not considered X-inefficiency. Similarly, if the optimal level cannot be achieved due to interventions other than those by management, it is also not classified as X-inefficiency. For example, consider inefficiency in the managerial inefficiency model introduced in Subsection 4.3.1. While management exercises control, employee unions and other groups may act to maximize their own interests, thereby preventing the firm from achieving the first-best optimal level. In such a case, a subset of the organization prioritizes its own benefit over maximizing the total organizational output, which satisfies the characteristics of X-inefficiency discussed in Section 4.1. However, under the definition based on the absence of control, this is not classified as X-inefficiency. Since it is always possible to interpret that management is optimizing at a second-best level by taking into account transaction costs associated with negotiations with the union, we do not classify this as X-inefficiency in order to avoid falling into the problem of the relativity of rationality.

[26] When uncontrolled inefficiency fluctuates in response to changes in the external environment, organizational members choose their own actions in order to optimize their individual interests. As a result, the productivity of the entire organization is impaired. In this case, control is present, but it takes the form of autonomous optimization by the organizational members. Here, the definition of X-inefficiency is based solely on whether control is exercised by management or by the entity responsible for decision-making for the organization as a whole, with the aim of maximizing the benefit accruing to the organization. This definition does not encompass all forms of control within the organization. Rather, the presence of X-inefficiency is determined by whether or not management engages in action to control inefficiency. Therefore, even if organizational members act lazily in pursuit of their own interests and the productivity of the organization is adversely affected, this alone does not establish the presence of X-inefficiency.

an optimal level commensurate with that cost, then the resulting inefficiency is not included in X-inefficiency as defined here. Conversely, if management does not pay attention to changes in efficiency caused by competitive pressure, or if it makes managerial efforts but those efforts are ineffective in influencing the level of competitive pressure as subjectively perceived by organizational members, then the observed inefficiency is considered X-inefficiency. This definition is not based on whether or not management has made an effort, but rather on whether effective control has been exercised.

Are the inefficiencies caused by the various factors introduced in Section 4.1 included in X-inefficiency under this definition based on the absence of control? In fact, this definition does not necessarily include all inefficiencies that arise from the reasons considered in the theory of X-inefficiency. Let us reconsider the managerial inefficiency model. In each process, inefficiency may arise from a prisoner's dilemma, or it may result from inertial behavior that has become incompatible with the new economic environment. From the perspective of causation, such inefficiencies would be classified as X-inefficiency. However, if, for example, there is a way for management to encourage employees to recognize the competitive economic environment through some form of managerial effort as described above, and if the level of inefficiency is thereby controlled, then the inefficiency is not considered X-inefficiency under this definition. As long as the level of inefficiency is controlled by management, regardless of its cause, it is not regarded as X-inefficiency. Even if we can prove that inefficiency exists, the fact that it is controlled leads us into the problem of the relativity of rationality. As a result, we cannot escape criticism from neoclassical theory, as has been repeatedly pointed out. In other words, proving the existence of controlled inefficiency does not mean that one has proven the existence of X-inefficiency. To avoid this problem, we have set the objective of identifying and testing the existence of phenomena that cannot be explained by neoclassical theory but can be explained by the concept of X-inefficiency. For this purpose, it is not necessary to define X-inefficiency in such a way that it includes all inefficiencies caused by the reasons considered in Section 4.1.

Next, we examine the following question: if the observed technical inefficiency is found to exhibit the properties of X-inefficiency under this definition, can that finding be regarded as proof of the existence of X-inefficiency in the commonly accepted sense? If X-inefficiency must be limited to inefficiencies arising from the causes introduced in the representative theory in Section 4.1, then confirming the existence of X-inefficiency under this definition does not constitute proof of the existence of X-inefficiency in the conventional sense. However, there remains a strong possibility that uncontrolled inefficiencies arise through mechanisms other than those discussed in Section 4.1. For example, in the misspecification inefficiency model presented in Subsection 4.2.1, inefficiency arises from deviations of unobserved factors of production from their optimal values. According to a cause-based classification, such inefficiency is regarded as allocative inefficiency rather than X-inefficiency. However, if these unobserved factors of production are not controlled and are merely dispersed, they fall within the scope of X-inefficiency as defined here.

To be sure, the definition based on the absence of control may diverge from the usual definition of X-inefficiency. However, is it not the case that X-inefficiency, as defined by the absence of control, represents a form of inefficiency that does not exist within the standard neoclassical economic model? In neoclassical models, all economic variables that affect the interests of economic agents must be treated either as strategic variables or as endogenous variables determined by other strategic variables. Variables that are not controlled are treated as environmental variables that are exogenously given. If X-inefficiency arises as an uncontrolled inefficiency, then the degree of X-inefficiency is a variable that has a significant impact on firm profits. Since it is not controlled, it is treated as an exogenous variable. However, the level of this variable is influenced by market structure variables such as competitive pressure. It is important to remember that competitive pressure is indirectly determined by firms' market behavior, including the interdependence of firm strategies. In other words, even if it is not directly controlled, it is variable and determined within the system, and is therefore essentially an endogenous variable. In a neoclassical microeconomic model, such uncontrolled endogenous variables are either unrecognized or ignored. These variables cannot be incorporated into standard neoclassical models, whether by considering factors such as leisure, as is commonly done, or by introducing managerial mechanisms within the firm. In other words, if it can be empirically demonstrated that explicitly incorporating variables related to uncontrolled inefficiency leads to appropriate model construction, then would this not constitute a type of inefficiency that cannot be explained by neoclassical theory, but can be explained by the theory of X-inefficiency?

The advantage of defining X-inefficiency as "inefficiency that is not controlled in any way by management effort" is not limited to its being an operational concept that avoids difficult conceptual questions such as "what is X" or "irrational behavior." If the level of X-inefficiency is controlled in some way, the effect of that control should appear as a characteristic of the distribution of inefficiency. Therefore, it may be possible to econometrically test whether inefficiency is controlled. If such a test is feasible and the null hypothesis that inefficiency is not controlled is not rejected, we can at least confirm that the proposition that uncontrolled inefficiency exists is not refuted by empirical evidence. In Chapters 5 and 6, we construct an econometric model to statistically identify X-inefficiency as defined above and attempt to test it using data from Japanese manufacturing industries.

4.6 Conclusion

Traditionally, technical inefficiency has been too optimistically regarded as a measurable concept corresponding to X-inefficiency. Unfortunately, the proposition of whether the existence of X-inefficiency can be empirically demonstrated by observing technical inefficiency has rarely been examined. As discussed in this chapter through various examples, testing for technical inefficiency alone does not constitute proof of the existence of X-inefficiency. Moreover, even if X-inefficiency does exist, it does not necessarily manifest as technical inefficiency. There can be technical inefficiency that is not X-inefficiency, and conversely, there can be X-inefficiency that does not appear as technical inefficiency. Therefore, X-inefficiency cannot yet be regarded as a concept whose existence has been empirically verified.

There has been a long-standing debate between X-inefficiency researchers and neoclassical microeconomists over the existence of X-inefficiency. These debates can be summarized as discussions about whether "irrational behavior" can be incorporated into economic analysis. Even if X-inefficiency is defined as the irrational behavior of economic agents, explaining how it arises and to what extent inefficiency occurs inevitably requires assuming some form of optimizing behavior—that is, rational behavior—at some point in the analysis. This dilemma is referred to here as the relativity of rationality. As long as the problem of the relativity of rationality exists, it is always possible to reinterpret apparently irrational behavior within a model of rational behavior. Moreover, neoclassical models of rational behavior are highly flexible and can accommodate a wide range of analytical cases by introducing various transaction costs. Therefore, actual inefficiencies can be explained without resorting to the concept of X-inefficiency. For this reason, econometric testing for technical inefficiency alone does not constitute proof of the existence of X-inefficiency. More generally, as long as X-inefficiency is defined as the result of irrational behavior—that is, in terms of its cause—it is impossible to claim that any statistically observable phenomenon constitutes empirical proof of the existence of X-inefficiency. In this sense, it has been shown that the existence of X-inefficiency cannot be directly tested through statistical methods.

These problems in confirming the existence of X-inefficiency arise because X-inefficiency is usually defined in terms of its causes. Therefore, this chapter examines whether there are any properties of X-inefficiency that can be tested through econometric analysis. If statistically testable properties of X-inefficiency exist, redefining X-inefficiency on the basis of such properties would be useful. If the redefined properties of X-inefficiency are observed in the statistical characteristics of technical inefficiency, this could be considered empirical evidence suggesting the existence of X-inefficiency. However, many alternative definitions of X-inefficiency fall into the problem of the relativity of rationality, and none has proven sufficient as an alternative definition.

In the course of this review, it was suggested that avoiding the problem of the relativity of rationality itself could serve as the basis for defining X-inefficiency. The relativity of rationality arises when the level of inefficiency is optimized at some point in the decision-making process. Therefore, it is useful to define X-inefficiency as inefficiency that is neither optimized nor controlled. Based on the above discussion, "inefficiency that is not controlled in any way by management effort" has been presented as a possible alternative definition of X-inefficiency.

This chapter has explained the impossibility of directly identifying X-inefficiency in econometric data, as well as the reasons why this is the case. On this basis, it proposes redefining X-inefficiency in terms of the absence of control, instead of the conventional cause-based definition. There is a certain conceptual gap between defining X-inefficiency based on the absence of control and defining it based on its causes. Unfortunately, the set of X-inefficiencies defined by the absence of control proposed here does not necessarily coincide with the set of X-inefficiencies defined by cause, nor does it fully meet the ideal condition of being both refutable and consistent with the traditional definition. In this sense, adopting the absence-of-control definition for empirical analysis should be considered a second-best approach. However, X-inefficiency, as defined by the absence of control, represents a type of inefficiency that has not been analyzed within the standard neoclassical framework. Its level is endogenously determined by market structure, such as the degree of competitive pressure, and it has a significant impact on firm profits. At the same time, in the sense that management does not control its level, X-inefficiency is treated as an exogenous variable. Such a variable is difficult to incorporate into standard neoclassical models, whether by considering factors such as leisure or a firm's internal management mechanisms. While this definition of X-inefficiency does not align with the traditional cause-based definition, it partially captures a key aspect of X-inefficiency—irrationality in decision-making—by representing it as the absence of control. Furthermore, as will be shown later, this definition allows for the construction of an econometric model that enables statistical testing. Indeed, in the subsequent chapters, an existence test for X-inefficiency will be conducted using input–output data from the Japanese manufacturing industries.

The discussion in this chapter may not necessarily advance the traditional discourse on X-inefficiency. Although Leibenstein provides a detailed description of X-inefficiency in numerous studies, this chapter does not attempt to capture its full scope. Rather, the discussion is framed as a conceptual overview, focusing specifically on how X-inefficiency can be interpreted.[27] This approach facilitates comparison with technical inefficiency as a typical interpretation. In addition, this chapter defines X-inefficiency in terms of the absence of control, aiming for an operationally useful definition. However, this definition inevitably includes allocative inefficiency and does not fully encompass all aspects of X-inefficiency considered by Leibenstein. It is a definition constructed solely for the purpose of making X-inefficiency amenable to econometric analysis. Even so, we adopt this definition and proceed with the analysis, based on the view that allowing measurement methods alone to advance while disregarding the conceptual distinction between technical inefficiency and X-inefficiency is not necessarily a desirable direction for progress.

References

Aigner D, Lovell CAK, Schmidt P (1977) Formulation and estimation of stochastic frontier production function models. J Econom 6(1):21–37

Caves RE, Associates (1992) Industrial efficiency in six nations. MIT press

Caves RE, Barton DR (1990) Efficiency in US manufacturing industries. MIT press

Colombi R, Kumbhakar SC, Martini G, Vittadini G (2014) Closed-skew normality in stochastic frontiers with individual effects and long/short-run efficiency. J Prod Anal 42(2):123–136

[27] Much of this interpretation follows Franz (1988).

Farrell MJ (1957) The measurement of productive efficiency. J R Stat Soc Ser A (General) 120(3):253–281
Førsund FR, Hjalmarsson L (1987) Analyses of industrial structure: a Putty-Clay approach. Almqvist & Wiksell International
Førsund FR, Lovell CAK, Schmidt P (1980) A survey of frontier production functions and of their relationship to efficiency measurement. J Econom 13(1):5–25
Franz R (1988) X-inefficiency: theory, evidence, and applications. Kluwer Academic Press
Hafner CM, Manner H, Simar L (2018) The "wrong skewness" problem in stochastic frontier models: a new approach. Econom Rev 37(4):380–400
Hatch J (1990) X-Efficiency and contestability theory: a clash of paradigms? In: Weiermair K, Perlman M (eds) Studies in economic rationality: x-efficiency examined and extolled. University of Michigan Press, pp 27–42
Hirakata N, Kido Y, Thum JL (2017) Empirical evidence on systemic as a herd: the case of Japanese Regional Banks. Technical report, Bank of Japan
Kumbhakar SC, Lai H-P (2022) Recent advances in the panel stochastic frontier models: heterogeneity, endogeneity and dependence. Int J Empir Econ 1(01):1–38
Kumbhakar SC, Lien G, Hardaker JB (2014) Technical efficiency in competing panel data models: a study of Norwegian grain farming. J Prod Anal 41:321–337
Leibenstein H (1966) Allocative efficiency vs. X-efficiency. Am Econ Rev 56(3):392–415
Leibenstein H (1976) Beyond economic man: a new foundation for microeconomics. Harvard University Press
Leibenstein H (1987) Inside the firm: the inefficiencies of hierarchy. Harvard university press
Meeusen W, van Den Broeck J (1977). Efficiency estimation from Cobb-Douglas production functions with composed error. Int Econ Rev 435–444
Nakagawa R (2008) Herd behavior by Japanese banks in local financial markets. RCSS Discuss Pap Ser 71:1–28
Nakagawa R, Oiwa H, Takeda F (2012) The economic impact of herd behavior in the Japanese loan market. Pacific-Basin Financ J 20(4):600–613
Stigler GJ (1976) The xistence of x-efficiency. Am Econ Rev 66(1):213–216
Timmer CP (1971) Using a probabilistic frontier production function to measure technical efficiency. J Polit Econ 79(4):776–794
Torii A (1992) Technical efficiency in Japanese industries. Ind Effic Six Nations 31–120
Tsionas EG, Kumbhakar SC (2014) Firm heterogeneity, persistent and transient technical inefficiency: a generalized true random-effects model. J Appl Econom 29(1):110–132
Weiermair K, Perlman M (1990) Studies in economic rationality: X-efficiency examined and extolled: essays written in the tradition of and to honor Harvey Leibenstein. University of Michigan Press
Zelenyuk V, Zheka V (2006) Corporate governance and firm's efficiency: the case of a transitional country, Ukraine. J Prod Anal 25:143–157

Chapter 5
X-inefficiencies Across Japanese Manufacturing Industries: Identification Based on a Vintage Capital Investment Model

In this chapter and the following Chap. 6, we adopt a refutable definition of X-inefficiency based on the absence of control. Specifically, we define it as "inefficiency that is not controlled in any way by the manager's managerial efforts," as introduced in Chap. 4. We develop a method to test for the existence of X-inefficiency under this definition and apply it to input–output data from 340 manufacturing industries in Japan to investigate whether X-inefficiency can be empirically confirmed. This chapter constructs an econometric model, based on a putty-clay type vintage capital investment framework, under the assumption that firms' decisions on facility renewal determine the observed distribution of productivity. Using this model, we estimate whether firms are making rational investment decisions.

This chapter does not attempt to demonstrate the existence of X-inefficiency merely by confirming the presence of technical inefficiency, as is often the case. In this context, the term "technical inefficiency" refers to an econometric concept that is estimated jointly with the production frontier function. Technical inefficiency is typically regarded, somewhat optimistically, as an econometric representation of X-inefficiency. However, even under rational decision-making, technical inefficiency can arise when adjustment costs exist, such as the cost of updating facilities to incorporate the latest technology. Therefore, confirming the existence of technical inefficiency does not provide a sufficient condition for confirming the existence of X-inefficiency. This proposition was discussed in detail in Chap. 4.

The discussion in Chap. 4 suggests that adopting the above definition of X-inefficiency based on the absence of control is useful for empirically verifying the existence of X-inefficiency. In this chapter, we follow this definition and attempt to test whether uncontrolled inefficiencies can be identified within the statistical properties of observed technical inefficiency. The inefficiencies examined here significantly impact firm profits but are not controlled by management and are not subject to firms' optimizing behavior. We aim to test whether such inefficiencies, which are not considered within the framework of neoclassical microeconomics, actually exist.

As an analysis of technical inefficiency, the empirical approach taken in this chapter is distinctive in its use of a cross-sectional framework covering a large num-

A. Torii, *Production Efficiency with the Stochastic Management Model*,
https://doi.org/10.1007/978-981-95-3501-9_5

ber of industries. Most previous empirical studies of technical inefficiency estimate input–output econometric models for a single industry or a small number of industries, assuming the presence of technical inefficiency and testing parameter values. In contrast, this chapter applies a uniform method to estimate input–output models across many industries and statistically examines whether the resulting technical inefficiencies exhibit common distributional properties. This enables an investigation into whether such properties are consistent with the existence of X-inefficiency.

Another feature of the empirical analysis in this chapter is that, unlike conventional approaches to estimating technical inefficiency, it does not assume *a priori* that the distribution of inefficiency levels follows a specific form, such as the half-normal distribution. When interpreting the estimation results, the implied distributional shape is situated within a family of distributions referred to in this book as the exponential power-type distribution. This family encompasses a wide range of distributional forms, including the half-normal and exponential distributions, depending on the values of its parameters. Since assumptions about the distribution type greatly affect the estimated level of technical inefficiency, they must be made with care to avoid arbitrariness. However, their importance is not limited to that. Given that the distributional characteristics of technical inefficiency across many industries are determined by the mechanism through which inefficiency arises, identifying the distributional form is essential for the purpose of this chapter, which is to analyze the nature of observed inefficiency. Information about the mechanism that generates technical inefficiency is embedded in the empirical distribution of the inefficiency term. As will be shown in this chapter, identifying the distributional form of the inefficiency term is equivalent to uncovering the mechanism by which inefficiency is generated.

The remainder of this chapter is organized as follows. Section 5.1 reviews the tests that have been conducted on the validity of the stochastic production frontier model assuming technical inefficiency, including those that test the assumptions about the distributional form. It also reviews estimation models that do not rely on specific distributional assumptions. Section 5.2 derives the condition that the distribution of technical inefficiency must satisfy when facility renewal intervals are controlled under the vintage capital investment model constructed in Chap. 3. If this condition is not satisfied, it suggests that the facility renewal intervals, which should be under managerial control, are in fact not being controlled. Section 5.3 presents a method for testing whether the distribution of observed inefficiencies satisfies this condition. In Sect. 5.4, this testing method is applied to the Japanese manufacturing industry using microdata from the Census of Manufacturers. We test the null hypothesis that facility renewal intervals are controlled and that X-inefficiency does not exist. This section also examines the appropriateness of common distributional assumptions for technical inefficiency, including the half-normal, truncated normal, and exponential distributions. Finally, Sect. 5.5 summarizes the conclusions and offers a brief discussion.

5.1 Test of Technical Inefficiency

5.1.1 *Validity of Econometric Models that Assume Technical Inefficiency*

Before discussing methods for testing X-inefficiency, we review various tests that have been conducted in the literature attempting to measure technical inefficiency. These tests primarily concern the validity of assuming a frontier production function. For example, when technical inefficiency is assumed to follow a half-normal distribution, testing the null hypothesis $H_0 : \sigma_u^2 = 0$ in the econometric model

$$y = f(x) + v - u, \quad v \sim N\left(0, \sigma_v^2\right), \quad u \sim \frac{\sqrt{2}}{\sqrt{\pi}\sigma_u} e^{-\frac{u^2}{2\sigma_u^2}}, \quad u \geq 0$$

serves as a test of the validity of the model formulation. If the null hypothesis $H_0 : \sigma_u^2 = 0$ is not rejected, then the model becomes indistinguishable from a standard linear regression model.

In Aigner et al. (1977), one of the earliest studies to estimate technical inefficiency under the assumption of half-normal and exponential distributions, and in Schmidt and Lovell (1979), which simultaneously estimated input allocative inefficiency and technical inefficiency, the validity of the econometric model is discussed based on the ratio of the MLE of σ_u^2 to its estimated variance. This indicates that the null hypothesis $H_0 : \sigma_u^2 = 0$ is tested using the Wald test.

Aigner et al. (1977) analyzed the U.S. metal refining industry (sample size: 28). They estimated the above econometric model under the assumption that technical inefficiency follows a half-normal distribution and obtained ML estimates of $\widehat{\sigma}_u^2 = 0.000686$ and $\widehat{\sigma}_v^2 = 0.0692$. Based on the fact that the asymmetric error component was substantially smaller than the symmetric component, and that the Wald statistics were 0.05 and 3.64, respectively, Aigner et al. concluded that only an insignificant asymmetric distribution could be identified, with negligible deviation from the production frontier.

Schmidt and Lin analyzed data from U.S. thermal power plants (sample size: 150) and obtained ML estimates of $\widehat{\sigma}_u^2 = 0.02483$ and $\widehat{\sigma}_v^2 = 0.001295$. The corresponding Wald statistics were 5.08 and 1.83, respectively, which they used as the basis for claiming the presence of inefficiencies of considerable magnitude. However, as later shown by Coelli (1995) through Monte Carlo simulations, the Wald test is not particularly effective when the sample size is small. Apart from the Wald test, Schmidt and Lin (1984) examined in detail how to test the same null hypothesis using the LM test. They reported that the information matrix becomes singular, making it impossible to compute the test statistic.

In the same paper, Schmidt and Lin suggested that, since the model becomes a standard regression model when the null hypothesis holds, the validity of an econometric model assuming inefficiency can be tested by examining the normality of the regression residuals. They proposed a method to assess normality using the skewness of the regression residuals. For this purpose, the method proposed by D'agostino and Pearson (1973) is useful. D'Agostino and Pearson presented a technique to approximate the distribution of sample skewness to a normal distribution through a variable transformation when the sample size ranges from 8 to 1000. They transformed the estimated skewness s as

$$X = \delta \sinh^{-1}(s/\lambda),$$

and provided a table of parameters $(\delta, 1/\lambda)$ for approximating the transformed values by a standard normal distribution.

For example, we select the JSIC 1421 Cotton Spinning Industry and the JSIC 1422 Chemical Fiber Spinning Industry from the estimates of technical inefficiency for Japanese four-digit manufacturing industries presented later in this chapter. The sample sizes (i.e., the number of establishment-level input–output observations used to estimate the frontier production function) for these industries are 51 and 66, and the skewnesses of the OLS regression residuals are -1.06281 and -0.07062, respectively. From the table provided by D'Agostino and Pearson, the corresponding values of $(\delta, 1/\lambda)$ for degrees of freedom 50 and 65 are (3.207, 1.0038) and (3.435, 1.0472), respectively. Using these values in the transformation formula, we obtain:

$$3.207 \sinh^{-1}(-1.06281 \times 1.0038) = -2.976,$$

$$3.435 \sinh^{-1}(-0.07062 \times 1.0472) = -0.2538.$$

These values can be evaluated using the standard normal distribution table. For the cotton spinning industry, the null hypothesis is rejected at the 1% significance level, while for the chemical fiber spinning industry, it cannot be rejected even at the 10% level. In other words, the assumption of a frontier production function incorporating technical inefficiency is supported for the cotton spinning industry but not for the chemical fiber spinning industry.

5.1.2 *Test of the Validity of the Distribution by Lee (1983)*

The above tests are based on various assumed distributions of technical inefficiency and aim to examine the validity of those assumptions. Although a wide range of distributions has been proposed for technical inefficiency, few studies have attempted to evaluate the relative superiority or inferiority of these distributions in order to determine which type is preferable. One notable exception is the work of Lee (1983), who introduced a general class of distributions known as the Pearson family to model technical inefficiency. This family includes the uniform, gamma, beta, Cauchy, and normal distributions, and its probability density function can be represented in the form:

$$\frac{d \ln f(u)}{du} = \frac{a + u}{b_0 + b_1 u + b_2 u^2}.$$

When $a = 0, b_1 = 0$, and $b_2 = 0$, this specification corresponds to the half-normal distribution; when $b_1 = 0$ and $b_2 = 0$, it corresponds to the truncated normal distribution. Therefore, the appropriateness of these distributional assumptions can be tested by examining whether the restrictions $a = 0, b_1 = 0, b_2 = 0$ or $b_1 = 0, b_2 = 0$ hold.

Lee derived the LM statistic to test these hypotheses and examined the validity of assuming a half-normal distribution for technical inefficiency using data from the Colombian food industry (sample size: 80) and the Indonesian textile industry (sample size: 50). For the Colombian food industry, the results were:

$$\widehat{\sigma}_u^2 + \widehat{\sigma}_v^2 = 0.6778, \quad \widehat{\sigma}_u^2/\widehat{\sigma}_v^2 = 1.476,$$

with estimated standard deviations of 0.1897 and 0.599, respectively, indicating a significant degree of technical inefficiency. The LM statistic was 179.48. Since this greatly exceeds the critical value of the chi-squared distribution with 3 degrees of freedom at the 1% significance level ($\chi^2_{3,0.01} = 11.34$), the null hypothesis is rejected, suggesting a model specification error. For the Indonesian textile industry, the estimates were:

$$\widehat{\sigma}_u^2 + \widehat{\sigma}_v^2 = 1.447, \quad \widehat{\sigma}_u^2/\widehat{\sigma}_v^2 = 1.889,$$

with standard deviations of 0.5875 and 1.253, respectively. The LM statistic in this case was 5.295. Compared to the chi-squared critical value of 6.25 with 3 degrees of freedom at the 10% significance level, the null hypothesis is not rejected. This result suggests that the assumption that technical inefficiency follows a half-normal distribution is valid in this case.

Even if testing the validity of assuming a specific distribution is not difficult, it is generally not easy to discuss which distribution should be chosen when several distributional hypotheses cannot be rejected. The only assertion that can be made based on such verification is that one distribution is more or less likely to be plausible than another. The difficulty of identifying the correct distributional form is not unique to hypotheses regarding technical inefficiency. For instance, similar challenges have historically arisen in identifying the size distribution of firms. Unless the sample size is extremely large, it is difficult to determine the underlying distribution from only several tens or hundreds of firms in a given industry.

5.1.3 Goodness-of-Fit Test by Wang et al. (2011)

Wang and Schmidt (2009) highlighted an important limitation in stochastic frontier models: the conditional expectation $\mathbb{E}[u_i|\hat{\epsilon}_i]$, which is often used to estimate technical inefficiency, has a distribution that differs from the true inefficiency u_i. This conditional expectation arises under the standard stochastic frontier model presented in Eq. (1.1), where $\epsilon_i = v_i - u_i$ and $\hat{\epsilon}_i$ is its estimated value. In the present book, the subscript i is used to denote industries, but in the original paper by Wang and Schmidt, i refers to individual sample units used in estimating a production function. Specifically, when the variance of the noise term σ_v^2 is large, $\mathbb{E}[u_i|\hat{\epsilon}_i]$ tends to shrink toward the mean inefficiency $\mathbb{E}[u_i]$, rather than accurately reflecting the heterogeneity in u_i. This "shrinkage effect" means that $\mathbb{E}[u_i|\hat{\epsilon}_i]$ cannot reliably be used to test assumptions about the distribution of u_i. This issue becomes particularly problematic when evaluating the validity of distributional assumptions about technical inefficiency in the model.

To address the limitations of using $\mathbb{E}[u_i|\hat{\epsilon}_i]$, particularly the shrinkage effect that causes inefficiency estimates to converge toward the mean and lose individual-specific information, Wang et al. (2011) proposed a bootstrap-based goodness-of-fit test. This method avoids the shrinkage issue by focusing not on $\mathbb{E}[u_i|\hat{\epsilon}_i]$ itself but on the distribution of the residuals $\hat{\epsilon}_i$. The procedure involves estimating parameters using maximum likelihood, generating bootstrap samples based on the assumed distributions of u_i and v_i, and applying the Kolmogorov–Smirnov (KS) test to compare the empirical and theoretical cumulative distribution functions of the residuals. In this way, the method provides a more direct and unbiased tool to evaluate the appropriateness of the assumed inefficiency distribution.

Wang et al. applied this method to two datasets: 25 state-level observations from Greene (2008) and 344 rice producers from Coelli et al. (2005). In the smaller sample, the test lacked statistical power and could not reject either the half-normal or exponential assumptions. In contrast, the larger sample revealed partial inconsistencies with the half-normal assumption, although the exponential distribution remained plausible. These results highlight that the bootstrap method performs better in larger samples but is still affected when the variance of the symmetric error term v_i is large, as the information from the asymmetric inefficiency term u_i is overwhelmed by noise. Thus, while the method offers a meaningful improvement in evaluating distributional validity, it is not universally robust, particularly when noise overwhelms the signal from technical inefficiency.

5.1.4 Without Assuming a Specific Distribution

The problem of statistically identifying the distributional form of technical inefficiency involves substantial difficulties, as described above. In response, several methods have been developed to estimate the frontier production function without assuming a specific distribution for technical inefficiency. Examples include the Distribution Free Analysis (DFA) proposed by Berger (1993) and the Thick Frontier Approach (TFA) introduced by Berger and Humphrey (1992). DFA builds upon the panel data framework of Schmidt and Sickles (1984), assuming that the random error component averages out over time and thus does not affect the estimation of the inefficiency term. In contrast, TFA begins by classifying the sample into size groups. Within each group, the top 25% of firms with the lowest average costs are selected. A cost function is then estimated using ordinary regression methods based on this subset of highly efficient firms.

TFA can only be applied when the sample size is sufficiently large. Accordingly, its application has been largely limited to the U.S. banking industry, where rich datasets are available. The main focus of these studies has been the relationship between regulatory intensity and efficiency in the banking sector. At the same time, many of them have conducted comparative analyses of frontier estimation methods, including DFA and TFA. Bauer et al. (1993) compared TFA with MLE under the standard half-normal assumption. They found that while the average inefficiency levels were similar (18% and 21%, respectively), the efficiency estimates for individual observations differed significantly, leading to divergent policy implications. Similarly, Berger and Mester (1997) compared DFA and the half-normal-based estimates using a profit function. Although the two methods yielded nearly identical efficiency levels, the goodness of fit to the half-normal distribution was found to be poor. Further extending these comparisons, Bauer et al. (1998) examined nine different methods, including both single-year and panel data approaches. They concluded that although parametric estimates tend to agree with each other, the results are not definitive and that researchers should explore and compare multiple methods. Finally, Cummins and Zi (1998) studied efficiency rankings across nine methods—each with different distributional assumptions—using data from life insurance companies rather than banks. They found high correlations among parametric estimates, including TFA and DFA, but low correlations between these estimates and those from nonparametric methods such as DEA, including the Free Disposal Hull (FDH) model by Tulkens (1993).

These comparative analyses share a common approach: they consider multiple estimation methods and adopt a particular method only when a consistent pattern is confirmed across those methods. This tendency is exemplified by Berger and Hannan (1998), who analyze the relationship between the efficiency of U.S. banks and the degree of market concentration in their local areas. They argue that their results are robust because, although the efficiency estimates for individual banks differ substantially between the conventional stochastic frontier model and DFA, the negative correlation between efficiency and the concentration index remains unchanged. Additional comparative studies on the effect of distributional assumptions have been conducted by Yuengert (1993) and Berger and DeYoung (1997). However, these studies merely report how the average efficiency level varies depending on the assumed distribution and do not involve formal hypothesis testing.

In recent years, Kneip et al. (2015) proposed a nonparametric method for simultaneously estimating the density function of technical inefficiency, the production frontier, and the noise variance in a stochastic frontier model. In their study, a penalized histogram-type estimator is particularly recommended as a practical approach. This estimator approximates the unknown density using a histogram structure and incorporates a penalization term to ensure smoothness, thereby enabling maximum likelihood estimation. The identifiability of the model is also theoretically established. Furthermore, Monte Carlo simulations confirm high estimation accuracy for sample sizes of 100 and 500. The method is also applied to data from the U.S. electricity industry, demonstrating its practical usefulness.

5.2 A Model for Testing X-inefficiency

As introduced in the previous section, most existing tests related to technical inefficiency have focused solely on verifying the presence of technical inefficiency by specifying the distribution of residuals using commonly assumed asymmetric forms, and then testing the appropriateness of the model specification based on observed data. However, in order to examine whether the observed inefficiency can be regarded as X-inefficiency, as intended in this book, it is essential to avoid arbitrary distributional assumptions and instead investigate the characteristics that the distribution is expected to exhibit, based on the mechanism by which inefficiency arises. To date, little attention has been paid to the dynamic process underlying the generation of inefficiency, such as the one suggested by the stochastic process model in Chap. 3. As a result, none of the existing methods are suitable for testing whether X-inefficiency is identifiable within the observed technical inefficiency.

In this section, we construct a theoretical model to evaluate whether firms make rational decisions regarding facility renewal, based on the assumption that such decisions determine the observed distribution of productivity. The model builds on the putty-clay vintage structure introduced in Chap. 3. Using this theoretical framework, we aim to capture the mechanism of technical inefficiency within a dynamic setting. By formulating a stochastic process that reflects the dynamic generation of technical inefficiency, we can derive a specific distribution for the level of inefficiency as the asymptotic steady-state distribution of the process. By testing whether this predicted distribution aligns with the empirically observed distribution of inefficiency, we aim to evaluate the plausibility and characteristics of the underlying model that explains the emergence of technical inefficiency.

5.2.1 Basic Configuration of the Vintage Model and the Rational Adjustment of the Facility Renewal Interval

The structure of this model follows the vintage model described in Chap. 3. In the industry under consideration, production technology advances at a constant Hicks-neutral productivity growth rate α. Since both the wage rate and the interest rate are constant, the optimal capital-labor ratio also remains constant, and all establishments construct their facilities in accordance with this ratio. We assume putty-clay type capital accumulation, meaning that when a facility is renewed, it adopts the most advanced technology available at that time (i.e., it attains the current frontier level of efficiency), and its productivity remains fixed until the next renewal. Let t_j denote the year in which the jth establishment was constructed. Then, the log deviation of its technology from the frontier at time τ is given by $\alpha(t_j - \tau) < 0$, where the frontier technology is normalized to 0. In other words, this corresponds to a state of inefficiency equal to $\alpha(\tau - t_j)$.

The optimal period for facility renewal generally varies across establishments. Let z_j denote the facility renewal interval for establishment j, which renews its facility periodically when inefficiency reaches the threshold level αz_j. At the moment of renewal, inefficiency resets to zero and then increases linearly at a rate of α per unit of time. Suppose that the distribution of renewal intervals across establishments is described by the probability density function $\phi(z)$. Under the assumption that the initial timing of renewal is uniformly distributed over time, the inefficiency level of an establishment observed at a randomly chosen point in time can be regarded as a random variable. The probability density function $\psi(x)$ of this inefficiency level is given by

$$\psi(x) = \int_{\frac{x}{\alpha}}^{\infty} \frac{\phi(z)}{\alpha z} \, dz. \tag{3.2}$$

When no management effort is made and each establishment selects its facility renewal interval randomly, the resulting distribution of renewal intervals is described by the probability density function $\xi(z)$. From this randomly chosen interval z, the actual renewal timing is assumed to be adjusted through management effort. This adjustment is represented by a transformation function $\zeta(w - z|z)$, which denotes the distribution of the modified renewal interval w conditional on the original randomly selected interval z. It is assumed that each establishment incurs an adjustment cost in order to recognize and implement its optimal renewal interval. When the renewal interval is controlled to some extent by management effort, each establishment compares the adjustment cost with the benefit obtained from optimally timing its renewal, and determines how accurately it estimates and follows the optimal renewal interval.

Here, z represents the facility renewal interval before adjustment, w represents the renewal interval after adjustment, and $\zeta(w - z|z)$ denotes the probability density that the original interval z is adjusted to a new interval w, conditional on the initial value z. Through this adjustment process, the probability density of the facility renewal interval is transformed from $\xi(z)$ to

$$\phi(w) = \int_0^{\infty} \zeta(w - z|z) \, \xi(z) \, dz.$$

The resulting probability density function for the level of inefficiency is then given by

$$\psi(x) = \int_{\frac{x}{\alpha}}^{\infty} \frac{\phi(w)}{\alpha w} \, dw = \int_{\frac{x}{\alpha}}^{\infty} \frac{1}{\alpha w} \left(\int_0^{\infty} \zeta(w - z|z) \, \xi(z) \, dz \right) dw. \tag{3.4}$$

5.2.2 Rational Adjustment of Facility Renewal Interval and PDF of Controlled Inefficiency

If the facility renewal period is adjusted according to the form shown in Eq. (3.4), then the resulting distribution of inefficiency levels, $\psi(x)$, reflects the control of X-inefficiency through this adjustment process. Therefore, a potential method to determine whether X-inefficiency is being controlled is to assess whether the observed inefficiency distribution $\psi(x)$ can be expressed in the form of Eq. (3.4), using an initial distribution of renewal periods $\xi(z)$ and an adjustment function $\zeta(w-z|z)$. However, since Eq. (3.4) is a fairly general formulation, it is often possible to construct an expression of this form for a wide range of inefficiency distributions by selecting suitable functions for $\zeta(w-z|z)$ and $\xi(z)$. Moreover, because $\psi(x)$ does not uniquely determine $\xi(z)$ and $\zeta(w-z|z)$, the fact that $\psi(x)$ can be expressed in the form of Eq. (3.4) does not necessarily imply that it actually results from such an adjustment process. Thus, the ability to express a given inefficiency distribution in this form alone is insufficient to conclude whether the generation of inefficiency has been subject to managerial control.

Therefore, assuming that all aspects of a firm's decision-making process regarding the facility renewal period are fully characterized by the transformation function $\zeta(\cdot)$, we examine the necessary conditions that this function must satisfy if the decision-making is rational. First, irrespective of whether the decision-making is rational or not, the transformation function must satisfy the following condition:

$$\int_0^\infty \zeta\left(w-z|z\right)dw = 1.$$

Aside from this condition, there are generally no *a priori* constraints imposed on the functions $\xi(z)$ and $\zeta(w-z|z)$.

Unless the distribution of optimal capital investment intervals is specified *a priori,* the adjustment function can take almost any form. However, as long as a positive cost is associated with facility renewal, the optimal renewal interval cannot be zero, since this would imply that it is always optimal to continuously update to the latest technology. Therefore, assuming the adjustment function is specified as above and that the initial timing of facility renewal is random, at least the following restrictions must be satisfied under rational decision-making.

Restrictions

(i) $\zeta\left(w-z|z\right) = 0$ for $z \geq 0$ and $w = 0$,
(ii) $\zeta(w-z|z) = 0$ for $w-z < 0$ in the neighborhood of $z = 0$,
(iii) $\xi(0)$ is bounded.

Condition (i) implies that the renewal interval will not remain at zero after adjustment. If the randomly given initial renewal interval is positive, it will not be adjusted to zero, since the optimal renewal interval is strictly positive for all establishments. Moreover, even if the initial renewal interval is zero, unless the cost of adjustment is infinite, it will be adjusted to increase by at least a small amount. Therefore, the renewal interval will not remain at zero after adjustment. Condition (ii) addresses a similar situation: since the optimal renewal interval is strictly positive for all establishments, as long as the randomly given initial renewal interval is sufficiently small, the optimal interval for almost all establishments will exceed this initial value. Consequently, the interval will not be adjusted downward to a value closer to zero. Furthermore, condition (iii) does not rule out the possibility that a facility renewal interval of zero is chosen without any management effort. However, it implies that the probability that such a choice occurs in a neighborhood of zero can be made arbitrarily small by selecting a sufficiently small neighborhood around zero. In other words, it is assumed that, even before the adjustment, no establishment persistently chooses $z = 0$. Since choosing $z = 0$ is clearly irrational as long as the cost of facility renewal is positive, this possibility can reasonably be ruled out regardless of how little management effort is exerted.

As long as the adjustment is carried out under rational decision-making, we consider that at least these three conditions must be satisfied. The next step is to examine what characteristics the probability density function of the inefficiency level will exhibit when the adjustment function satisfies these three conditions.

If the above-mentioned conditions (i) and (ii) are satisfied, then in the neighborhood of $w = 0$, the probability density function of the adjusted facility renewal interval is given by

$$\phi(w) = \int_0^w \zeta\left(w - z|z\right)\xi(z)dz. \tag{5.1}$$

Using this equation, we can identify the following characteristics of the distribution density function of the facility renewal interval $\phi(w)$, as well as that of the inefficiency level $\psi(x)$, which is expressed in Eq. (3.4).

Proposition 5 (Characteristics of controlled inefficiency)
If the adjustment function $\zeta(w - z|z)$ and the initial facility renewal interval distribution density function $\xi(z)$ satisfy conditions (i), (ii), and (iii), then the probability density function $\phi(w)$ of the facility renewal interval and the probability density function $\psi(x)$ of inefficiency given by Eq. (3.4) *have the following properties.*

(iv) $\phi(0) = 0,\ \phi'(0) = \zeta\left(0|0\right)\xi(0) = 0.$
(v) $\psi'(x) \leq 0,$ *for* $x \geq 0.$
(vi) $\psi'(0) = 0.$

See Appendix for the proof.

Note that Eq. (5.1) holds only in the neighborhood of $w = 0$, but this expression is used solely to derive property (vi). Property (iv) shows that the probability that firms have an optimal facility renewal interval of zero is zero. Moreover, since the renewal interval is not adjusted toward zero, the probability of such an outcome remains close to zero when the inefficiency level is sufficiently small.[1] Property (v) is valid for all $x \geq 0$, and it is required for the distribution of inefficiency regardless of the distribution type of the optimal facility renewal intervals. Low efficiency arises stochastically in the vintage model as technology becomes obsolete for establishments with a slower facility renewal rate. A lower level of efficiency is caused only by establishments with slower renewal rates (i.e., longer facility renewal intervals). Therefore, given a certain distribution of facility renewal intervals, the lower the efficiency level, the fewer the establishments that generate such inefficiency, resulting in a monotonically decreasing probability density. Property (vi), on the other hand, must be satisfied in the neighborhood of zero inefficiency, unlike property (v). As shown in property (iv), firms attain such low inefficiency levels only immediately following a renewal investment. Right after a renewal, inefficiency begins to increase at a certain rate rather than being reset again. This implies that the probability density remains unchanged for small deviations from zero inefficiency.

5.2.3 Testing for Controlled Inefficiency

If the distribution of given or observed technical inefficiency levels is confirmed to satisfy the minimum requirements for rational decision-making, as stated in Proposition 5, then the null hypothesis that all inefficiency is controlled—that is, that there is no X-inefficiency as defined by the absence of control in Chap. 4—is not rejected. Thus, the existence of X-inefficiency can be verified by testing whether the technical inefficiency distribution satisfies the characteristics shown in Proposition 5.

However, as far as SFA is employed, what is observed as a deviation from the frontier is not the distribution of inefficiency u, but the convolution $v - u$ with the symmetric error term v. Therefore, it is not possible to directly verify whether the distribution of deviations from the frontier production function satisfies the properties (v) and (vi) for the distribution of the inefficiency level u. This is because when using the method of moments or the maximum likelihood method, it is not possible to separate the convoluted distribution into u and v distributions unless the functional form is specified or the parameters of either distribution are given *a priori*.

Therefore, we propose the following systematic approach to assess whether the observed technical inefficiency can be interpreted as being controlled.

Procedure 1: Among the distributional forms proposed as inefficiency distributions, reject those that fail to satisfy either property (v) **or property** (vi)**, no matter what values their parameters take.** For example, suppose that the distribution type A does not satisfy either property (v) or property (vi). This means that, no matter what distribution the initial facility renewal intervals of each establishment follow, the inefficiency distribution cannot take the form of type A. Thus, assuming *a priori* that inefficiency follows distribution type A is equivalent to presupposing that the observed technical inefficiency cannot be regarded as controlled inefficiency.

[1] In Sect. 3.1.7, which discusses the vintage model under competitive pressure, it is shown that under positive facility renewal costs, the probability of facility renewal becomes zero within a certain range near zero inefficiency.

Therefore, unless the mechanism explaining how X-inefficiency forms distribution type A can be provided, assuming *a priori* that inefficiency follows distribution type A is not appropriate for the purpose of identifying the existence of X-inefficiency.

Procedure 2: A generalized distribution type B is created by extending the distribution type that satisfies both property (v) **and property** (vi). By construction, for some parameter values under certain conditions, this generalized distribution type B satisfies properties (v) and (vi), but it does not necessarily satisfy them in all cases. If the observed technical inefficiency is a controlled inefficiency, then the observed parameters will be such that distribution type B satisfies properties (v) and (vi). Conversely, if the inefficiency is considered "uncontrolled inefficiency," then the observed parameters do not necessarily have to satisfy properties (v) and (vi).

Procedure 3: In the generalized distribution type B, identify the parameter region G that satisfies both property (v) **and property** (vi). **Then, assuming that the observed inefficiencies follow distribution type B, we test the hypothesis that the estimated parameter lies in region G as the null hypothesis, and that it lies in the complement set G^C as the alternative hypothesis.** If the null hypothesis is rejected at an appropriate level of significance, then we cannot confirm a property that must be satisfied if the observed technical inefficiency is controlled. In other words, the results support the hypothesis that X-inefficiency exists and that inefficiency is not controlled. Conversely, if the null hypothesis is not rejected, then we cannot reject the possibility that the observed technical inefficiencies are at least to some extent controlled. In other words, we would not be able to reject the claim that observed inefficiencies may be technical inefficiencies but not necessarily X-inefficiencies.

Thus, the above-mentioned procedures allow us to test the hypothesis that "observed technical inefficiency is not necessarily controlled inefficiency" using input–output data of enterprises.

5.2.4 Procedure 1: Examination of Four Typical Distribution Types

The four distribution types introduced in Chap. 2—half-normal, exponential, gamma distribution, and truncated normal distribution—are the most frequently assumed distributions in the technical inefficiency estimation literature. In this subsection, to implement Procedure 1 described in the previous subsection, we examine whether these four distribution types satisfy properties (v) and (vi). In the following sections, we denote the distribution density function as $\psi(u)$.

Half-Normal Distribution

The property (v) is satisfied because

$$\psi'(u) = -\frac{2u}{\sigma_u^3}\sqrt{\frac{2}{\pi}}\exp\left(-\frac{u^2}{2\sigma_u^2}\right) \leq 0.$$

From this derivative, since $\psi'(0) = 0$, the property (vi) is also satisfied.

Exponential Distribution

The property (v) is satisfied because

$$\psi'(u) = \frac{\exp\left(-\frac{u}{\eta}\right)}{\eta^2} < 0.$$

As $\psi'(0) = -1/\eta^2$, the property (vi) is not satisfied.

Gamma Distribution

As

$$\psi'(u) = \frac{u^{m-1}}{\Gamma(m+1)\alpha^{m+1}}\left(m - \frac{u}{\alpha}\right)e^{-u/\alpha},$$

for any $m > 0$, there necessarily exists a region in $u \geq 0$ such that $\psi'(u) > 0$, violating property (v), which must hold for all $u \geq 0$. Moreover, as

$$\psi'(0) = \lim_{u \to 0} \frac{mu^{m-1}}{\Gamma(m+1)\alpha^{m+1}},$$

$\psi'(0)$ diverges to infinity when $m < 0$, so property (vi) is not satisfied. The case $m = 0$ reduces to the exponential distribution.

Truncated Normal Distribution

As

$$\psi'(u) = -\frac{u - \mu}{\sqrt{2\pi}\sigma_u^3\left(1 - \Phi\left(-\frac{\mu}{\sigma_u}\right)\right)}e^{-\frac{(u-\mu)^2}{2\sigma_u^2}},$$

for any $\mu > 0$, there exists a region in $u \geq 0$ such that property (v) is violated. Here, $\Phi(\cdot)$ represents the CDF of the standard normal distribution. Moreover, unless $\mu = 0$, property (vi) is also not satisfied. The case $\mu = 0$ corresponds to the half-normal distribution.

As shown above, the half-normal distribution satisfies both properties (v) and (vi), whereas the exponential distribution fails to satisfy property (vi). The gamma distribution necessarily fails to satisfy at least one of properties (v) or (vi), depending on the parameter values. The truncated normal distribution does not satisfy property (vi), except in the special case where it reduces to the half-normal distribution. Thus, both properties (v) and (vi) are satisfied only by the half-normal distribution.

Therefore, technical inefficiencies that follow a half-normal distribution cannot be ruled out as a pattern resulting from rational decision-making by individual establishments regarding their facility renewal intervals, since they satisfy the necessary conditions under the basic requirements specified in conditions (i), (ii), and (iii). Conversely, any technical inefficiency model that assumes a distribution other than the half-normal distribution, insofar as it explains inefficiencies using the vintage model, in effect presumes from the outset that these basic requirements are not satisfied in the determination of facility renewal intervals.

Given the distribution $\psi(x)$ of technical inefficiency, differentiating equation (3.2) with respect to x gives

$$\phi(w) = -\alpha^2 w \psi'(\alpha w),$$

which represents the distribution of facility renewal intervals that generate the inefficiency distribution. For example, assuming a half-normal distribution for technical inefficiency is equivalent to assuming that the PDF of facility renewal intervals is

$$\phi(w) = -\alpha^2 w \psi'(\alpha w) = \frac{\alpha^3 w^2}{\sigma_u^3}\sqrt{\frac{2}{\pi}} \exp\left(-\frac{\alpha^2 w^2}{2\sigma_u^2}\right). \tag{5.2}$$

As a result of rational decision-making by each establishment, if the facility renewal interval is adjusted to w, which is distributed by the density function (5.2), then the technical inefficiency will be distributed according to a half-normal distribution. It is possible that the optimal facility renewal interval for each establishment is distributed according to (5.2), and if each establishment realizes this optimal interval, then the resulting level of technical inefficiency would follow a half-normal distribution.

Figure 5.1 illustrates the distribution of facility renewal intervals derived in this manner, which leads to technical inefficiency following a half-normal distribution.

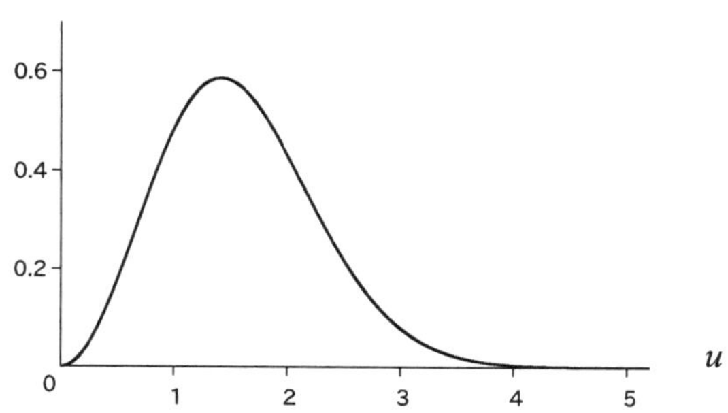

Fig. 5.1 Example of the distribution of facility renewal intervals when technical inefficiency follows a half-normal distribution. *Notes* Parameters are set as $\sigma_u^2 = 1$ and $\alpha = 1$

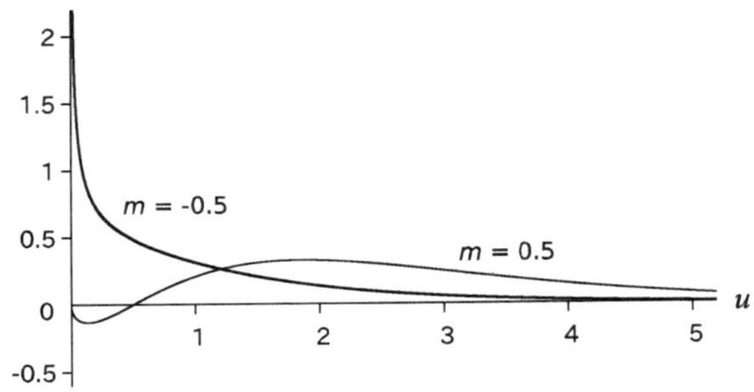

Fig. 5.2 Example of the distribution of facility renewal intervals when technical inefficiency follows a gamma distribution. *Notes* Thick line: $m = -1/2$, thin line: $m = 1/2$

Assuming that technical inefficiency follows a half-normal distribution is equivalent to assuming that the facility renewal interval follows a distribution close to a symmetric shape, as shown in the figure. In this case, both properties (v) and (vi) are satisfied.

On the other hand, if we assume that technical inefficiency follows a gamma distribution with $m = -1/2$ or $m = 1/2$, which does not satisfy property (vi), then the facility renewal interval follows the distribution shown in Fig. 5.2. When $m = -1/2$, the distribution is asymmetric, has a mode at 0, and exhibits a very long tail. This suggests that in the industry, some establishments continuously pursue high productivity through frontier technology, resulting in an almost infinite facility renewal speed, while others with low productivity rarely renew their facilities but still survive. According to the proposed method, such a distribution for facility renewal intervals is not expected as long as each establishment makes rational decisions and adjusts its renewal speed accordingly. When $m = 1/2$, there exists a region in the facility renewal interval where the probability density becomes negative. This implies that no adjusted facility renewal interval distribution can explain the observed technical inefficiency distribution. In such industries, we assume the existence of uncontrolled inefficiencies, or X-inefficiencies, and conduct a test for their presence.

5.2.5 Procedures 2 and 3: Extension of Half-Normal Distribution and Null Hypothesis to Be Tested

Next, we extend and generalize the half-normal distribution, which retains the possibility that it results from rational decision-making. There are two directions in this generalization, represented by the introduction of parameters p and μ in the following equation:

$$\psi(u) = C \exp\left(-\frac{(u-\mu)^{1+p}}{K}\right), \qquad (\text{If } p < 0, \text{ then } \mu < 0).$$

The introduction of parameter p represents generalization in a direction that includes exponential distributions, while the introduction of parameter μ represents generalization in a direction that includes truncated normal distributions. However, it is not necessary to consider generalization in both directions when conducting the test. The reasons for this are explained below. First,

$$\psi'(0) = -\frac{C(1+p)(-\mu)^p}{K}\exp\left(-\frac{(-\mu)^{1+p}}{K}\right),$$

which implies that property (vi) is not satisfied when $\mu \neq 0$. Furthermore, when $\mu = 0$, we have

$$\psi'(u) = -\frac{C(1+p)u^p}{K}\exp\left(-\frac{u^{1+p}}{K}\right),$$

so property (v) is satisfied for all positive values of u, but property (vi) requires that $p > 0$. Thus, both properties (v) and (vi) are satisfied only when $(p > 0) \wedge (\mu = 0)$. Therefore, the existence of X-inefficiency should be tested using the null hypothesis $H_0 : (p > 0) \wedge (\mu = 0)$, which does not contradict the assumption that the facility renewal interval is rationally determined.

If we consider the alternative hypothesis based on the distribution generalized with respect to the parameter p,

$$\psi(u) = C\exp\left(-\frac{u^{1+p}}{K}\right), \tag{5.3}$$

then the alternative hypothesis becomes $H_1 : p \leq 0\ (\mu = 0)$. Even if the distribution is further generalized to include the truncated normal distribution, the null hypothesis remains unchanged as H_0, since only the case $\mu = 0$ can be explained as the outcome of rational decision-making. In this case, the alternative hypothesis expands to $H_2 = H_1 \cup \{\mu \neq 0\}$.[2] Clearly, $H_1 \subset H_2$, so rejecting H_0 in favor of H_1 also implies rejection in favor of H_2. For this reason, we test the null hypothesis $p > 0$ against the alternative hypothesis $p \leq 0$ within the distributional form of technical inefficiency given by (5.3).[3]

Distribution (5.3) includes not only the half-normal distribution when $p = 1$, but also the exponential distribution when $p = 0$. Assuming that the probability density function $\psi(u)$ of the inefficiency distribution follows distribution (5.3) is equivalent to assuming that the density function $\phi(w)$ of the adjusted facility renewal interval is given by

---

[2] Note that the case $(p < 0, \mu > 0)$ does not arise, so writing H_2 in terms of $\mu \neq 0$ is equivalent to considering $\mu < 0$ or $(\mu > 0, p \geq 0)$.

[3] Even if the truncated normal distribution is considered a generalized form of the half-normal distribution, the resulting test remains essentially the same. For details, see footnote 4 in this chapter.

$$\phi(w) = -\alpha^2 w \psi^{'}(\alpha w) = C^{'} w^{1+p} \exp\left(-\frac{(\alpha w)^{1+p}}{K}\right), \tag{5.4}$$

where C' is a constant.

The advantage of assuming distribution (5.3) goes beyond merely enabling hypothesis testing about whether the observed technical inefficiencies result from a controlled mechanism. As discussed in detail in Sects. 3.1.4 and 3.1.5 of Chap. 3, the vintage inefficiency model allows for an economic interpretation of the parameter p, which indicates the extent to which an establishment's likelihood of upgrading its facilities is proportional to a power of its level of inefficiency. For example, a half-normal distribution implies that the probability of an establishment upgrading its facilities is proportional to its inefficiency level, whereas an exponential distribution implies that this probability remains constant regardless of the inefficiency level.

In general, when p is positive, inefficient establishments are more likely to renew their facilities, which may be consistent with firms' rational decision-making. For example, we have already seen that when $p = 1$, where technical inefficiency follows a half-normal distribution and facility renewal is proportional to the inefficiency level, this case can be interpreted as the outcome that arises when the probability density of facility renewal intervals, adjusted through rational decision-making, is given by (5.2), which is close to a symmetric distribution.

On the other hand, when p is negative, less efficient establishments tend to be less likely to renew their facilities. As discussed in this section, such a situation cannot arise if we assume that each establishment optimally controls its facility renewal. In this case, more efficient establishments are more likely to renew their facilities. However, if this tendency persists near zero inefficiency, it implies the existence of establishments that renew their facilities at an infinite rate. Therefore, when p is negative, property (vi) is no longer satisfied. Accordingly, if the observed distribution of technical inefficiency suggests a negative value for p, then, assuming that inefficiency is generated through the vintage model, this indicates that the observed inefficiencies include uncontrolled inefficiencies, that is, X-inefficiencies as redefined in Chap. 3.

Intuitively, one might think that the more inefficient an establishment is, the greater the cost-saving incentive from upgrading; therefore, it would be unlikely for rational decision-making to result in a tendency to neglect upgrading. Certainly, a negative value of p implies that the more inefficient an establishment is, the higher the probability that its optimal facility renewal interval is longer. However, strictly speaking, this does not necessarily mean that such a tendency cannot exist; rather, it can arise when the distribution of optimal facility renewal intervals happens to be particularly long-tailed. Such a possibility cannot be ruled out without imposing strong assumptions on the shape of the optimal facility renewal distribution. Nevertheless, if we assume that this distribution is continuous, then at the point of zero inefficiency, its shape becomes one that cannot occur unless we allow for adjustments such that the optimal renewal interval becomes zero.

Figure 5.3 shows an example of the density function for the facility renewal interval when $p = -0.5$. As in the distribution shown in Fig. 5.2, it is asymmetric, has a mode close to zero, and exhibits a long tail. When the facility renewal interval is

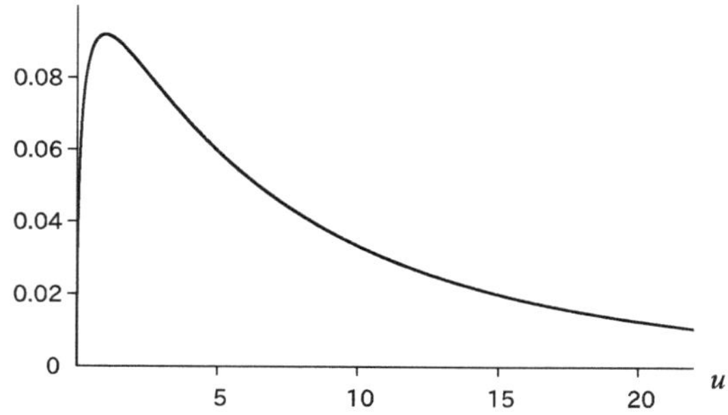

Fig. 5.3 An example of the distribution of facility renewal intervals when inefficiency distributes by the exponential power-type distribution with $p = -0.5$. *Notes* the PDF (5.4) with $p = -0.5, \alpha = 1, K = 1, C' = 0.25$

adjusted through the establishment's decision-making and exhibits such a distribution, the parameter p in the distribution of technical inefficiency takes a negative value. Note that the slope of this density function becomes infinite when inefficiency is zero. As can be seen from Eq. (5.1), this slope indicates the direction of adjustment, which in this case reflects the intensity of the adjustment toward a facility renewal interval of zero. Therefore, when p is negative, the adjustment toward a facility renewal interval of zero becomes infinite.

In the example of the facility renewal interval distribution with a negative value of p shown in Fig. 5.3, some establishments tirelessly pursue high productivity with frontier technology, while others rarely renew their facilities. Moreover, there appears to be no tendency for low-productivity establishments to be eliminated. According to the method defined here, such an industry is considered to exhibit uncontrolled inefficiencies, or X-inefficiencies.

5.3 A Method for Testing X-inefficiency

In the previous section, assuming that technical inefficiency arises according to the vintage model, we identified an adjustment process in facility renewal intervals that would not occur if inefficiency were controlled. We then determined the characteristics that would appear in the distribution of technical inefficiency if such an adjustment process existed, and expressed these characteristics as conditions on the distributional parameters. By testing these conditions, we can verify the existence of uncontrolled inefficiency, or X-inefficiency, as redefined in Chap. 4.

Based on the discussion in the previous subsection, we assume distribution (5.3) as the distribution for technical inefficiency. This distribution generalizes the half-normal distribution. Since it is a probability density function, its integral over the defined domain must be equal to one. This condition determines the value of C, and by substituting $K = (p + 1)/\theta$, we obtain the normalized distribution:

$$\rho(u;\theta,p)=\frac{(1+p)^{\frac{p}{1+p}}\theta^{\frac{1}{1+p}}}{\Gamma\left(\frac{1}{1+p}\right)}\exp\left(-\frac{\theta}{1+p}u^{1+p}\right), \tag{2.1}$$

which corresponds to the exponential power-type distribution analyzed in Chap. 2.

Under the exponential power-type distribution, if the null hypothesis $p > 0$ is not rejected, we cannot rule out the possibility that the observed distribution of technical inefficiency arises from rational control. Conversely, if the null hypothesis is rejected in favor of the alternative hypothesis $p \leq 0$, this suggests that the observed inefficiency may not result from control and instead indicates the existence of X-inefficiencies. In this section, we present a method to conduct this test.

5.3.1 Formulation of Hypotheses for Testing X-inefficiency

To test the hypothesis concerning the parameter p of the exponential power-type distribution, we use the relationship among moments explained in Chap. 2:

$$M_4 - 3M_2^2 = K_h\,|M_3|^{\frac{4}{3}}\,. \tag{2.3}$$

As discussed in Chap. 2, asymmetric distributions such as the half-normal and exponential distributions are generally used to represent technical inefficiency. For a random variable u following one of these distributions, there exists a relationship among its second-, third-, and fourth-order central moments that is independent of the parameters characterizing the variance magnitude of the distribution, as expressed in (2.3). Furthermore, as shown in the Appendix of Chap. 1, this relationship remains unchanged when the variable u is convolved with a symmetric stochastic error term v that follows a normal distribution, resulting in the composed error term $v - u$.

In the case of an exponential power-type distribution, the relationship presented in (2.3) also holds among the second-, third-, and fourth-order central moments of the convolution $v - u$, where u follows the distribution density (2.1) and the error term follows $v \sim N(0, \sigma_v^2)$. For an exponential power-type distribution, the constant K_h is given by

$$K_h=\frac{g_5g_1^3\;-\;4g_4g_2g_1^2\;+\;12g_3g_2^2g_1\;-\;6g_2^4\;-\;3g_3^2g_1^2}{\left(g_4g_1^2\;-\;3g_3g_2g_1\;+\;2g_2^3\right)^{4/3}}, \tag{2.5}$$

where $g_j \equiv \Gamma(j/(1+p))$. This constant K_h depends only on the parameter p, which determines the shape of the distribution, and does not depend on the parameters θ and σ_v^2, which represent the magnitude of the variance.

For $p > -1$, K_h is a monotonically decreasing function of p with a value range of $[-\infty, +\infty]$, as shown in Fig. 2.2 in Chap. 2. Therefore, if we estimate the value of the coefficient K_h in Eq. (2.3) via econometric analysis, we can use Eq. (2.5) to estimate the value of p and uniquely determine the tendency of establishments to invest in renewal on average in proportion to a power of the degree of inefficiency. Furthermore, using the properties of the estimators of K_h and p analyzed in Chap. 2, we can test the null hypothesis $p > 0$ for the value of p.[4]

5.3.2 *Inter-Industry Cross-Sectional Analysis*

The coefficient K_h can be obtained by estimating Eq. (2.3) for the relationship among central moments up to the fourth order, but determining the distribution of the estimates of K_h analytically is difficult. Therefore, even if we hypothesize that K_h takes a value within a certain range for an individual industry and estimate K_h directly using the calculated moment values as

$$\widehat{K}_h = \frac{M_4 - 3M_2^2}{|M_3|^{4/3}},$$

it remains challenging to test the hypothesis. However, a different approach is possible if the hypothesis is formulated not for the value of K_h in an individual industry but rather as a general tendency across many industries. If the hypothesis states that there exists a relationship

$$M_4 - 3M_2^2 = K_h\,|M_3|^{4/3},$$

with a particular value of K_h as a tendency across many industries, then testing becomes feasible. As a cross-sectional relationship across many industries, we estimate Eq. (2.3) and test the hypothesis regarding the coefficient value.

Thus, Eq. (2.3) is estimated econometrically to test a hypothesis when a sufficient number of moment estimates are available for samples that are expected to follow the same mechanism. Accordingly, the estimation of coefficients is conducted cross-sectionally across many industries rather than through independent empirical analyses for individual industries, as in previous studies.

---

4 In Sect. 5.2.1 of this chapter, when the half-normal distribution is generalized for testing the null hypothesis, $\psi(u) = C\exp(-u^{1+p}/K)$ is assumed. Although $\psi(u) = C\exp(-(u-\mu)^{1+p}/K)$ is a more general extension, we assume that the case $\mu = 0$, which considers a more restrictive alternative hypothesis, is sufficient for testing the null hypothesis $p > 0$. Numerical analysis shows that when $p > 0$, K_h is a decreasing function of μ, whereas when $p < 0$, it is an increasing function. In both cases, as μ becomes sufficiently small ($\mu \to -\infty$), K_h converges to the exponential case of approximately 2.38. In this sense, considering the case where $\mu < 0$ serves as an interpolation between the exponential distribution and the half-normal distribution. If the observed value of K_h is smaller than the exponential case of approximately 2.38, it is not possible to distinguish whether this results from a large μ or $\mu = 0$, $p > 0$. However, if the observed value of K_h is greater than approximately 2.38, then $\mu = 0$, $p > 0$ is not a possibility, since regardless of the value of μ, K_h exceeds the exponential case only when $p \leq 0$. Thus, to test the null hypothesis $p > 0$, one can assume $\mu = 0$ and conduct the test without any practical limitations.

When estimating inefficiency, the advantages of using cross-sectional analysis across many industries are not limited to technical issues. In Sect. 5.1.2, we introduced Lee's (1983) test, which examines the appropriateness of selecting a distribution function for technical inefficiency. Lee (1983) conducted tests on the distribution of technical inefficiency for specific industries. In fact, in one of the cases tested in the paper, the half-normal distribution is rejected, while in another, it is not. Does this imply that different mechanisms for the generation of technical inefficiency dominate in each industry? Furthermore, if different distributions of inefficiency arise under different mechanisms, a question emerges: Does it make sense to apply a common measure of technical inefficiency across different industries and compare them? In general, the estimated level of inefficiency depends on the assumed distribution type. Therefore, if one were to examine the suitability of specific distributions for individual industries, the level of inefficiency would be estimated according to different criteria for each industry. If so, should the parameters of different distributions be considered comparable indicators? These issues can be avoided by conducting a cross-sectional analysis across many industries.

In Chap. 1, we introduced the idea that the wrong skewness problem can be viewed as an issue arising from sampling from the population. When estimating higher-order moment values from a sample set drawn from the population, the variance of these estimates tends to be large. As a result, even if the wrong skewness problem does not exist in the population, it is not necessarily unlikely that a given sample set exhibits the characteristics of wrong skewness. Here, we consider an individual industry as a sample set, meaning a collection of establishments, drawn from a broader population of establishments in a wider region or the economy as a whole. By doing so, we aim to explore the overall tendencies in the distribution of inefficiency.

In a vintage model, parameters can only be compared as representing the tendency for establishments to retain inefficiency once the same tendency has been confirmed across industries. The value of the parameter p in the exponential power-type distribution indicates the shape of the distribution of technical inefficiency, but it does not by itself determine the average magnitude of inefficiency. In the context of the stochastic facility renewal model described in Chap. 3, the value of p represents the functional form of the probability that a facility will be renewed, expressed as a function of the degree of inefficiency. However, the average efficiency can only be calculated when both the shape parameter p and the parameter θ, which indicates the degree to which a certain proportion of establishments renew their facilities, are given. If it is confirmed that the parameter p, which determines the shape of the function, is common across industries, then comparing the values of θ, which reflect the extent of facility renewal, is directly meaningful for comparing the degree of inefficiency.[5] On the other hand, if the shape of the function is assumed to differ across industries, it becomes difficult to assign meaning to comparisons of the parameter θ across different functional forms. This is because, when the value of p differs, the order of magnitude of the θ values does not necessarily correspond to the order of

---

[5] In general, the larger the value of θ, the smaller the variance and the smaller the inefficiency.

magnitude of the average degree of inefficiency. In such cases, it becomes necessary to introduce a concept such as average efficiency for comparison.

5.3.3 Employing MOLS

To estimate Eq. (2.3) in an inter-industry cross-sectional setting, we need the moments of the deviations from the frontier production functions for each industry. This, in turn, requires estimating the frontier production function itself. Two major estimation approaches are available for this purpose: the ML method and the MOLS method.

The ML approach to estimating the frontier production function requires specifying the distributional form of the residuals *a priori*. Once a specific distribution is chosen, a likelihood function is constructed for the observed sample, and the parameters of the frontier production function are estimated by maximizing this likelihood. Although it is theoretically possible to estimate the parameter p jointly with the other production function parameters for each individual industry, the present approach assumes that p is common across all industries. Therefore, joint estimation of p and the production function parameters within each industry is not feasible. One possible alternative is to adopt an iterative procedure: starting from a starting value for p, one estimates the production function and residual moments for each industry, aggregates the moments across industries, and then estimates p using Eq. (2.3). This new value of p can then be used as the next starting value, and the procedure repeated until convergence. While such an iterative estimation method is theoretically possible, it is not practically feasible when applied across hundreds of industries.

Therefore, we use the MOLS approach instead of ML. First, OLS is applied to estimate the slope coefficients of the frontier production function. Next, the regression residuals are calculated, and their second-, third-, and fourth-order central moments are computed. Note that although we refer to the method as MOLS, it is equivalent to standard OLS in this context, since the constant term does not affect the central moments used for estimation. Let M_{2i}, M_{3i}, and M_{4i} denote the second-, third-, and fourth-order central moments of the OLS residuals for industry i. Using these moment values across industries, we estimate the coefficient K_h by regressing

$$M_{4i} - 3M_{2i}^2 = K_h \, |M_{3i}|^{4/3} + \varepsilon_i .$$

The estimated values of K_h from these regressions are then used to test theoretical implications regarding the distributional characteristics of technical inefficiency across industries.

When the results are interpreted based on the vintage inefficiency model, the value of the parameter p, which defines the shape of the distribution of technical inefficiency, is uniquely determined once the coefficient K_h is given. MOLS also has the advantage of providing a consistent estimator in a much simpler manner than ML. Moreover, the estimators obtained are sufficiently efficient compared to the MLE, as confirmed by Olson et al. (1980). In addition, the OLS-based moment estimates used to test for the existence of X-inefficiency have been shown to be empirically robust to misspecification of the production function, as demonstrated by Torii (1992).

5.4 Test of X-inefficiency Existence in the Japanese Manufacturing Industries

In this section, we econometrically confirm the existence of X-inefficiency in the Japanese manufacturing industry using the method presented in the previous section. Under the vintage model, when we obtain a distribution of technical inefficiency that cannot be explained by assuming that facility renewal intervals are somehow controlled, we cannot rule out the existence of X-inefficiency as "uncontrolled inefficiency." To perform this test, we estimate the frontier production functions for more than 300 industries in Japan and simultaneously determine the deviations of establishment-level performance from these functions as regression residuals. Next, a regression analysis is conducted to examine whether the relationship presented in Eq. (2.3) holds among the second-, third-, and fourth-order moments of the residuals. Based on the estimated regression coefficient K_h, we test the hypothesis for the distribution parameter p. As a result of this sequence of analysis, we not only test for the existence of X-inefficiency as described above, but also generate information that could potentially serve as a basis for cross-industry and international comparisons of technical inefficiency. However, such comparative analyses lie beyond the scope of this book and are not pursued further here.

5.4.1 Estimation Model of Technical Inefficiency

Stochastic Production Frontier Model

As a model of technical inefficiency, we adopt a parametric method to estimate the stochastic production frontier. The first reason for selecting this method is its consistency with the assumption of a smoothly differentiable production frontier. In nonparametric estimation, several of the most productive samples are used as benchmarks, and efficiency is measured as the deviation of other samples from these benchmarks. As a result, multiple samples have an efficiency score of one, creating non-differentiable points on the frontier. By contrast, because the vintage model assumes continuous time, obsolescence begins immediately after a facility is renewed, and the probability that inefficiency is exactly zero at any moment is effectively zero. For these reasons, nonparametric estimation is not a suitable modeling approach for the objectives of this chapter.

Second, to estimate second- or higher-order moments, either stochastic or deterministic models can be used, as long as the estimation method is parametric. However, as shown in Chap. 2 through Monte Carlo simulations, the resulting estimators are significantly affected by the magnitude of the random noise component. Therefore, it is preferable to adopt a stochastic model that explicitly incorporates random noise. Aside from technical estimation issues, the essential difference between stochastic and deterministic models lies in how faithfully the production frontier reflects the concept of a "maximum possible" output. In a deterministic model, efficiency equals one only when all production conditions are ideally and simultaneously satisfied. In contrast, the vintage model assumes that any establishment can reach full efficiency by renewing its facilities, thereby embodying the latest available frontier technology. For this reason, the vintage model is not well aligned with the assumptions underlying deterministic frontier models.

In addition, if the objective is to obtain an index of technical efficiency for inter-industry or international comparison, there are several additional technical advantages worth noting. First, technical inefficiency can be estimated while eliminating errors due to measurement issues or omitted variables, which helps reduce the variance of the estimated inefficiency level. If the goal is to construct comparable indices of technical inefficiency, it is preferable to prioritize the reliability of the inefficiency estimates rather than to pursue a production function that strictly conforms to a theoretical definition. Second, in the stochastic production frontier model, the parameters of the distribution assumed for the inefficiency term u can be obtained in a form directly comparable to those of the symmetric noise term v. For example, the variance σ_v of v can be estimated simultaneously with the variance σ_u of u, allowing the magnitude of technical inefficiency to be expressed relative to the magnitude of the noise. Third, as discussed in Chap. 1, a limitation of the stochastic production frontier model is that it only allows estimation of technical inefficiency at the industry level, not at the individual DMU level. However, this limitation poses no issue when the objective is to compare technical inefficiency across industries or countries.

Trans-Log Production Function

We adopt a translog production function, which is among the most flexible functional forms commonly used in production analysis. This choice allows us to avoid imposing strong assumptions regarding Allen's partial elasticity of substitution and strong separability. More importantly, it also enables us to avoid the assumption that the production function is homothetic with respect to scale.[6]

Specifically, we use two types of production functions, as shown below. These functional forms follow the approach proposed by Caves (1982) for the purpose of international comparison. The dependent variable in the production function is value added (VA). The explanatory variables, or input factors, are tangible fixed assets (K) and labor input (L), where labor input is measured by total cash wages. To explicitly capture the effect of scale, all variables on both sides of the equation are normalized by labor input. Equation (5.6) differs from Eq. (5.5) in that it includes additional explanatory variables, X_1 through X_4, which serve as controls for various

[6] The properties of translog production functions were analyzed by Christensen et al. (1973).

adjustments, such as differences in the services provided to production by production versus non-production workers, or variations between energy-intensive and energy-saving technologies.

$$\log(VA_j/L_j) = a_0 + a_1 \log(K_j/L_j) + a_2\{\log(K_j/L_j)\}^2 + a_3 \log(L_j) + a_4\{\log(L_j)\}^2 + a_5 \log(K_j/L_j)\log(L_j) + v_j - u_j \tag{5.5}$$

$$\log(VA_j/L_j) = a_0 + a_1 \log(K_j/L_j) + a_2\{\log(K_j/L_j)\}^2 + a_3 \log(L_j) + a_4\{\log(L_j)\}^2 + a_5 \log(K_j/L_j)\log(L_j) + a_6 X1_j + a_7 X2_j + a_8 X3_j + a_9 X4_j + v_j - u_j \tag{5.6}$$

where each variable denotes the value for the jth establishment:

VA_j: value added,
K_j: tangible fixed assets,
L_j: labor input (measured by total cash wages),
$X1_j$: ratio of energy costs to total material cost,
$X2_j$: ratio of inventory to total tangible assets,
$X3_j$: index of enterprise diversification (defined as the ratio of shipments of the largest product classified at the 6-digit JSIC level; lower values indicate greater diversification),
$X4_j$: ratio of commissioned production costs to total material cost.

Data Resource and Details of Variables

The materials used and the definitions of each variable are as follows:

Data:
Individual data from the Census of Manufacture in 1993 and 1995.

Establishments:
Establishments with 30 or more employees (Table *Kou*).

Unit for estimating the production function:
Cross-sectional analysis of establishments in the 4-digit JSIC manufacturing industry.

Calculation of each variable:

VA = Total shipments - (Raw materials usage + Decrements of raw materials and fuel inventory + Decrements of inventory of goods in process).

K = Tangible assets at the beginning of the year + (Tangible fixed assets acquired - Tangible assets removed - Depreciation)/2 + (Inventory at the beginning of the year + Inventory at the end of the year)/2.

L = Total cash wage payroll.

$X1$ = (Fuel usage + Electricity usage)/Total raw materials usage.

$X2$ = (Inventory at the beginning of the year + Inventory at the end of the year)/(2 K).

$X3$ = Shipments of the largest product in the 6-digit classification/Total shipments.

$X4$ = Commissioned production cost/Total material cost.

Variations in the Estimation

Variations left in the production function estimation

Whether to include $X_1 \sim X_4$ as explanatory variables
It is not known *a priori* whether the inclusion of these control variables improves the fit of the production function. This decision corresponds to the choice between Eqs. (5.5) and (5.6).

Whether to perform a weighted regression analysis
There is a choice between using standard OLS to obtain unbiased coefficient estimates and performing a weighted regression. In the latter, OLS is first applied to obtain residuals, and then the observations are weighted by the inverse of the squared residuals before applying OLS again.

Whether to exclude extremely large establishments
When estimating technical inefficiency, the regression residuals play an important role. For this reason, it is necessary to avoid the influence of a small number of extremely large establishments on the estimation results. One approach is to exclude, in advance, samples likely to be outliers. This is done by removing samples whose values for key variables, such as value added and capital, fall outside the range defined by the mean plus or minus 4.5 times the standard deviation. However, it should be noted that the stochastic production frontier model has a built-in mechanism to mitigate the influence of outliers. Thus, this option concerns whether to implement an additional precautionary step to exclude potential outliers. The same reasoning also applies to the decision regarding weighted regression in item 2 above. This procedure should be understood not as a statistical outlier detection and removal method, but as a preventive measure to limit the effect of extreme values treated as noise within the v component. Nevertheless, for convenience, we refer to this process as "outlier elimination" in the following discussion.

The variations in the production function estimation are denoted by the symbols summarized in Table 5.1. Since there is no prior information indicating which of these variations is most suitable for estimating the production function in the Japanese manufacturing industry, the estimation results for all variations are presented below to the extent possible.

Table 5.1 Variations of the frontier production function estimation

	X_i Adjustment Factor	Regression Analysis	Filter for Production Factors
IWD	Include	Weighted OLS	Delete outliers
IWR	Include	Weighted OLS	Retain outliers
IOD	Include	OLS	Delete outliers
IOR	Include	OLS	Retain outliers
EWD	Exclude	Weighted OLS	Delete outliers
EWR	Exclude	Weighted OLS	Retain outliers
EOD	Exclude	OLS	Delete outliers
EOR	Exclude	OLS	Retain outliers

Table 5.2 Distribution of establishments in valid industries

Number of establishments	Number of valid industries	
	1993	1995
21 ~ 29	48	53
30 ~ 49	85	83
50 ~ 69	38	46
70 ~ 99	41	39
100 ~ 149	43	49
150 ~ 199	36	33
200 ~ 499	46	49
500 ~	20	18
Total	357	370

Conditions for Eliminating Inappropriate Samples of Establishments and Estimating Production Functions

The following establishments were excluded:

(i) The value of tangible assets at the beginning or end of the year is 0.
(ii) The total amount of cash wage payroll is 0.
(iii) The number of permanent workers is 0.
(iv) The total shipments are 0.
(v) The number of permanent production workers is 0.
(vi) The value added is less than or equal to 0.
(vii) The total material cost is 0.
(viii) The total cash wage payroll for production workers is less than or equal to 0.

To preserve the degrees of freedom in the regression analysis, the production function was estimated only for industries with 20 or more valid establishments remaining after exclusions. These industries are hereafter referred to as "valid industries." Out of 406 industries, production functions were ultimately estimated for 357 manufacturing subdivisions in 1993 and for 370 in 1995. Table 5.2 shows how the number of establishments is distributed among the valid industries.

The descriptive statistics for the number of establishments in the sample are as follows: For 1993,

Minimum: 21, Maximum: 2351, Mean: 148.8, Median: 74, Standard Deviation: 240.3, Skewness: 5.2

and for 1995,

Minimum: 21, Maximum: 2293, Mean: 137.8, Median: 72, Standard Deviation: 210.4, Skewness: 5.7

5.4.2 *Test for the Existence of X-Inefficiency*

Descriptive statistics for the moments of the regression residuals for each estimation variation are summarized in Tables 5.3 and 5.4. These tables show that the moments of the regression residuals do not vary substantially across different variations of the regression analysis. In the rows labeled "> 0" for the third-order moment, the numbers indicate the number of industries in which the third-order moment is positive. In these industries, the distribution of residuals from the production function is positively skewed. However, for all distributional assumptions typically imposed on technical inefficiency, the third-order moment is expected to be negative. Therefore, in these industries, the method of moments cannot provide estimates of distribution parameters. As discussed in Chap. 1, these cases are referred to as "Type 1 failures" by Olson et al. (1980), and more recently as instances of "wrong skewness." Approximately one-quarter of industries fall into this category. In contrast, the remaining three-quarters of industries exhibit negative third-order moments, which are consistent with the distributional assumptions commonly used in the estimation of technical inefficiency.

Relationship Between Moments of Residuals

To estimate the coefficient K_h in Eq. (2.3), the following equations are established. These are identical to Eqs. (2.7) and (2.8), which were used in Chap. 2 to evaluate the properties of the estimator of K_h through Monte Carlo experiments. The reason for testing K_h as a regression coefficient, rather than as the direct ratio of excess kurtosis to skewness raised to the 4/3 power, is that the third central moment often takes values close to zero in a non-negligible number of samples. This leads to large variability in the ratio and makes direct inference problematic. By contrast, the regression framework allows for more stable estimation and hypothesis testing.

$$M_{4i} - 3M_{2i}^2 = K_1 \text{sign}\left(-M_{3i}\right) \left|M_{3i}\right|^{\frac{4}{3}} + \epsilon_i \tag{R1}$$

$$\log\left(M_{4i} - 3M_{2i}^2\right) = \log\left(K_2\right) + \frac{4}{3}\log\left(-M_{3i}\right) + \epsilon_i \tag{R2}$$

Equation (R2) applies only to samples such that

$M_{4i} - 3M_{2i}^2 > 0$ and $M_{3i} < 0$.

The log-log OLS estimation Eq. (R2) is introduced because the explanatory variables in the original OLS Eq. (R1) exhibit skewed distributions, raising concerns that the estimated coefficients may be unduly influenced by industry samples with large third-order moments. Figure 5.4 shows scatter plots of $(\text{sign}(-M_{3i})|M_{3i}|^{4/3}, M_{4i} - 3M_{3i}^2)$ for the IWD case in 1993 and 1995, respectively. When the variables are log-transformed, this problem is alleviated, as shown in the scatter plots in Fig. 5.5. However, for about one-third of the industries, $M_{4i} - 3M_{3i}^2$ is negative, and the

Table 5.3 Descriptive statistics of estimated moments Part I

In 1993		Regression variation			
		IWD	IWR	IOD	IOR
Second moment	Maximum	1.322	1.284	1.304	1.270
	Minimum	0.020	0.026	0.020	0.026
	Mean	0.228	0.245	0.226	0.243
	s.d.	0.145	0.149	0.143	0.148
Third moment	Maximum	0.136	0.239	0.124	0.152
	Minimum	−6.717	−6.580	−6.026	−5.957
	Mean	−0.149	−0.138	−0.135	−0.126
	s.d.	0.469	0.466	0.420	0.421
	>0	84	105	84	103
Fourth moment	Maximum	44.952	44.310	39.348	39.271
	Minimum	0.001	0.002	0.001	0.002
	Mean	0.753	0.819	0.686	0.752
	s.d.	2.868	2.858	2.550	2.573
		EWD	EWR	EOD	EOR
Second moment	Maximum	1.341	1.294	1.329	1.284
	Minimum	0.021	0.029	0.021	0.029
	Mean	0.244	0.262	0.243	0.261
	s.d.	0.151	0.155	0.150	0.154
Third moment	Maximum	0.160	0.345	0.134	0.326
	Mimimum	−6.414	−6.354	−6.139	−6.070
	Mean	−0.156	−0.142	−0.147	−0.135
	s.d.	0.476	0.477	0.455	0.456
	>0	84	114	86	113
Fourth moment	Maximum	42.708	42.728	40.296	40.267
	Minimum	0.002	0.003	0.001	0.002
	Mean	0.810	0.886	0.773	0.846
	s.d.	2.884	2.894	2.743	2.755

Notes s.d. indicates standard deviation. " > 0" indicates that the number of samples for the third moment is greater than zero.

logarithms of the variables are not defined. Therefore, estimation using regression Eq. (R2) is limited to samples for which $M_{4i} - 3M_{3i}^2 > 0$. At the same time, under the assumption of a positive constant K_h, this condition implies that $-M_{3i} > 0$. As a result, samples in which the third-order moment takes a positive value are also excluded. As shown by the results of the Monte Carlo experiments in Chap. 2, the estimates of K_h obtained from the two regression equations exhibit different bias tendencies. Therefore, it is essential to use both sets of estimates in a complementary manner when conducting hypothesis testing.

In the regression analysis shown in Eq. (R1), the constant term was fixed at zero, and in the log-log OLS estimation in Eq. (R2), the regression coefficient was fixed at

Table 5.4 Descriptive statistics of estimated moments Part II

in 1995		Regression variation			
		IWD	IWR	IOD	IOR
Second moment	Maximum	0.942	0.942	0.933	0.933
	Minimum	0.021	0.036	0.021	0.036
	Mean	0.235	0.251	0.233	0.248
	S.d.	0.136	0.140	0.134	0.139
Third moment	Maximum	0.434	0.406	0.328	0.377
	Mimimum	−2.261	−2.281	−2.178	−2.204
	Mean	−0.147	−0.134	−0.135	−0.123
	S.d.	0.298	0.291	0.277	0.272
	>0	84	97	87	99
Fourth moment	Maximum	12.428	12.027	12.301	11.942
	Minimum	0.001	0.004	0.001	0.003
	Mean	0.687	0.736	0.639	0.687
	S.d.	1.423	1.425	1.354	1.363
		EWD	EWR	EOD	EOREOR
Second moment	Maximum	1.033	1.033	1.026	1.026
	Minimum	0.030	0.040	0.029	0.040
	Mean	0.253	0.269	0.251	0.268
	S.d.	0.144	0.148	0.143	0.147
Third moment	Maximum	0.541	0.489	0.479	0.470
	Mimimum	−2.642	−2.642	−2.428	−2.428
	Mean	−0.157	−0.140	−0.148	−0.132
	S.d.	0.323	0.318	0.308	0.304
	>0	90	112	91	110
Fourth moment	Maximum	13.647	13.260	13.636	13.269
	Minimum	0.004	0.004	0.003	0.004
	Mean	0.772	0.825	0.735	0.790
	S.d.	1.573	1.579	1.518	1.530

Notes s.d. indicates standard deviation. " > 0" indicates that the number of samples for the third moment is greater than zero.

one, assuming the analysis is interpreted as an OLS. Figure 5.5 presents several theoretical relationships between $\log(M_{4i} - 3M_{2i}^2)$ and $\log((-M_{3i})^{4/3})$, corresponding to different values of $\log(K_2)$, each represented by a different dashed line. These dashed lines correspond respectively to the cases of the half-normal distribution, the exponential distribution, the case $K_1 = 3.0$ used for the test in Chap. 6, and the estimated value from Eq. (R2) under variation IWD. All of these dashed lines have a slope of one. The fact that the industry-level samples are generally distributed along these lines indicates that excess kurtosis and skewness raised to the 4/3 power are approximately proportional, thereby supporting the hypothesis that the value of K_h is constant.

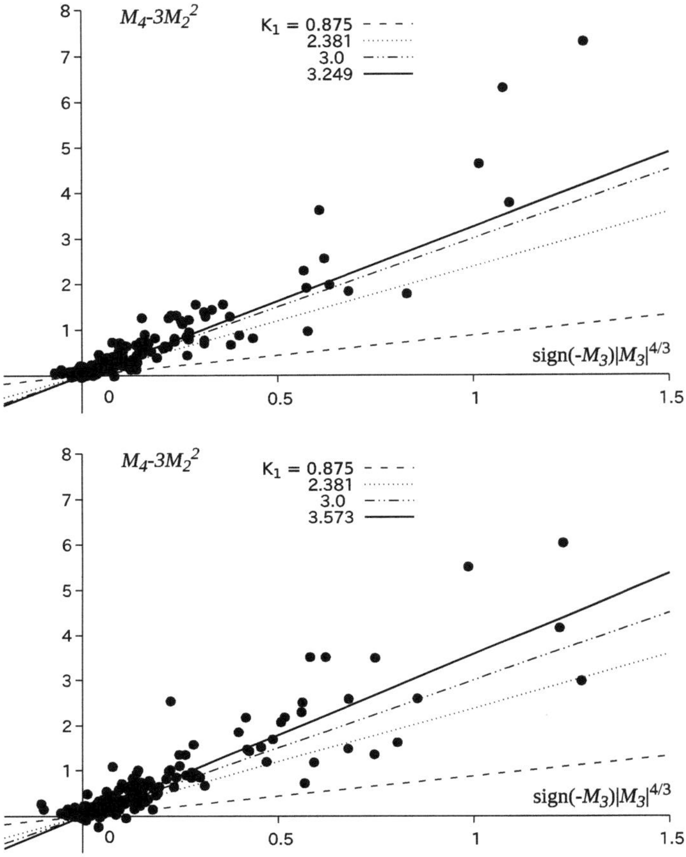

Fig. 5.4 Scatter Plot and Regression Line Based on Equation (R1).
Notes The upper panel shows the IWD case based on 1993 data, and the lower panel shows the IWD case based on 1995 data. The bold solid lines in the two panels represent the OLS regression lines from Eq. (R1), where the intercept is fixed at zero

The results of the regression analysis are summarized in Tables 5.5 and 5.6. In 1993, the estimated value of K_1 is approximately 3.3. When the log transformation is applied, the estimated value of $\log(K_2)$ is around 1.4 when outliers are excluded, and approximately 1.7 when they are included. These correspond to K_2 values of about 4.0 and 5.4, respectively. In 1995, the estimated value of K_1 ranges from approximately 3.5–3.6. With log transformation, K_2 is approximately 4.1 when outliers are excluded, and around 4.5 when they are included.

According to the Monte Carlo experiments presented in Chap. 2, estimation using Eq. (R1) reveals a systematic downward bias (as shown in Tables 2.1–2.7): when the value of σ_v is relatively large, the estimated value of K_h tends to approach zero due to random noise, making it difficult for the model to capture the information contained

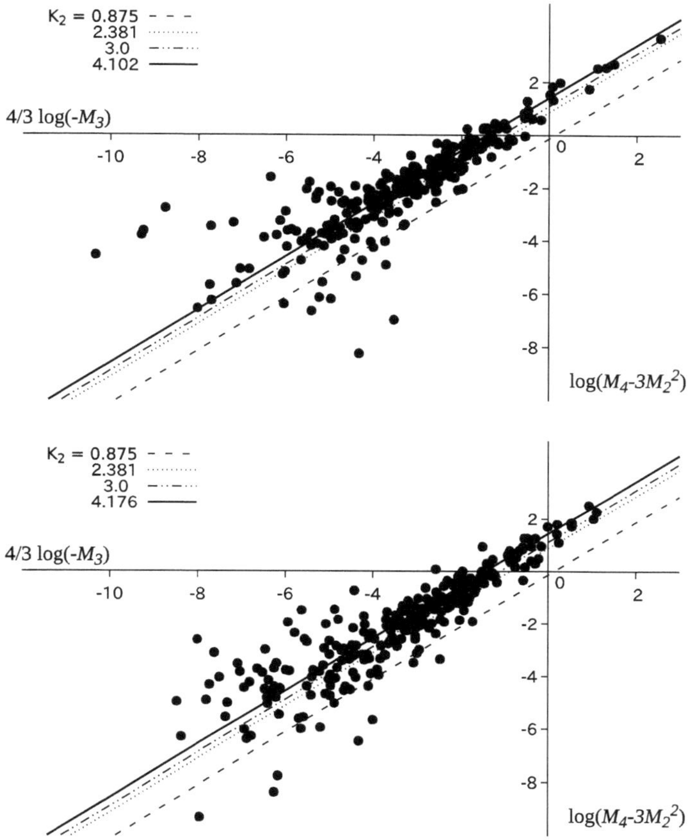

Fig. 5.5 Log-log Scatter Plot and Regression Line Based on Equation (R2).
Notes The upper panel shows the IWD case based on 1993 data, and the lower panel shows the IWD case based on 1995 data. Due to the log transformation of both axes, observations with non-positive values are excluded. As a result, 323 out of 357 observations are retained in 1993, and 343 out of 370 in 1995. The bold solid lines represent OLS regression lines based on Eq. (R2), applied to the log-transformed data, with the slope fixed at one

in the asymmetric technical inefficiency term u. However, in the present results, all estimates of K_h exceed 3, suggesting that the downward bias observed in the Monte Carlo experiments does not arise and that the asymmetric component is sufficiently large compared with the symmetric component. The Monte Carlo experiments in Chap. 2 also showed that when estimation is conducted using the log-log OLS specification (Eq. R2), the results in Tables 2.8–2.14 indicated a systematic upward bias in the estimated values when σ_v is large. This upward bias in the estimated value of $\log(K_2)$ creates an identification problem: it becomes difficult to determine whether the high estimate reflects a genuinely large value of the parameter p, or merely the influence of substantial noise from σ_v. However, since the value of K_1 obtained

Table 5.5 Estimation results for K_1 and $\log(K_2)$ based on Equations (R1) and (R2)

Variations	1993			
	(R1)	(R2)	(R3)	(R4)
IWD	3.249	1.411	3.250	1.144
	(0.103)	(0.066)	(0.104)	(0.050)
	357	323	210	208
IWR	3.321	1.764	3.322	1.295
	(0.113)	(0.075)	(0.115)	(0.050)
	357	323	167	165
IOD	3.290	1.392	3.290	1.173
	(0.134)	(0.067)	(0.138)	(0.047)
	357	304	181	178
IOR	3.369	1.697	3.370	1.298
	(0.146)	(0.077)	(0.149)	(0.053)
	357	308	165	161
EWD	3.277	1.476	3.277	1.186
	(0.117)	(0.071)	(0.119)	(0.050)
	357	324	208	205
EWR	3.343	1.759	3.346	1.273
	(0.113)	(0.087)	(0.116)	(0.070)
	357	327	164	162
EOD	3.278	1.426	3.279	1.147
	(0.129)	(0.073)	(0.131)	(0.059)
	357	318	205	201
EOR	3.353	1.715	3.355	1.283
	(0.127)	(0.077)	(0.131)	(0.065)
	357	318	159	155

Notes “Variations” refer to alternative specifications of the production function estimation. White’s heteroskedasticity-robust standard errors for the OLS estimates based on Eq. (R1) are reported in parentheses. In addition, standard errors from the log-log OLS estimation in Eq. (R2), where the slope is fixed at one, are also presented. Note that these standard errors refer not to the estimate of K_2 itself, but to that of $\log(K_2)$. Estimations (R3) and (R4) report the results of Eqs. (R1) and (R2), respectively, using only industries for which skewness is less than or equal to–0.4. The bottom row indicates the number of industries included in each estimation.

from the OLS estimation (Eq. R1) is sufficiently large, the possibility of a relatively large σ_v is unlikely. As a result, the estimated value of $\log(K_2)$ can reasonably be interpreted as conveying meaningful information about the shape of the distribution.

Tables 2.1–2.7 indicate that the OLS-based estimation using Eq. (R1) generally tends to produce upward-biased estimates, while Tables 2.8–2.14 show that the log-log OLS estimation using Eq. (R2) tends to yield downward-biased estimates. However, in the actual estimation results presented in Tables 5.5 and 5.6, the mean of the estimates of K_2 obtained using Eq. (R2) is 3.31 in 1993 and 3.60 in 1995,

Table 5.6 Estimation results for K_1 and $\log(K_2)$ based on Eqs. (R1) and (R2)

Variations	1995			
	(R1)	(R2)	(R3)	(R4)
IWD	3.573	1.429	3.584	1.147
	(0.286)	(0.072)	(0.306)	(0.045)
	370	343	208	204
IWR	3.645	1.529	3.672	1.235
	(0.300)	(0.066)	(0.325)	(0.053)
	370	346	193	190
IOD	3.674	1.417	3.679	1.096
	(0.310)	(0.074)	(0.331)	(0.051)
	370	319	202	195
IOR	3.744	1.452	3.765	1.167
	(0.320)	(0.067)	(0.345)	(0.058)
	370	328	191	185
EWD	3.464	1.344	3.486	1.157
	(0.287)	(0.064)	(0.311)	(0.047)
	370	341	210	207
EWR	3.534	1.556	3.570	1.266
	(0.308)	(0.070)	(0.341)	(0.053)
	370	339	193	190
EOD	3.551	1.362	3.570	1.163
	(0.302)	(0.067)	(0.327)	(0.048)
	370	326	206	201
EOR	3.610	1.486	3.646	1.266
	(0.321)	(0.075)	(0.353)	(0.054)
	370	329	190	185

Notes See notes to Table 5.5.

which is lower than the corresponding estimates of K_1 obtained using Eq. (R1), 4.86 in 1993 and 4.25 in 1995. There are exceptions to the upward bias observed in the regression analysis based on Eq. (R1); when the parameter p takes negative values, the bias becomes downward. This is clearly illustrated in Tables 2.15 and 2.16, which present the results of a more detailed Monte Carlo experiment conducted with $N = 100$, a value close to the typical number of establishments within a Japanese industry. The contrast in bias directions between the Monte Carlo simulations using Eqs. (R1) and (R2) and the observed reversal in the actual estimates suggest that the true value of the parameter p may be negative. Another possible explanation for this divergence lies in the variation in the number of establishments across industries. In the Monte Carlo experiments presented in Chap. 2, the number of establishments per industry was fixed at predetermined values, such as 100 or 200. In contrast, as shown in Table 5.2, the actual Japanese manufacturing industries analyzed here vary considerably in their number of establishments, ranging from fewer than 30 to more than 2,000. This heterogeneity in sample size is likely to explain the differing bias tendencies between the Monte Carlo results and the actual estimation outcomes.

Comparing the results of the Monte Carlo experiments with a fixed sample size of 100, shown in Tables 2.15 and 2.16, with the average residual skewness for each case presented in Tables 2.20 and 2.21, we find that the estimated values of K_h tend to deviate more from their theoretical values as the average residual skewness approaches zero. This deviation is likely caused by the increasing influence of noise from the symmetric error term. Figure 5.6 presents scatter plots of the deviation of the estimated K_h from its theoretical value against the average residual skewness for each combination of p and σ_v. Except in several cases where the parameter p is small and the theoretical value of K_h is especially high, the deviation tends to remain small when the average residual skewness is below approximately -0.4.[7]

Based on this finding, Eqs. (R1) and (R2) were re-estimated for Japanese manufacturing industries, excluding those industries with residual skewness greater than -0.4, since in these samples, the influence of the symmetric error term is presumed to substantially distort the information regarding technical inefficiency. The results are presented in the columns labeled (R3) and (R4) in Tables 5.5 and 5.6. In the results shown as (R3), despite the number of industries being reduced by roughly half, the estimated values changed surprisingly little. In particular, the estimates for 1993 are identical up to the second significant digit. This suggests that in industries where the residual skewness exceeds -0.4 and the influence of symmetric noise is presumed to be large, both the skewness and excess kurtosis tend to be small, and when the intercept is fixed at zero, the regression coefficient is more strongly determined by samples with large skewness and excess kurtosis. Thus, the estimation results obtained from a regression model assuming a zero intercept, such as Eq. (R1), are hardly affected. This implies that the estimation method based on this regression specification is robust to the influence of symmetric noise.

In contrast to the results for (R3), where the exclusion of industries with skewness greater than -0.4 had little effect on the estimated value of K_h, the estimation results for (R4), which apply the same exclusion under the specification of Eq. (R2), differ substantially from those obtained directly using Eq. (R2). This difference arises because the excluded samples tend to exhibit lower excess kurtosis and smaller skewness, making their log-transformed values more negative and of larger absolute magnitude. Although such samples carry less information about technical inefficiency due to the dominance of symmetric noise, they exert a disproportionately large influence on the regression when the slope is fixed and only the intercept is estimated. Consequently, removing them enhances the precision of the estimated value of K_h. This effect is clearly illustrated in the scatter plot in Fig. 5.7, where both axes are log-transformed: the observations for each industry lie approximately along a straight line with a slope of one. It is important to emphasize that the production frontier function is estimated separately for each industry. The observation that a common distributional property of technical inefficiency emerges across many

[7] Although similar discrepancies are observed even when skewness is around -0.75, we focus on the threshold of -0.4 here in order to ensure a sufficient number of observations.

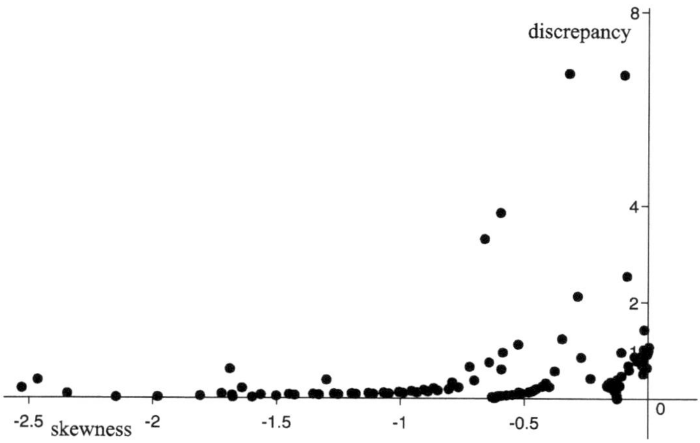

Fig. 5.6 Scatter plot showing the relationship between residual skewness and deviations of Kh estimates.

Note The horizontal axis represents the average residual skewness for each combination of the specified values of p and σ_v in the Monte Carlo experiments with a fixed sample size of 100, as reported in Tables 2.15, 2.16, 2.20, and 2.21. The vertical axis shows the ratio of the deviation of the estimated value of K_h from its theoretical value for the same combinations

independently estimated industries suggests that technical inefficiency is generated by a shared underlying mechanism.

5.4.3 Test of the Hypothesis of Half-Normal and Exponential Distribution

The estimated values of K_h, which exceed 3 as shown in Tables 5.5 and 5.6, raise concerns about the validity of the conventional distributional assumptions regarding technical inefficiency used in previous studies. For instance, under the assumption of a half-normal distribution, the theoretical value of K_h is given by $8(\pi - 3)/(2^{2/3}(4 - \pi)^{4/3})$, which evaluates to approximately 0.875. In the case of an exponential distribution, the theoretical value is $3/2^{1/3}$, which is approximately 2.381. In comparison, the estimated values reported in Tables 5.5 and 5.6 are substantially higher. Figures 5.4 and 5.5 include reference lines corresponding to these theoretical values, labeled $K_1 = 0.875$ and $K_2 = 0.875$, respectively, under the half-normal distribution assumption. These plots visually indicate that the half-normal distribution may not adequately capture the distributional characteristics of the observed data, even in the absence of formal statistical testing.

Next, we test the validity of the exponential distribution assumption. Based on the results in Tables 5.5 and 5.6, we examine the null hypothesis that the OLS regression coefficient from Eq. (R1) equals the theoretical value implied by the exponential

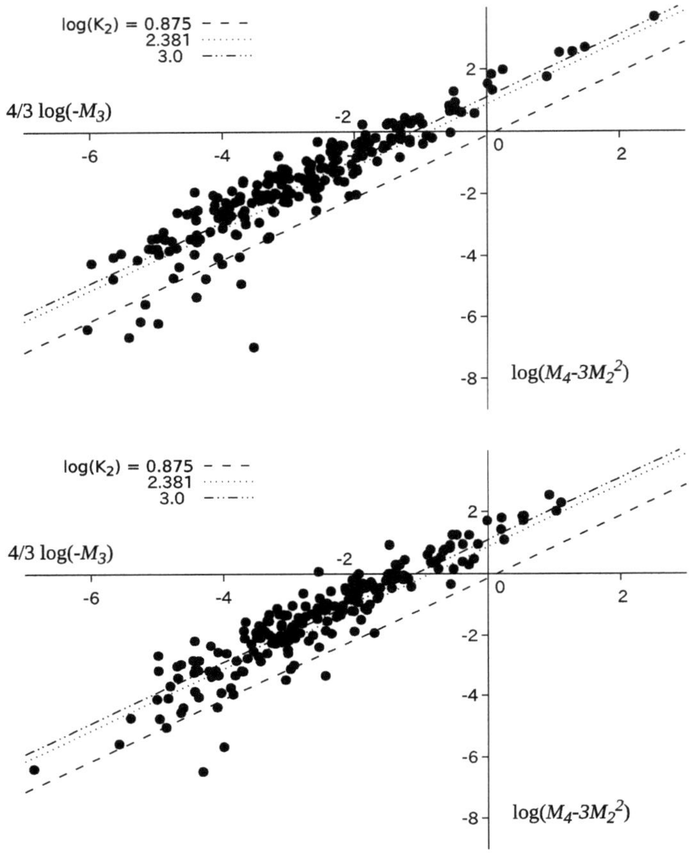

Fig. 5.7 Scatter plot based on the Log-log OLS estimation (R2).
Notes The upper panel shows the IWD case based on 1993 data, and the lower panel shows the IWD case based on 1995 data. Due to the log transformation of both axes, observations with non-positive values are excluded. Furthermore, industries with skewness greater than -0.4 are also excluded. As a result, 208 out of 357 observations are retained in 1993, and 204 out of 370 in 1995. The lines representing the OLS regression based on Eq. (R2), applied to the log-transformed data, are not shown because they nearly overlap with the line corresponding to $\log(K_2) = 3.0$

distribution. This hypothesis is rejected in all cases. In the 1993 results, the Wald statistics (based on the χ_1^2 distribution) range from 44.53 (IOD) to 72.96 (EWR), depending on the variation. In the 1995 results, they range from 13.98 (EWR) to 18.13 (IOR). In addition, Wald statistics are computed for testing the null hypothesis $\log(K_2) = \log(2.381)$, using the intercept and its standard error estimated from the log-log OLS estimation in Eq. (R2). In the 1993 results, the values of these Wald statistics range from 59.24 (EOD) to 144.41 (IWR), while in the 1995 results, they range from 53.91 (EOD) to 100.54 (IWR). Tables 5.7 and 5.8 summarize the Wald statistics for these tests, along with the results of additional hypothesis tests discussed in the remainder of this section.

As indicated by the results of the Monte Carlo experiment in Chap. 2, Sect. 2.3, bias in the OLS estimates of K_h is unavoidable when the number of establishments in each industry is around 100. Therefore, instead of directly testing the null hypothesis that the estimated value of K_h equals the theoretical value under the half-normal or exponential distribution, we test a revised null hypothesis based on Monte Carlo results: that the estimated value of K_h equals the mean of the biased estimates observed in the Monte Carlo experiments for each distribution, using the corresponding standard deviation also obtained from the Monte Carlo results. First, we refer to Table 2.15 in Chap. 2 for the case where $p = 1$, which corresponds to the half-normal distribution within the exponential power-type family, assuming a sample size of 100. This size is close to both the median (72) and the mean (138) number of establishments in the actual dataset. Even in the case with the largest estimate ($\sigma_v = 0.25$), the mean of the OLS estimates is 1.090, and the standard deviation is 0.138. Compared with the estimates of K_1 shown in Tables 5.5 and 5.6, the hypothesis that inefficiency follows a half-normal distribution is clearly rejected, even without conducting a formal test.

Next, we refer to Table 2.16 for the case where $p = 0$, corresponding to an exponential distribution, also assuming a sample size of 100. When $\sigma_v = 0.25$, the mean of the estimates is 2.460, and the standard deviation is 0.220. The Wald statistics for the null hypothesis that the estimates obtained using regression model (R1) equal 2.460 range from 10.29 (IOD) to 12.76 (EWR) for the 1993 data, and from 7.71 (EWR) to 10.93 (IOR) for the 1995 data. Even in the smallest case, the null hypothesis is rejected at the 5% significance level under a two-tailed test. Since $\chi^2_{1,0.995} = 7.879$, only one case in the 1995 results (EWD) falls just short of the critical value for rejection at the 1% level. It should be noted that both the mean and standard deviation of the Monte Carlo results vary depending on the value of σ_v. However, when smaller values of σ_v, such as 0.1 or 0.05, are used, the results remain nearly identical to those for $\sigma_v = 0.25$. Therefore, the hypothesis that technical inefficiency follows an exponential distribution is rejected at the 5% significance level under a two-tailed test.

Next, we conduct hypothesis tests using the estimation results (R3) and (R4) in Tables 5.5 and 5.6, which exclude industry samples with skewness greater than -0.4, on the grounds that these samples, due to a relatively large value of σ_v compared with σ_u, are unlikely to retain sufficient information about the distribution of inefficiency. First, for the estimation results (R3) based on Eq. (R1), we test the null hypothesis that the estimated value equals 2.46 with a standard deviation of 0.22, corresponding to the case of $\sigma_v = 0.25$ previously referenced. The Wald statistics for this hypothesis range from 10.22 (IOD) to 12.68 (EWR) for the 1993 data, and from 7.27 (EWD) to 10.17 (IOR) for the 1995 data. In two cases for the 1995 data (EWD and EWR), the null hypothesis cannot be rejected at the 1% significance level under a two-tailed test. However, in all variations, the null hypothesis is rejected at the 5% significance level under a two-tailed test. For the estimation results (R4) based on Eq. (R2), we again test the null hypothesis corresponding to the case of $\sigma_v = 0.25$, where the expected value of $\log(K_2)$ is 0.359 with a standard deviation of 0.062. The Wald statistic takes a minimum value of 84.52 (EOD) for the 1993 data, and 84.61 (IOD) for the 1995 data. Accordingly, in all variations, the null hypothesis is rejected at the 1% significance level under a two-tailed test.

Since the sample size may not be sufficiently large to ensure the normality of the estimates, hypothesis testing is conducted using the 2.5% and 97.5% quantiles reported in Tables 2.17 and 2.18. These tables clearly indicate that, in all the cases reported in Tables 5.5 and 5.6, both the null hypothesis that the asymmetric error term follows an exponential distribution and the hypothesis that it follows a half-normal distribution are rejected.

As shown by the test results presented above, the hypothesis that the asymmetric error term follows an exponential distribution is not supported, at least in the case of the Japanese manufacturing industry. This finding also suggests that the truncated normal distribution, which is often assumed in recent empirical studies, is likewise inappropriate for describing the observed inefficiency. The theoretical value of the coefficient K_h is given in Eq. (2.4), and as explained in the previous chapter, this value depends on the shape parameter and reaches at most the theoretical value under the exponential distribution, $3/2^{1/3} \simeq 2.381$. The above analysis shows that the estimated values of K_h are significantly greater than this upper bound. Therefore, the truncated normal distribution cannot account for the observed values of K_h for any value of the shape parameter.

5.4.4 *Identification of X-Inefficiency Using the Vintage Model*

Assuming the vintage model, the existence of X-inefficiency is confirmed when the distribution of the observed asymmetric error term cannot be explained as the result of rational adjustment in each establishment's choice of facility renewal intervals. A necessary condition for interpreting the observed distribution of the asymmetric error term as being rationally controlled is that $p > 0$ when the distribution is modeled using an exponential power-type distribution. The value of K_h corresponding to the boundary case $p = 0$ is approximately 2.381, which is equal to the value under the exponential distribution. As explained above, the null hypothesis $p = 0$ is rejected in nearly all of the regression analyses using Eqs. (R1) and (R2). Since this test concerns whether the asymmetric error term follows an exponential distribution, a two-tailed test is applied. In contrast, to verify the existence of X-inefficiency, we conduct a one-tailed test of the null hypothesis $p > 0$, which implies rational control, against the alternative hypothesis $p \leq 0$, which implies the absence of control. Because all the estimated values of p fall in the region $p \leq 0$, the rejection of the null hypothesis $p = 0$ in a two-tailed test implies that the null hypothesis $p > 0$ is also rejected in a one-tailed test at the same significance level. Therefore, a separate test for the hypothesis $p > 0$ is unnecessary. Although the null hypothesis $p = 0$ is not rejected at the 1% level in some cases under a two-tailed test (with the critical value $\chi^2_{1,0.99} = 6.635$), it is still rejected at the 1% level under a one-tailed test. Accordingly, the null

Table 5.7 Results of Wald Statistics Part I

In 1993		Regression variation			
Model	Hypothesis	IWD	IWR	IOD	IOR
(R1)	Theoretical Value	71.589	68.804	44.533	45.775
	Monte Carlo Result ($\sigma_v = 0.25$)	10.567	12.100	10.287	11.847
	Monte Carlo Result ($\sigma_v = 0.1$)	11.879	13.641	11.204	12.955
	Monte Carlo Result ($\sigma_v = 0.05$)	12.356	14.165	11.568	13.359
(R2)	Theoretical Value	67.092	144.412	60.961	115.773
	Monte Carlo Result ($\sigma_v = 0.25$)	134.200	209.798	127.694	182.922
(R3)	Monte Carlo Result ($\sigma_v = 0.25$)	10.545	12.040	10.218	11.702
(R4)	Monte Carlo Result ($\sigma_v = 0.25$)	97.496	137.083	110.012	131.715
		EWD	EWR	EOD	EOR
(R1)	Theoretical Value	58.481	72.961	48.696	58.713
	Monte Carlo Result ($\sigma_v = 0.25$)	10.733	12.760	10.314	12.357
	Monte Carlo Result ($\sigma_v = 0.1$)	11.930	14.459	11.308	13.786
	Monte Carlo Result ($\sigma_v = 0.05$)	12.370	15.022	11.694	14.276
(R2)	Theoretical Value	73.703	103.993	59.239	121.769
	Monte Carlo Result ($\sigma_v = 0.25$)	140.701	170.642	124.976	188.739
(R3)	Monte Carlo Result ($\sigma_v = 0.25$)	10.683	12.676	10.252	12.235
(R4)	Monte Carlo Result ($\sigma_v = 0.25$)	107.885	95.317	84.519	106.642

Notes The "Model" column refers to the estimation results tested in Tables 5.5 and 5.6. In the "Hypothesis" column, "Theoretical Value" indicates that the null hypothesis tests whether the estimated value is equal to the theoretical value of 2.381, which corresponds to the case where $p = 0$. "Monte Carlo Result" indicates that the null hypothesis tests whether the estimated value equals the mean obtained from the Monte Carlo experiments, using the standard error of the estimate and the standard deviation from the Monte Carlo results. Items in parentheses indicate additional conditions.

hypothesis $p > 0$, which must hold if the observed technical inefficiency is to be interpreted as rationally controlled rather than X-inefficiency, is rejected in all cases. This result shows that the existence of X-inefficiency in Japanese manufacturing cannot be statistically ruled out, and supports the interpretation that the observed technical inefficiency reflects the presence of X-inefficiency. In addition, Table 2.19 presents the 95% quantile values estimated from the Monte Carlo experiment, which further confirm that the null hypothesis $p > 0$ is rejected under the one-tailed test.

Here, we have presented the case in which the null hypothesis is set as $p > 0$. However, even if the null hypothesis were set as $p \leq 0$ and the alternative hypothesis as $p > 0$, the same conclusion would follow: since the null hypothesis $p = 0$ has already been rejected in a two-tailed test, it would also be rejected in a one-tailed test at the same significance level. Thus, we again arrive at the conclusion that the existence of X-inefficiency cannot be statistically ruled out.

Using the results from Tables 2.15 and 2.16, bias-corrected theoretical values of K_h can be obtained through interpolation-based adjustment. Focusing on the case with the smallest symmetric error term, $\sigma_v = 0.05$, the relationship between the theoretical and estimated values of K_h for $p \in [0.0, -0.6]$ is used to perform bias

Table 5.8 Results of Wald Statistics Part II

in 1995		Regression variation			
Model	Hypothesis	IWD	IWR	IOD	IOR
(R1)	Theoretical Value	17.404	17.806	17.420	18.134
	Monte Carlo Result ($\sigma_v = 0.25$)	9.528	10.165	10.206	10.928
	Monte Carlo Result ($\sigma_v = 0.1$)	9.499	10.137	10.153	10.887
	Monte Carlo Result ($\sigma_v = 0.05$)	9.606	10.243	10.253	10.990
(R2)	Theoretical Value	60.542	100.540	54.632	75.545
	Monte Carlo Result ($\sigma_v = 0.25$)	126.484	167.025	119.465	142.799
(R3)	Monte Carlo Result ($\sigma_v = 0.25$)	8.886	9.524	9.401	10.167
(R4)	Monte Carlo Result ($\sigma_v = 0.25$)	106.261	115.764	84.610	90.844
		EWD	EWR	EOD	EOR
(R1)	Theoretical Value	14.237	13.975	15.009	14.693
	Monte Carlo Result ($\sigma_v = 0.25$)	7.710	8.036	8.524	8.748
	Monte Carlo Result ($\sigma_v = 0.1$)	7.571	7.875	8.399	8.599
	Monte Carlo Result ($\sigma_v = 0.05$)	7.648	7.945	8.479	8.672
(R2)	Theoretical Value	55.870	95.856	53.911	68.801
	Monte Carlo Result ($\sigma_v = 0.25$)	122.689	163.022	120.048	135.060
(R3)	Monte Carlo Result ($\sigma_v = 0.25$)	7.269	7.475	7.953	8.121
(R4)	Monte Carlo Result ($\sigma_v = 0.25$)	104.799	123.149	105.202	121.365

Notes Refer notes of Table 5.7

correction via the Lagrange interpolation method. For instance, in the case of variation IWD, the estimated values of K_h for the 1993 data are corrected to 3.274 and 4.112 under estimations (R1) and (R2), respectively. For the 1995 data, the corresponding corrected values are 3.873 and 4.396. Using these bias-corrected values of K_h, the corresponding values of p that satisfy the theoretical relationship given in Eq. (3.8) can be derived. The resulting estimates of p are -0.276 and -0.417 for (R1) and (R2), respectively, in 1993, and -0.384 and -0.450 in 1995. The estimate for variation IWD in 1993 represents the smallest among the K_h values reported in Tables 5.5 and 5.6, and accordingly, the corresponding estimate of p, -0.276, is the largest (least negative) among the inferred values in that table. Furthermore, applying the Lagrange interpolation method to the 2.5% and 97.5% quantiles of the estimated K_h values reported in Tables 2.17 and 2.18, the 95% confidence interval for K_h is obtained as (2.756, 4.310), and the corresponding 95% confidence interval for p is estimated as $(-0.441, -0.138)$.

The hypothesis testing conducted here is based on the recognition that the estimates of the ratio K_h, obtained through simple regression analysis, are subject to bias. Nevertheless, the hypothesis is evaluated using the results of the Monte Carlo experiments, which account for this known bias. Among standard methods for constructing confidence intervals for the ratio of two random variables, it is well known that when the denominator—the skewness value—is small, the resulting intervals become wide, making these methods difficult to use for hypothesis testing. Table 5.9 presents the 95% confidence intervals estimated using both Fieller's theorem and the delta

Table 5.9 Estimation of the 95% confidence interval for K_h based on Fieller's theorem and the delta method

Variations	1993		1995	
	Fieller	Delta	Fieller	Delta
IWD	8.893	5.807	5.884	5.055
	1.652	2.114	2.593	2.892
IWR	10.021	6.350	6.820	5.722
	1.934	2.514	2.974	3.376
IOD	9.059	5.902	5.986	5.124
	1.690	2.172	2.544	2.843
IOR	10.214	6.451	6.930	5.794
	1.965	2.564	2.927	3.328
EWD	8.343	5.697	5.829	5.007
	1.742	2.181	2.620	2.923
EWR	9.587	6.300	6.890	5.755
	2.040	2.609	3.043	3.467
EOD	8.516	5.751	5.941	5.090
	1.735	2.187	2.617	2.925
EOR	9.770	6.357	6.997	5.832
	2.033	2.614	3.037	3.464

Notes "Variations" refer to different specifications of the production function estimation. The column labeled "Fieller" reports the 95% confidence interval for K_h based on Fieller's theorem, while the column labeled "Delta" reports the interval based on the delta method. In both columns, the upper row indicates the upper bound of the 95% confidence interval, and the lower row indicates the lower bound.

method. For the 1993 data, the intervals are too wide to allow for meaningful hypothesis testing. However, for the 1995 data, despite the broad confidence intervals, the null hypothesis that the asymmetric error term follows an exponential distribution, i.e., $K_h \simeq 2.381$, is still rejected.

Assuming the mechanism of inefficiency based on the vintage model, a negative value of p cannot be explained if facility renewal intervals are even partially controlled, let alone perfectly optimized. Intuitively, as discussed in detail in Sect. 5.2.5, a negative value of the parameter p implies a tendency whereby the more inefficient an arbitrarily selected establishment is, the lower the probability that it undertakes facility renewal. This tendency alone makes it difficult to interpret the observed pattern as the outcome of rational decision-making.[8] For example, Fig. 5.8 illustrates the distribution of facility renewal intervals corresponding to the regression estimate $p = -0.276$ for case IWD based on Eq. (R1). This distribution is characterized by a mode close to zero and a very long upper tail. This suggests a pattern in which some establishments repeatedly renew their facilities in an effort to maintain productivity

[8] It has already been explained that such a distribution of renewal intervals is unlikely to emerge even after each establishment adjusts its renewal timing toward the optimal value. However, it may arise if the distribution of renewal intervals is entirely idiosyncratic.

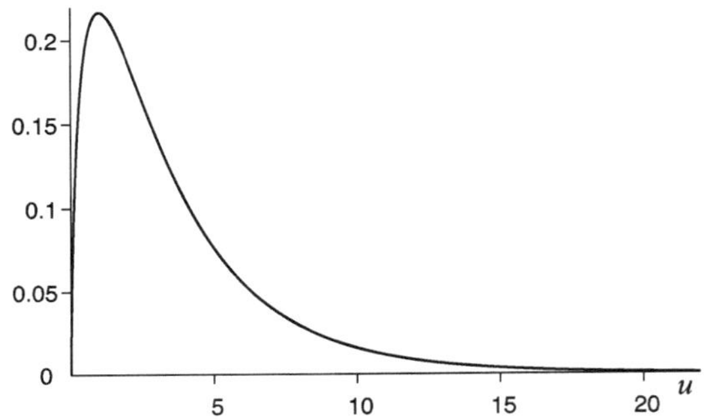

Fig. 5.8 Distribution of facility renewal intervals when inefficiency distributes by the exponential power-type distribution with p = −0.276. *Notes* the PDF (5.4) with $p = -0.276$, $\alpha = 1$, $K = 1$, $C' = 0.589$

at the frontier level, possibly regardless of whether such renewal is economically justified, while many other establishments rarely implement renewal-based productivity improvements.

5.5 Conclusion and Discussion

Based on the technical inefficiency estimates for the Japanese manufacturing industry, we demonstrate that the existence of X-inefficiency-defined as the absence of control-cannot be statistically ruled out. The model examined in this chapter assumes that technical inefficiency arises from differences in the vintage of each firm. We begin by identifying the conditions that the distribution of technical inefficiency must satisfy if facility renewal intervals are rationally adjusted, based on an analysis of the adjustment model. We then examine distributional forms such as the half-normal and exponential distributions that have been employed in the literature, and confirm that only the half-normal distribution satisfies these conditions. Next, we consider the half-normal distribution as a special case of the exponential power-type distribution and find that the condition is satisfied only when the shape parameter p is positive. As long as facility renewal intervals are controlled, the distribution of technical inefficiency must satisfy $p > 0$. Accordingly, we conduct a hypothesis test of $p > 0$, which corresponds to the null hypothesis that facility renewal intervals are controlled and that X-inefficiency, as defined by the absence of control, does not exist in the Japanese manufacturing industry. This test is implemented using establishment-level data from the 1993 and 1995 Censuses of Manufactures in Japan.

The test employs a method developed in Chap. 2, in which the parameter K_h is estimated by fitting the relationship between moments expressed as

$$M_4 - 3M_2^2 = K_h \, |M_3|^{4/3} \, .$$

This implies that if the null hypothesis $K_h < 2.381$ in this equation is not rejected, then the null hypothesis that $p > 0$, concerning the distribution type, is also not rejected. The frontier production function is estimated for each of over 300 four-digit manufacturing industries in Japan using MOLS, and the moments of the residual distribution, which result from the convolution of the technical inefficiency term and a symmetric error term, are obtained from the regression residuals. Next, the value of K_h is estimated via cross-sectional analysis across industries, and hypothesis tests are conducted using the results of the Monte Carlo experiments presented in Chap. 2. An advantage of the method described in this chapter is that, even when production functions or other structural details vary by industry, the results can still be interpreted as general tendencies across the entire manufacturing sector, as long as the generation structure of technical inefficiency is assumed to be the same.

As a result, we could not reject the possibility that the observed distribution of technical inefficiency does not satisfy the condition $p > 0$, which must hold if facility renewal intervals are controlled. In this sense, the existence of X-inefficiency in the Japanese manufacturing industry cannot be ruled out. At the same time, it became evident that the assumptions of the half-normal, exponential, and truncated normal distributions are not appropriate for modeling technical inefficiency in the Japanese manufacturing sector. These distributions have frequently been used in empirical studies due to their asymmetry and analytical tractability. The choice of distributional assumption has a substantial impact on the estimated level of technical inefficiency and therefore requires careful consideration. Despite this, distributions such as the half-normal have often been adopted without adequate justification or empirical validation.

Several points should be considered when evaluating the conclusions presented in this chapter. First, these conclusions are based on the assumption that all observed technical inefficiencies arise from differences in the vintage distributions across establishments. The model does allow for the possibility that an establishment's observed productivity may deviate from the level predicted solely by its facility vintage. Thus, the vintage model does not require that all variations in productivity be fully explained by differences in vintage alone. However, it must be acknowledged that the generation of technical inefficiency heavily depends on the assumptions of the putty-clay model. For example, the model assumes that facility renewal exclusively involves investment in the latest available technologies and does not account for incremental improvements achieved through smaller-scale investments. In reality, the cost of investment typically varies depending on the extent of technological advancement achieved through renewal. If such variation is incorporated, the underlying stochastic process would change, and as a result, the asymptotic distribution would also differ.

Second, in certain industries, the vintage of production facilities may be a major determinant of productivity, whereas in others, it may not be a particularly important factor. In such cases, the mechanism by which inefficiencies arise would not accurately reflect whether the facility renewal decisions were appropriate. The empirical analysis in this chapter proceeds under the assumption that differences in vintages resulting from facility renewal decisions are a source of inefficiency and that this relationship holds uniformly across all industries. Unfortunately, the method presented in Chap. 2 does not allow us to test whether the hypothesis that the distribution of observed inefficiencies follows an exponential power-type distribution is valid. The exponential power-type distribution has a shape parameter that determines the distribution type, and this analysis tests whether the value of that parameter falls within a specific range. However, this approach does not allow us to test the appropriateness of assuming the exponential power-type distribution itself. In other words, it does not test the broader assumption that the vintage model, through this distribution, fully accounts for the degree of technical inefficiency.

Third, it should be noted that the regression coefficients examined in this chapter are derived from the moments of the regression residuals up to the fourth order. As such, the properties of the sample distribution cannot be directly analyzed. Because the analysis involves testing the ratio of random variables, the inference relies on estimates obtained from a biased simple regression. Consequently, the hypothesis testing conducted in this chapter relies heavily on the Monte Carlo experiments presented in Chap. 2. The reliability of these Monte Carlo results, in turn, depends on the quality of the random number generation.

With regard to the first issue, the analysis presented in this chapter may be valid to some extent, as the statistical tests conducted here depend particularly on the distributional characteristics of technical inefficiency near zero. Nevertheless, a more direct analysis of the distributions of facility vintages and technical efficiency is still necessary for an appropriate interpretation of the results. This is especially important for addressing the second issue raised earlier. For example, Førsund and Hjalmarsson (1987) supplemented their vintage model-based analysis of technical efficiency with a detailed case study of the cement industry. To assess the appropriateness of the vintage model, it is essential to examine a specific industry in which facility vintages can be clearly identified and to verify the model's assumptions through in-depth empirical investigation. Although we had intended to include such a case study in this chapter, the limited availability of data on the vintages of Japanese capital equipment made this difficult to implement. Nonetheless, Caves and Barton (1990) partially explored the relationship between vintage and inefficiency using U.S. data. Torii (2009) also confirmed the productivity-enhancing effects of store renovations, consistent with the predictions of the vintage model, using store-level panel data from Japanese food supermarkets. Through similar empirical investigations, it would be possible to deepen our understanding of whether technical inefficiency actually arises from differences in facility vintages, and whether the absence of competitive pressure leads to suboptimal vintage distributions that hinder the realization of potential productivity. Furthermore, with regard to the second issue, as explained in detail in Chap. 3, when there is both a uniform tendency for costs to rise and a mechanism that counteracts this tendency by promoting efficiency, the vintage model generally represents the asymptotic state to which the resulting dynamic process converges. As long as inefficiency exists, even if it does not arise from differences in vintages, the vintage model may still retain a certain degree of validity, provided that such a dynamic process is expected to be at work.

The results presented here may merely reflect the possibility that the vintage model falls short of fully capturing the mechanisms by which inefficiency arises across industries. Explaining the outcomes of non-rational behavior is inherently difficult. Nevertheless, even in such cases, it remains meaningful to consider the economic implications suggested by the observed facts. For example, Fig. 5.7 shows that the moments of the residuals from the estimated production functions tend to exhibit consistency across industries, and that the ratio of excess kurtosis to the skewness raised to the power of 4/3 appears to be nearly constant. This finding suggests that, as a general trend across industries, the distribution of technical inefficiency tends to exhibit substantially greater excess kurtosis relative to skewness than the distributions traditionally assumed in previous studies.

Appendix: Proof of Proposition 5

Proof

Directly substituting $w = 0$ into (5.1) yields the first half of condition (iv). Next, differentiating both sides of (5.1) with respect to w gives

$$\phi'(w) = \zeta\left(0\middle|w\right)\xi(w) + \int_0^w \frac{\partial}{\partial w}\zeta\left(w - z\middle|z\right)\xi(z)dz.$$

Substituting $w = 0$ on both sides of the equation, together with conditions (i) and (iii), leads to the second half of property (iv). Since $\phi(w)$ is a probability density function, it satisfies $\phi(w) \geq 0$. Differentiating the left-hand side and the middle term of Eq. (3.4) with respect to x gives

$$\psi'(x) = -\frac{\phi(x/\alpha)}{\alpha x},$$

which leads to property (v). Taking the limit $x \to 0$ on both sides of this differentiated equation, we obtain

$$\psi'(0) = \lim_{x\to 0} -\frac{\phi\left(\frac{x}{\alpha}\right)}{\alpha x} = \lim_{x\to 0} -\frac{\frac{1}{\alpha}\phi'\left(\frac{x}{\alpha}\right)}{\alpha} = -\frac{\phi'(0)}{\alpha^2} = -\frac{1}{\alpha^2}\zeta\left(0\middle|0\right)\xi(0).$$

Thus, by the second half of property (iv), we obtain property (vi). □

References

Aigner D, Lovell CAK, Schmidt P (1977) Formulation and estimation of stochastic frontier production function models. J Econ 6(1):21–37

Bauer PW, Berger AN, Ferrier GD, Humphrey DB (1998) Consistency conditions for regulatory analysis of financial institutions: a comparison of frontier efficiency methods. J Econ Bus 50(2):85–114

Bauer PW, Berger AN, Humphrey DB (1993) Efficiency and productivity growth in US. Banking. In: The measurement of productive efficiency: techniques and applications. Oxford University Press

Berger AN (1993) "Distribution-free" estimates of efficiency in the US banking industry and tests of the standard distributional assumptions. J Prod Anal 4(3):261–292

Berger AN, DeYoung R (1997) Problem loans and cost efficiency in commercial banks. J Bank Financ 21(6):849–870

Berger AN, Hannan TH (1998) The efficiency cost of market power in the banking industry: A test of the "quiet life" and related hypotheses. Rev Econ Stat 80(3):454–465

Berger AN, Humphrey DB (1992) Measurement and efficiency issues in commercial banking. In: Output measurement in the service sectors. University of Chicago Press, pp 245–300

Berger AN, Mester LJ (1997) Inside the black box: what explains differences in the efficiencies of financial institutions? J Bank Financ 21(7):895–947

Caves RE (1982) Estimation of stochastic production frontiers and measures of technical inefficiency

Caves RE, Barton DR (1990) Efficiency in US manufacturing industries. MIT Press

Christensen LR, Jorgenson DW, Lau LJ (1973) Transcendental logarithmic production frontiers. Rev Econ Stat 28–45

Coelli T (1995) Estimators and hypothesis tests for a stochastic frontier function: a Monte Carlo analysis. J Prod Anal 6:247–268

Coelli TJ, Prasada Rao DS, O'donnell CJ, Battese GE (2005) An introduction to efficiency and productivity analysis. Springer Science & Business Media

Cummins JD, Zi H (1998) Comparison of frontier efficiency methods: an application to the US life insurance industry. J Prod Anal 10:131–152

D'agostino RALPH, Pearson ES (1973) Tests for departure from normality. Empirical results for the distributions of b_2 and $\sqrt{b_1}$. Biometrika 60(3):613–622

Førsund FR, Hjalmarsson L (1987) Analyses of industrial structure: a putty-clay approach. Almqvist & Wiksell International

Greene WH (2008) Econometric analysis, 6th edn

Kneip A, Simar L, Van Keilegom I (2015) Frontier estimation in the presence of measurement error with unknown variance. J Econ 184(2):379–393

Lee L (1983) On maximum likelihood estimation of stochastic frontier production models. J Econ 23(2):269–274

Olson JA, Schmidt P, Waldman DM (1980) A Monte Carlo study of estimators of stochastic frontier production functions. J Econ 13(1):67–82

Schmidt P, Lin T-F (1984) Simple tests of alternative specifications in stochastic frontier models. J Econ 24(3):349–361

Schmidt P, Lovell CAK (1979) Estimating technical and allocative inefficiency relative to stochastic production and cost frontiers. J Econ 9(3):343–366

Schmidt P, Sickles RC (1984) Production frontiers and panel data. J Bus Econ Stat 2(4):367–374

Torii A (1992) Technical efficiency in Japanese industries. Ind Effic Six Nations 31–120

Torii A (2009) Dynamic analysis of the mechanism behind technical inefficiency: evidence from panel data on Japanese food supermarkets (in Japanese). Yokohama Bus Rev 30(1):31–54

Tulkens H (1993) On FDH efficiency analysis: some methodological issues and applications to retail banking, courts, and urban transit. J Prod Anal 4(1):183–210

Wang WS, Amsler C, Schmidt P (2011) Goodness of fit tests in stochastic frontier models. J Prod Anal 35:95–118

Wang WS, Schmidt P (2009) On the distribution of estimated technical efficiency in stochastic frontier models. J Econ 148(1):36–45

Yuengert AM (1993) The measurement of efficiency in life insurance: estimates of a mixed normal-gamma error model. J Bank Financ 17(2–3):483–496

Chapter 6
X-inefficiencies in the Japanese Manufacturing Industries II: Identifying X-inefficiencies assuming the Existence of Inefficiency Unobserved Production Factors

In this chapter, following Chapter 5, we conduct another existence test for X-inefficiency, defined as the absence of control. Unlike the vintage model used in Chapter 5, the test here is based on a different assumption regarding the mechanism by which inefficiency is generated. It assumes that an unobserved but important production factor exists, and that the input level of this factor, or its input ratio relative to other factors, varies across establishments, resulting in dispersion in observed productivity. Due to the curvature of the production function, such dispersion gives rise to asymmetric deviations in output, which are observed as technical inefficiency. In other words, because this factor is unobservable, the production function is misspecified, and the resulting error manifests as apparent technical inefficiency.

If the unobserved input is recognized by an establishment's management and controlled to some extent, such control would influence the distribution of technical inefficiency. Therefore, by identifying how the distribution is affected by this control, we can test whether the unobserved input is being managed, that is, whether technical inefficiency is rationally controlled. If the null hypothesis that the unobserved factor is not controlled is not rejected in the test of the distributional form of technical inefficiency, then the existence of X-inefficiency cannot be ruled out. For the purposes of this analysis, X-inefficiency refers to inefficiency that is not subject to managerial control, as redefined in Chapter 4 to address the standard critique posed by neoclassical microeconomics. Accordingly, this chapter tests whether the distributional characteristics of technical inefficiency reflect the presence of X-inefficiency. This approach is fundamentally the same as that taken in the previous chapter. Although the hypotheses and distributional assumptions differ from those based on the vintage model, the approach remains consistent in that it avoids imposing arbitrary distributional forms and instead explicitly analyzes the mechanism by which inefficiency arises.

Strictly speaking, this form of inefficiency is classified as allocative inefficiency under Farrell's definition. However, since the input responsible for the variation is not a major factor of production, such as capital or labor, the resulting inefficiency

A. Torii, *Production Efficiency with the Stochastic Management Model*,
https://doi.org/10.1007/978-981-95-3501-9_6

does not stem from incorrect choices among technologies, as is typically implied by allocative inefficiency. Since technical inefficiency is defined as a one-sided deviation from the production frontier, it can be represented by introducing a new axis and an associated variable z, along with a smooth and continuous function that passes through the frontier and attains its local maximum when $z = 0$. In this formulation, this setup enables us to associate the value of the variable z with the corresponding level of technical inefficiency. If inefficiency is assumed to be subject to control, then the degree of inefficiency can be interpreted as the outcome of controlling the variable z along this new axis. Under this conceptualization, there is essentially no substantive difference between allocative inefficiency and technical inefficiency, except in cases where allocative inefficiency arises from differing combinations of major inputs such as capital and labor.

In Sect. 6.1, we begin by examining how such production factors, if they exist, influence productivity and how they might contribute to the occurrence of technical inefficiency. Section 6.2 introduces a testing methodology that builds on the properties derived in Sect. 6.1 and assesses whether the unobserved production factor, which is assumed to be the source of technical inefficiency, is being controlled. In Sect. 6.3, we apply this test to the Japanese manufacturing industry, testing the null hypothesis that the unobserved production factors responsible for technical inefficiency are not controlled. If this null hypothesis is rejected, we cannot rule out the alternative hypothesis that the level of inefficiency is rationally controlled with consideration of the cost of such control within the framework of neoclassical microeconomics. This interpretation remains valid even if the inefficiency appears to result from causes that are conventionally attributed to X-inefficiency. Conversely, if the null hypothesis is not rejected, we cannot rule out the possibility that the unobserved production factors responsible for technical inefficiency are indeed left uncontrolled. In that case, the presence of X-inefficiency cannot be denied.

6.1 A Model Assuming an Unobserved Production Factor

In this section, we present a conceptual model that explicitly describes how asymmetrically distributed inefficiencies arise in frontier production function models, under the assumption that unobserved production factors exist. As with the vintage model, this conceptual framework offers insights into which type of distribution is appropriate for representing technical inefficiency.

The conceptual model presented here assumes the existence of an unobserved production factor. Although it is not dynamic like the vintage inefficiency model, it nonetheless explains how technical inefficiency can be observed. If the input–output relationship that includes this unobserved factor is estimated using an econometric model based solely on observable inputs, the production function becomes misspecified. We demonstrate that the resulting error structure exhibits the same structural characteristics as those found in a standard input–output model with technical inefficiency, i.e., the two are isomorphic in terms of their error-generating mechanisms.

This implies that when such misspecification occurs due to the omission of an unobserved factor, estimating the model within a technical inefficiency framework will still yield what appears to be technical inefficiency. Therefore, the observed technical inefficiency in such cases can be interpreted as arising from the presence of a dispersed unobserved production factor. Furthermore, if this unobserved factor is controlled, the model parameters should fall within a certain range. When the estimated parameter lies outside this range, it indicates that the factor is not being controlled. Based on this relationship, we construct a statistical test to assess whether the unobserved factor is subject to control.

6.1.1 Input–Output Model with Controlled, Unobserved Production Factor

The basic model builds on the misspecification inefficiency model developed in Chapter 4, Sect. 4.2.1. Assume that the twice-differentiable frontier production function for industry i is given by $Y = F^i(L, K, z)$, where Y denotes output, K is capital, L is labor, and z is an unobservable factor of production. For example, z may represent managerial effort to implement QMP practices, such as workforce management or supplier involvement. Alternatively, it may correspond to the level of employees' superego, as introduced in Sect. 4.1 of Chapter 4 in the context of X-inefficiency theory. In general, a higher level of superego leads to higher output for a given input bundle. The resource associated with this unobservable input is tentatively referred to as resource M.

The second-order partial derivative of the frontier production function with respect to z is assumed to take a constant negative value b^i for each industry:

$$F^i_{zz}(L, K, z) = b^i < 0.$$

Here, the subscript z in expressions such as F_z and F_{zz} denotes partial differentiation with respect to z (not an index such as in z_0). Let q_j denote the opportunity cost per unit of resource M for the jth establishment. For example, if resource M represents superego, then q_j corresponds to the opportunity cost of managerial efforts aimed at enhancing the level of employees' superego. As in previous notational conventions in this book, when a value pertains to the jth establishment in industry i, the industry subscript i is omitted for simplicity. We assume that the values of q_j are symmetrically distributed around their mean value q^0, and represent them as:

$$q_j = q^0 + \Delta q.$$

We assume that the input quantities K_j and L_j are historically predetermined and thus exogenous with respect to current unobserved productivity shocks. This assumption allows us to abstract from the intractable difficulties often embedded in the regression residuals when estimating a production function that incorporates technical inefficiency. Accordingly, the analysis can focus on the structural properties of the estimation method proposed in this study.

First, we consider the input–output relationship that would be observed if the input of resource M were controlled. Resource M is not observable from outside the firm; in other words, an external observer cannot identify the level of its input. However, the manager of the enterprise is aware of its existence, knows the opportunity cost of allocating it to production activities, and chooses the input level z_j to maximize profit, taking that opportunity cost into account. The first-order conditions for profit maximization by the jth enterprise are:

$$F_z^i\left(L_j, K_j, z_j\right) = q_j. \tag{6.1}$$

Let $z_0^i(q_j; L_j, K_j)$ be the solution for z_j that satisfies the condition (6.1). We assume that a solution to this condition exists. As q_j is assumed to distribute symmetrically, establishments choose

$$\begin{aligned} z_0^i(q^0 + \Delta q; L_j, K_j) &= z_0^i(q^0; L_j, K_j) + \frac{1}{F_{zz}^i}\Delta q \\ &= z_0^i(q^0; L_j, K_j) + \frac{1}{b^i}\Delta q. \end{aligned}$$

Here, Δq is assumed to be sufficiently small so that the approximation remains valid. The term $\Delta q/b^i$ captures the variation arising from the dispersion in the opportunity cost q_j of resource M. In addition to this, we consider another source of variation stemming from the unobservability of resource M. Because managers must rely on noisy estimates of both costs and marginal products when allocating such unobservable inputs, it is inherently difficult to make optimal decisions. As a result, decision errors are inevitable. Therefore, the actual dispersion in the choice of z_j across establishments reflects not only the effect of $\Delta q/b^i$, but also the additional variation caused by these decision errors. We denote the total deviation in z_j arising from both sources as Δz. Thus,

$$z_j = z_0^i(q^0; L_j, K_j) + \Delta z.$$

The input–output relationship is then observed as

$$Y = F^i\left(K_j, L_j, z_0^i(q^0; L_j, K_j) + \Delta z\right).$$

Expanding this relation around $z_i^0(q^0; L_j, K_j)$ with respect to the variable z for each observed K and L gives

$$\begin{aligned} Y =& F^i\left(L_j, K_j, z_0^i\left(q^0; L_j, K_j\right)\right) + F_z^i\left(L_j, K_j, z_0^i\left(q^0; L_j, K_j\right)\right)\Delta z \\ &+ F_{zz}^i\left(L_j, K_j, z_0^i\left(q^0; L_j, K_j\right)\right)\frac{(\Delta z)^2}{2} + o\left(\Delta z^3\right). \end{aligned} \tag{6.2}$$

With the first-order condition (6.1), the definition of function $z_0^i(\cdot)$, and the assumption $F_{zz} = b^i$, we obtain the following econometric model:

$$Y = F^i\left(L_j, K_j, z_0^i\left(q^0; L_j, K_j\right)\right) + a\Delta z + b\frac{(\Delta z)^2}{2} + \epsilon. \tag{6.3}$$

where a and b are structural parameters of the econometric model, and ϵ is a random error term. If this econometric model is actually estimated using input–output data, it is expected that $a = q^0$ and $b = b^i$.

Thus, if the input of z is controlled with consideration of the opportunity cost of resource M, and the realized input z is distributed around the optimal input $z_0^i(L_j, K_j, q_j)$, then inefficiency is observed according to Eq. (6.3). The first term represents the production frontier, the second term $a\Delta z$ is a symmetric deviation component, and the third term $b(\Delta z)^2/2$ is an asymmetric component that reflects deviation only in the negative direction, since it is expected that $b < 0$. This structure corresponds to the stochastic frontier production model, an econometric specification used to estimate the input–output relationship under the assumption of technical inefficiency:

$$y_j = f^i(\boldsymbol{x}_j; \boldsymbol{\beta}^i) + v_j - u_j. \tag{1.1}$$

However, in this econometric model, the symmetric and asymmetric error components are not independent but are deterministically related through a common underlying variable Δz, since the asymmetric term is a nonlinear transformation of the same source of variation. This contrasts with the standard SFA model, in which the error terms are typically assumed to be independent. In this sense, the model implicitly assumes a specific copula structure that imposes functional dependence between the two error components.[1] Although in actual estimation the symmetric error term is likely to include various sources of noise independent of Δz, as explained in Proposition 1 in Chapter 1, this does not pose a problem when conducting hypothesis tests based on the relationships among the moments of the regression residuals.

Thus, when an input–output relationship is estimated using an econometric model that accounts for technical inefficiency, even if the null hypothesis of no technical inefficiency is not rejected, it is possible for the model to fit the data well due to the presence of unobserved production factors. In other words, the observed technical

[1] The model implicitly assumes a dependence structure that closely resembles a co-monotonic copula. Although strict co-monotonicity does not hold globally, each component of the error structure exhibits co-monotonic behavior with respect to a common underlying variable. This allows the model to approximate a co-monotonic copula-based specification in a piecewise fashion. For other examples of copula-based analyses in SFA, see Amsler et al. (2014, 2016), and Haschka (2024), all of which model the dependence between the symmetric and asymmetric error components using various copula structures.

inefficiency may result from a misspecification of the production function caused by omitting such a factor. Since we have so far assumed that managers optimally choose the input level of resource M, it is important to note that technical inefficiency can be observed even when X-inefficiency is not present. That is, the observed inefficiency arises not from irrational managerial behavior or a lack of effort, but from the model's failure to account for an important unobserved input.

6.1.2 Characteristics of Managerial Resource Input

In Sect. 6.1.1, we showed that when there exists an important but unobservable production factor that varies across establishments, this factor, referred to as resource M, can generate an effect that appears as technical inefficiency in the input–output relationship. In this subsection, we further specify resource M as managerial effort devoted to business resources such as QMP at the establishment level, and discuss how the input of this factor differs in nature from that of other production inputs. Based on this preliminary consideration, we then examine a method for testing the hypothesis of X-inefficiency, where X-inefficiency is defined as a situation in which, despite the significant impact that the allocation of managerial resources has on productivity, the input level of such resources is not controlled.

Let us begin by assuming, as explained in Sect. 1.5.2 of Chapter 1, that managerial input can be viewed as a resource allocated by establishments to various types of QMP. According to Flymn et al. (1995), the activities that constitute QMP are diverse and include top management support, workforce management, quality information, supplier involvement, product design, process management, and customer involvement. As shown in international comparative studies such as Phan et al. (2011), the levels of these activities are quantified based on questionnaire responses collected from establishments. These responses are typically measured using a five- or seven-point Likert scale. While the Likert scale enables the quantification of respondents' perceptions regarding corporate activities, it does not directly measure objective realities. Consequently, the level of managerial practices can only be described through such relative and subjective indicators. Naturally, firms are likely to implement a variety of QMP activities in combination. However, because it is difficult to capture these activities with a single comprehensive indicator, managerial input tends to remain unobservable.

Since managerial effort is itself a production input, it is only to be expected that it entail a cost corresponding to its input level. This cost arises as an opportunity cost, given the limited availability of managerial resources within the firm. The capacity of upper management to supply managerial effort is inherently constrained not only because managerial attention and decision-making capacity are scarce but also because the size of such resources cannot be easily adjusted in the short term. These limited managerial resources must be allocated across various managerial activities, such as quality control, strategic planning, personnel management, and external coordination. As a result, opportunity costs inevitably arise from the need to prioritize among competing uses.

For other production inputs such as labor or capital, the associated costs are typically recorded under specific accounting categories. These accounting costs are not identical to the corresponding opportunity costs, but because labor and capital markets are generally well-developed and competitive, the accounting costs tend not to deviate significantly from the actual opportunity costs. In contrast, for managerial resources, although activities to implement QMP entail various expenditures, these costs are not necessarily consolidated under a unified accounting category that reflects their opportunity cost. Some of these expenditures appear as operating expenses, such as payments to consulting firms or R&D expenditures. Others are recorded as non-operating expenses, including support for Quality Control (QC) circle activities or promotional expenses used to incentivize employees. Although all of these expenses are associated with the use of managerial resources, they do not directly reflect the opportunity cost of allocating limited internal managerial capacity to specific efforts.

In addition, because the alternative uses of managerial input within the firm are diverse and context-dependent, it is difficult to infer an implicit price for any particular allocation. No internal market exists to support such valuation, nor is there a well-established and competitive external market for managerial resources. As a result, the opportunity cost of managerial input can substantially diverge from the actual operating expenses incurred when implementing managerial efforts. Consequently, it is difficult for managers to accurately assess the opportunity cost of allocating managerial resources across different types of managerial activities.

For example, if an establishment succeeds in reducing inefficiencies such as slack by strengthening process control, the cost associated with process management will likely increase to some extent. However, as productivity improves, the unit cost of production may decline, potentially leading to a reduction in overall accounting costs. In such cases, the change in total costs at the establishment level does not necessarily reflect the price of managerial resource input. Conversely, if an establishment allocates an excessive amount of managerial resources to a specific business project, the project itself may generate a profit, while the overall profitability of the establishment may decline, possibly resulting in a substantial increase in total costs. In general, the opportunity costs associated with the use of managerial resources are rarely recorded explicitly as business expenses in accounting records. More likely, only a portion of these costs is captured by observable accounting items. Therefore, it is difficult to estimate the level of managerial input based solely on recorded expenditures. This difficulty is one of the reasons why managerial resource allocation remains largely invisible.

The absence of a well-functioning market for managerial effort not only causes a divergence between opportunity costs and accounting costs, as discussed earlier, but also leads to substantial differences in factor prices of managerial input across firms. Since the unit cost of such input largely depends on the personal attributes of individual managers, inputs associated with higher costs than those in other firms may persist without adjustment. Therefore, as assumed in Sect. 6.1.1 in the analysis of the invisible effects reflected in input–output relationships, the actual factor prices of managerial resources are considered to be dispersed across establishments.

Since measuring the input level is challenging, achieving the optimal input level with precision is difficult, even if such an optimum exists. Furthermore, because the exact input price of managerial resources is hard to determine, the optimal level itself is also uncertain. For these reasons, the actual input level is expected to be dispersed around the optimal value. This assumption has already been made in the previous Subsection.

On top of these factors, the invisibility of managerial input leads to a situation in which the observed product is effectively considered net of the input costs associated with managerial resources. For other production factors, managers are generally expected to recognize output and factor costs separately, and to maximize the residual by subtracting the latter from the former. However, in the case of managerial resources, even if managers are able to accurately assess the quantity of input, the associated costs, as explained earlier, tend to appear in various forms and are not consolidated into a specific accounting category. As a result, the output reflected in value added likely excludes a portion of the costs related to managerial effort.

For example, expenses incurred from outsourcing system analysis to external vendors for supply chain management, or from using external IT platforms to enhance coordination with suppliers, are recorded as operating expenses and thus deducted from value added. These expenses clearly represent part of the factor costs associated with managerial resource input. However, as discussed earlier, they do not capture the full factor price of such input. Accordingly, following the notation used in the previous Sect. 6.1.1, the observed output takes the form:

$$F^i(L_j, K_j, z_j) - \tilde{q}_j z_j > F^i(L_j, K_j, z_j) - q_j z_j,$$

where $\tilde{q}_j$ denotes the portion of the unit cost q_j that is recorded as an accounting expense and therefore deducted in the calculation of value added, with $\tilde{q}_j < q_j$.[2]

[2] It should be noted, however, that the portion of managerial input costs not recorded as accounting expenses will inevitably affect productivity in the long run. In this sense, the production function estimated here should be regarded as a short-run production function. For instance, a project that requires substantial managerial resources and involves high opportunity costs may exert its influence over a longer time horizon, altering the shape of the long-run production function. Such effects are not necessarily captured by the short-run production function, which reflects only short-term managerial inputs.

6.1.3 *Absence of Control over Managerial Resources*

Existence of X-inefficiency and Absence of Control over Managerial Input

In the theory of X-inefficiency, if resource M were superego, then the productivity dispersion caused by differences in the level of superego would indeed be regarded as X-inefficiency, since it results from differences in the level of superego, which is treated as a causal factor. However, from the perspective of neoclassical microeconomics, which presents a critique of the X-inefficiency argument, we need to consider the problem referred to in Chapter 4, Sect. 4.3.1 as the "relativity of rationality." With regard to resource M, the issue can be framed as follows: "As long as resource M is a factor of production, its use entails an opportunity cost, even if it is unobservable. Therefore, when the optimal input level is determined by comparing the unit opportunity cost with the marginal productivity of resource M, the economic agent should be regarded as making a rational choice. Even if the input level of resource M is low, resulting in apparently low productivity, this reduction in productivity may reflect a rational decision rather than the presence of inefficiency."

As explained in the previous Sect. 6.1.1, when the input of an invisible resource M is properly controlled, technical inefficiency may be observed in the input–output relationship. However, such inefficiency is distinct from X-inefficiency, which implies a form of "irrational" behavior. Even if differences in productivity arise from variations in the realized input levels of resource M, these differences are difficult to interpret as X-inefficiency if the input levels result from rational managerial decisions made with due consideration of the opportunity cost of resource M.

However, if the input of resource M is not appropriately controlled, the neoclassical critique based on the relativity of rationality does not apply. In such a case, observed inefficiency arises because resource M, despite being an important determinant of productivity, is left uncontrolled and follows an exogenously given distribution, leading to disparities in productivity. This type of inefficiency lies outside the scope of conventional criticisms rooted in neoclassical microeconomics. According to the redefinition provided in Chapter 4, such inefficiency can be interpreted as X-inefficiency in the sense that it reflects an "absence of control." In this way, whether the input of resource M is controlled or not leads to fundamentally different interpretations of the observed inefficiency. If it is controlled, then the resulting inefficiency is the outcome of rational decision-making. The observed deviation merely reflects a misspecification in the estimated production function due to the invisibility of resource M. Technical inefficiency does exist, but its extent is determined by managerial decisions regarding the input level of resource M. By contrast, if the input of resource M is not controlled, the same deviation, although still stemming from a misspecification of the production function, can be interpreted as X-inefficiency, as redefined in Chapter 4, in the sense that the degree of technical inefficiency is not itself subject to control.

Input–Output Relation in the Absence of Control

The proposition that managerial input z is controlled is empirically testable using the basic model presented in the previous Sect. 6.1.1. If the input of resource M is in fact controlled, and consequently the level of productivity is also regulated, then the control variable must possess an implicit price. As long as the input of resource M is under control, this implicit price becomes observable as the marginal productivity of resource M. In the input–output relationship (6.2), the marginal productivity of resource M is given by $F_z^i(L_j, K_j, z_j)$, and in the econometric model (6.3), this value is reflected in the estimated coefficient a.

As discussed in the first half of this subsection, since part of the output generated by managerial input is offset by operating expenses associated with the use of managerial resources, the output actually observed is $F^i(L_j, K_j, z_j) - \tilde{q}_j z_j$. Accordingly, when the input–output relationship is estimated using the econometric model (6.3), the estimated coefficient $\hat{a}$ is given by

$$\hat{a} = F_z^i(L_j, K_j, z_0^i(q^0, L_j, K_j)) - \tilde{q}^0 > F_z^i(L_j, K_j, z_0^i(q^0, L_j, K_j)) - q^0.$$

Here, as in the case of q_j, we assume that $\tilde{q}_j$ is symmetrically distributed around its mean $\tilde{q}^0$, where $\tilde{q}^0 < q^0$. If the input level of managerial resources is optimally controlled, the first-order condition $F_z^i(L_j, K_j, z_0^i(q^0)) = q^0$ holds. This implies that the estimated coefficient $\hat{a}$ is expected to be positive. Therefore, if resource M is a scarce resource with a positive opportunity cost q_j and is under control, it is unlikely that the estimate $\hat{a}$ would be zero.

Now, suppose that in the estimation of the econometric model (6.3), the null hypothesis $a = 0$ is not rejected. How should such a result be interpreted? The possible explanations are as follows. First, resource M may not be a scarce resource. Second, resource M may be an exogenous environmental factor that cannot be controlled. Third, although resource M may be a scarce good with a positive opportunity cost, it may simply not be subject to control.

First, one might assume that resource M is not a scarce resource and is utilized in production until it reaches saturation. However, if that were the case, differences in the input of resource M would not lead to differences in productivity across establishments, which would contradict the observed technical inefficiency.

Second, it might be assumed that resource M is not an input in the usual sense, but rather a natural environmental factor that influences productivity. For example, some production processes may be affected by outdoor humidity, where productivity decreases if the humidity deviates either above or below an optimal level. It is indeed possible that such a specific factor like humidity exists in a particular industry and that this factor is omitted when estimating the input–output relationship. Such an omission could lead to a misspecification of the production function and result in the appearance of technical inefficiency. This possibility should be carefully taken into account. In such a case, the observed technical inefficiency is merely the apparent result of a “technical” issue in model specification. However, it is difficult to assume that a common exogenous environmental factor influences production in the same way across many industries. While this may be plausible in agriculture, where production depends heavily on natural conditions, such a possibility is unlikely in general manufacturing industries. It is also implausible that specification errors in identifying the relevant factors of production would occur in nearly the same pattern across a wide range of manufacturing sectors. If it is confirmed that technical inefficiency tends to appear in a similar way across many industries, then we must acknowledge the general existence of resource M across those industries.[3] Thus, it is important to distinguish whether the observed technical inefficiency reflects a general phenomenon across many industries or a specific factor observed only in some of them. This distinction must be carefully considered when designing an econometric analysis.

As both the first and second possibilities are rejected, the third possibility must be considered if the null hypothesis $a = 0$ is not rejected in the estimation of the econometric model (6.3). That is, even if resource M is a scarce good with a positive opportunity cost, it may not be subject to control. This possibility can be illustrated by the following situation: although resource M is scarce and an opportunity cost q_j exists, managers do not take this cost into account when allocating managerial resources. As a result, there is no well-defined production frontier with respect to managerial input. In such a case, managerial resources are not allocated through deliberate managerial effort. Instead, the opportunity cost is realized passively as a loss in output. Because the input of resource M is not perceived as a controllable variable, the resulting productivity loss is recognized by management only as an unintended and unexplained decline.

To capture this situation formally, consider the following model. Suppose that the production function $F^i(L_j, K_j, z_j)$ is separable into a component F^{0i} that depends on the production factors L_j and K_j, and a component F^{1i} that depends on z_j:

$$F^i(L_j, K_j, z_j) = F^{0i}(L_j, K_j) \cdot F^{1i}(z_j).$$

Furthermore, the execution of managerial efforts can be divided into individual QMP activities, each indexed by m, with the complete set of indices denoted by S. Let σ denote a subset of S ($\sigma \subset S$). For each m-th QMP, let λ_m be the opportunity cost incurred, $\tilde{\lambda}_m$ the portion recorded as an operating expense and deducted from output ($\lambda_m > \tilde{\lambda}_m$), ω_m the productivity improvement achieved prior to this deduction, and $\Lambda(\sigma)$ the function representing the amount of resource M consumed by the set of QMP activities σ. Here, λ_m, $\tilde{\lambda}_m$, and ω_m are all assumed to be additively effective. Under these assumptions, the production frontier $F^{1i}(z)$ with respect to the input level z can be expressed as the result of an optimal selection as follows:

$$F^{1i}(z) \equiv \sum_{m \in \sigma^*} \omega_m, \text{ where } \sigma^* = \underset{\sigma \subset S,\ \Lambda(\sigma) \leq z}{\operatorname{argmax}} \sum_{m \in \sigma} \left(\omega_m F^{0i} - \lambda_m\right),$$

[3] However, if such special factors exist only in a limited number of industries, the method used in this chapter might mistakenly interpret them as a general tendency. This issue concerns the estimation method rather than the question of whether resource M is, in fact, an environmental factor. See the concluding section of this chapter.

and let $m^* \in \sigma^*$ be such that

$$q \equiv \lambda_{m^*}, \quad \tilde{q} \equiv \tilde{\lambda}_{m^*}, \quad \omega_{m^*} - \lambda_{m^*} \leq \omega_{m'} - \lambda_{m'}, \quad \forall m' \in \sigma^*. \tag{6.4}$$

In this case,

$$F_z^i(z) = \omega_{m^*} F^{0i} \geq \lambda_{m^*} = q > \tilde{\lambda}_{m^*} = \tilde{q}.$$

So, when the input–output relationship is estimated using the econometric model (6.3), the estimated coefficient $\hat{a}$ is given by

$$\hat{a} = F_z^i(L_j, K_j, z_0^i(q^0, L_j, K_j)) - \tilde{q}^0 = q^0 - \tilde{q}^0 > 0.$$

In contrast, if managers do not attempt to evaluate the opportunity costs associated with each QMP, and instead make their choices solely based on the anticipated productivity gains in order to increase apparent productivity, then $F^{1i}(z)$ would be given by:

$$F^{1i}(z) \equiv \sum_{m \in \sigma^{**}} \omega_m, \text{ where } \sigma^{**} = \underset{\sigma \subset S,\ \Lambda(\sigma) \leq z}{\operatorname{argmax}} \sum_{m \in \sigma} \left(\omega_m F^{0i} - \tilde{\lambda}_m \right),$$

and let $m^{**} \in \sigma^{**}$ be such that

$$\tilde{q} \equiv \tilde{\lambda}_{m^{**}}, \quad \omega_{m^{**}} - \lambda_{m^{**}} \leq \omega_{m'} - \lambda_{m'}, \quad \forall m' \in \sigma^{**}. \tag{6.5}$$

In this case,

$$F_z^i(z) = \omega_{m^{**}} F^{0i} \geq \tilde{\lambda}_{m^{**}} = \tilde{q},$$

and the estimated coefficient $\hat{a}$ is such that $\hat{a} = F_z^i - \tilde{q}^0 \geq 0$.

Alternatively, the manager may choose σ regardless of λ and $\tilde{\lambda}_m$. Even if the choice is not rational, it would still be based on some sort of criterion. Without assuming the existence of such a selection criterion, the analysis itself would be invalid, so we consider that some arbitrary selection is being made. This can be expressed as the case that the range of QMP activities from which the choice is made is unintentionally restricted, and only a biased subset is available (denoted as $S' \subset S$). In such cases, the production function observed through the input–output relationship would be shrunken or downward-shifted relative to the case in which the optimal selection is made. In this case, the estimated coefficient $\hat{a}$ in Eq. (6.3) is derived as:

$$\hat{a} = \mathbb{E}_{m \in S'} \left[\omega_m F^{0i} - \lambda_m \right], \qquad S' \subset S.$$

where m is a QMP activity arbitrarily selected from the subset $S' \subset S$. When the number of elements in the subset S' is considerably small, this value is expected to be distributed around 0. If managers fail to properly recognize the opportunity cost in their decision-making, the range of possible QMP activities is likely to become either narrowed or biased, and the production function becomes either contracted or shifted downward. Accordingly, $F^{1i}(z)$, the component of the production function reflecting the outcome of managerial effort, is also expected to be lower. This superficially appears as if the choice implied a marginal product of zero.

If the input of resource M is controlled and the production function is expressed as in Eq. (6.2), then the estimated value of parameter a in the econometric model (6.3) is not expected to be zero. On the other hand, if the input is not controlled, although it is possible that $a \neq 0$, it is also entirely possible that $a = 0$. This contrast provides a basis for hypothesis testing. Specifically, if we estimate model (6.3) and fail to reject the null hypothesis $a = 0$, then we cannot reject the hypothesis that resource M is not controlled. In that case, the observed technical inefficiency may be interpreted as reflecting the presence of X-inefficiency. Conversely, if the null hypothesis is rejected in favor of the alternative hypothesis $a > 0$ in the econometric analysis of technical inefficiency using model (6.3), we cannot rule out the possibility that resource M is being controlled, and that the observed technical inefficiency reflects controlled inefficiency.

In conclusion, if the null hypothesis $a = 0$ cannot be rejected as a general tendency across many industries, we must acknowledge the possibility that the observed technical inefficiency is a manifestation of X-inefficiency, that is, inefficiency arising from the absence of control over resource M.

6.2 Method for Testing the Existence of X-inefficiency

Based on the discussion in Sect. 6.1, when the following econometric model is estimated across many industries,

$$Y_j \equiv F^i(L_j, K_j) + a\Delta z_j + b(\Delta z_j)^2 + \epsilon_j, \tag{6.6}$$

the outcome of the hypothesis test for $a = 0$ provides a basis for determining whether the unobserved production factor z is a controlled or uncontrolled variable. Here, ϵ_j denotes a standard symmetric error term.

If the null hypothesis $a = 0$ is rejected in favor of the alternative $a > 0$, then this provides support for the interpretation that the input–output relationship is expressed in the form of Eq. (6.2), implying that the input of resource M is controlled. In this case, if the actual input of resource M deviates from the optimal input determined as a function of factor prices, the deviation from the production function can be represented as the sum of a symmetric error term and an asymmetric inefficiency term. It is therefore plausible to interpret the resulting discrepancy as technical inefficiency. The observed technical inefficiency arises from input allocation inefficiency due to the failure to account for a controlled production factor, caused by the misspecification of the production function. Moreover, since this production factor is distributed around the optimal input level determined by factor prices, it can be considered as controlled in this sense.

On the other hand, if the null hypothesis $a = 0$ is not rejected, it is unlikely that the unobserved production factor causing technical inefficiency is being controlled. This is because, in the input–output relationship expressed by Eq. (6.2), $a = 0$ implies that the factor price of resource M, that is, the net opportunity cost after subtracting the portion of accounting expenses associated with the use of managerial resources, is zero. This suggests that the input of resource M is inherently expected to have an effect beyond the portion of costs that arise directly and explicitly from its use, yet such an effect is not observed. In other words, managerial decisions are not made with proper regard for the opportunity cost of resource M. If the opportunity cost is not properly taken into account, it may be expected that resource M would be over-utilized. However, as indicated in Eq. (6.5), since the target of managerial effort itself is expected to have degenerated, both the actual input level and its effect are considered to be small. Thus, in this case, the observed technical inefficiency may reflect X-inefficiency in the sense of an "absence of control," as discussed in Chapter 4.

In this section, we introduce a method for testing the hypothesis concerning the value of parameter a in the econometric model (6.3). The testing procedure follows the approach introduced in Chapter 2, which identifies relationships among statistical moments.

6.2.1 Square Normal-Type Distribution

To perform the test, we further assume that Δz follows a normal distribution. Under this assumption, the second term on the right-hand side of Eq. (6.6) is normally distributed, while the third term follows a χ_1^2 distribution. Therefore, if higher-order terms in Δz beyond the third are ignored, the resulting distribution of productivity becomes a convolution of a normal distribution and a χ_1^2 distribution. Assuming that $\Delta z \sim N(0, \sigma_u^2)$, the distribution of the deviation term from the frontier function, $u = a\Delta z + b(\Delta z)^2$, corresponds to the square normal-type distribution analyzed in detail in Chapter 2. Its density function is given by:

$$\rho(u) = \frac{\exp\left(-\frac{\left(\sqrt{u+\frac{a^2}{4b}}-\frac{a}{2}\right)^2}{2b^2\sigma_u^2}\right) + \exp\left(-\frac{\left(\sqrt{u+\frac{a^2}{4b}}+\frac{a}{2}\right)^2}{2b^2\sigma_u^2}\right)}{2\sqrt{2\pi}b\sigma_u\sqrt{u+\frac{a^2}{4b}}}. \tag{2.2}$$

The square normal-type distribution reduces to a χ_1^2 distribution when $a = 0$; therefore, testing the hypothesis $a = 0$ is equivalent to testing whether technical inefficiency follows a χ_1^2 distribution. As in the case of the vintage model, the test for the existence of X-inefficiency is closely related to the question of which distribution is appropriate to assume for technical inefficiency.

6.2.2 Test Using the Relation Between Moments

To test hypotheses about the parameter a in the square normal-type distribution, this section adopts the same approach used for testing the vintage model. Specifically, we apply the method presented in Chapter 2 for identifying relationships among moments. For many of the distributional forms assumed for technical inefficiency, a simple relationship exists among the second-, third-, and fourth-order moments of the distribution obtained by convolving the inefficiency term with the symmetric normal error term. Furthermore, the parameter values characterizing these relationships provide information about the characteristics of the technical inefficiency distribution.

Let u be a random variable representing an asymmetric component of technical inefficiency, such as one that follows a half-normal distribution, and let v be a symmetric error term that follows a normal distribution. Denote the second-, third-, and fourth-order moments of the distribution of $v - u$ as M_2, M_3, and M_4, respectively. Then, in general, the following relationship holds:

$$M_4 - 3M_2^2 = K_h \, |M_3|^{\frac{4}{3}} . \tag{2.3}$$

The coefficient K_h, which is the ratio of kurtosis to the absolute value of skewness raised to the power of $4/3$, takes a constant value when the distribution type is fixed, such as in the case of the half-normal distribution. If the distribution has two or more parameters, K_h becomes a function of the parameter(s) that determine the shape of the distribution. This relationship can be used to estimate distributional parameters by first obtaining an econometric estimate of K_h.

In the case of the square normal-type distribution, the relationship among the moments can also be expressed in the form of Eq. (2.3), where the constant K_h is given by

$$K_h = 3\left(1 + \frac{a^2}{b^2\sigma_u^2}\right) \Big/ \left(1 + \frac{3a^2}{4b^2\sigma_u^2}\right)^{4/3} \leq 3. \tag{2.6}$$

The value of K_h reaches its maximum of 3 when $a = 0$, regardless of the value of b, and it is a monotonically decreasing function of $a^2/(b^2\sigma_u^2)$ for $a > 0$. Therefore, once K_h is estimated, it can be used to test hypotheses concerning the value of the parameter a.

When the null hypothesis $a = 0$ cannot be rejected, we cannot reject the hypothesis that the invisible factor of production causing technical inefficiency is not controlled. According to Eq. (2.6), this null hypothesis can be equivalently tested by examining the value of K_h: the null hypothesis $K_h = 3$ versus the alternative hypothesis $K_h < 3$, since $K_h = 3$ holds if and only if $a = 0$, while $K_h < 3$ holds when $a \neq 0$.

Note that the value of the other parameter b^i of the distribution does not affect the equivalence between the null hypothesis $a = 0$ and the null hypothesis $K_h = 3$. In Eq. (2.6), the value of K_h equals 3 when $a = 0$, regardless of the value of b^i. Therefore, even if individual production functions or their second derivatives differ, the validity of the test is unaffected by the specific form of the production function.

This enables the hypothesis to be tested by identifying a general relationship across many industries.

Employment of MOLS

As with the vintage model, this test is conducted cross-sectionally across many industries, rather than as separate tests for each individual industry. As discussed in Sect. 6.1.3, even if a tendency toward $a = 0$ is observed in a single industry, this alone does not clarify whether it stems from uncontrollable environmental factors unique to that industry or from more general structural factors, such as X-inefficiency. It is indeed possible that a specific environmental factor is omitted from the production function in a particular industry, leading to the observation of a χ_1^2 distribution with $a = 0$. However, it is unlikely that such special environmental factors would consistently operate in the same pattern across many industries.

To estimate Eq. (2.3) across many industries, we must first obtain the values of the moments that characterize the deviation from the frontier production function. This requires estimating the frontier itself. As in the case of the vintage model, the MOLS method is employed for this purpose. Specifically, the coefficients $\boldsymbol{\beta}^i$ of the frontier production function, including the constant term, are first estimated using OLS. Then, based on the resulting regression residuals, the second-, third-, and fourth-order central moments are calculated. It is important to note that differences in the constant term do not affect these central moments. Let M_{2i}, M_{3i}, and M_{4i} denote the second-, third-, and fourth-order central moments of the OLS residuals for industry i. Using this set of moment values, we estimate the following cross-sectional regression model across industries to obtain the value of K_h as a coefficient:

$$M_{4i} - 3M_{2i}^2 = K_h \, |M_{3i}|^{\frac{4}{3}} + \epsilon_i. \tag{6.7}$$

The estimated value of K_h is then used to test several theoretical hypotheses.

Note that Δz is uncorrelated with L_j and K_j in the econometric model (6.3), which is derived from the basic model in Sect. 6.1 to estimate technical inefficiency. This lack of correlation follows directly from the assumption that L_j and K_j are exogenously given. Furthermore, since Δz is also assumed to be independent of the factor prices w, r, and q, which in turn determine the values of L_j and K_j, this independence is further reinforced. As a result, the MOLS method yields unbiased estimators.[4]

[4] It should also be noted that when resource M is completely uncontrolled, the function $z_0^i(q, L_j, K_j)$ does not exist. Consequently, the production function in the econometric model (6.3) takes the form $F^i(L_j, K_j, z_j)$. In this case, one might suspect that the residual term is correlated with the explanatory variables in the MOLS estimation, potentially leading to biased estimates. Specifically, the values of Δz may influence the marginal productivity of capital and labor, which in turn affects the realized input levels L_j and K_j, thereby creating correlation between these inputs and Δz. However, suppose that decision-makers are aware that the marginal productivity of labor depends on z_j, taking the form $F_L^i(L_j, K_j, z_j)$, and that they make their input choices based on this

Tests Considering the Properties of the K_h Estimator Under OLS

When technical inefficiency follows a square normal-type distribution with $a = 0$, that is, when it follows a χ_1^2 distribution, the properties of the estimator for the coefficient K_h, obtained via OLS using the econometric model (6.7) across many sample groups, are verified through Monte Carlo simulations in Sect. 2.4 of Chapter 2. The results are presented in Tables 2.26 and 2.27. These tables show that when technical inefficiency follows a square normal-type distribution with $a = 0$, the estimated value of K_h has an upper bound of approximately 3, which depends on the number of establishments in each quasi industry. They also reveal that the greater the variance of the asymmetrically generated technical inefficiency term relative to that of the symmetrically generated random error term, the larger the estimated value of K_h. This latter relationship is illustrated in Fig. 2.3 in Chapter 2, which further shows that when the variance of the random error term is sufficiently large compared to that of the technical inefficiency term, the estimated value of K_h approaches zero.

When adopting a model that assumes the existence of unobserved factors of production, the objective is to test the hypothesis that the parameter a, which is expected to capture the implicit price of unobserved production factors not recorded as explicit accounting costs associated with the use of managerial resources, is equal to zero. As shown in Eq. (2.6), the coefficient K_h reaches its maximum value of 3 when $a = 0$, and decreases monotonically with respect to a in the domain $a > 0$. Therefore, as previously noted, the hypothesis $a = 0$ corresponds to the null hypothesis $K_h = 3$, and the alternative hypothesis becomes $K_h < 3$. Under the alternative hypothesis $a > 0$, it is thus expected that $K_h < 3$ will be observed. Moreover, we must consider the bias confirmed through Monte Carlo simulations. Specifically, even when $a = 0$, if σ_v, the standard deviation of the symmetric random noise, is relatively large and non-negligible, the estimated K_h will fall below 3. In the case where $a > 0$, the estimated value of K_h becomes even smaller than the theoretically predicted value, and will necessarily satisfy $K_h < 3$.

Therefore, when estimating the value of K_h using regression Eq. (6.7), observing a value of K_h less than 3 may indicate that $a > 0$, that the magnitude of random noise σ_v is non-negligible, or both. On the other hand, if the hypothesis $K_h = 3$ is not rejected, it must be the case that $a = 0$ and that the magnitude of σ_v is relatively small compared with σ_u. Thus, even in the presence of a random noise term, if the estimated value of K_h is not significantly different from 3 after accounting for potential bias, then the hypothesis $a = 0$ cannot be rejected and may be regarded as supported by the result.

---

knowledge. In that case, the situation is equivalent to assuming that z_j is observable. Nevertheless, when resource M is not controlled, it is more appropriate to regard z_j as a stochastically varying variable rather than a fixed value specific to each establishment. In such a case, the marginal productivity of labor perceived by managers corresponds to $\mathbb{E}_z[F_L^i(L_j, K_j, z_j)]$, the expected value over the distribution of z_j. As a result, the selected input quantities L_j and K_j are not correlated with Δz, and thus no estimation bias arises in the MOLS procedure.

6.3 The Existence of X-inefficiency in the Japanese Manufacturing Industries

This section aims to apply the test method described in Sect. 6.2 to data from the Japanese manufacturing industries, in order to examine whether the unobserved input factors thought to underlie the observed technical inefficiency are in fact controlled. In other words, it seeks to empirically assess the existence of X-inefficiency in Japanese manufacturing. If the hypothesis that the implicit price of an input—not recorded as an explicit accounting cost associated with the use of managerial resources—is equal to zero cannot be rejected despite its effect on productivity, this raises doubts as to whether such an input is truly being controlled. In this sense, the result can be interpreted as supporting the existence of X-inefficiency, understood as "uncontrolled inefficiency" as defined in Chapter 4.

To perform this test, we estimate the frontier production function across as many industries as possible, derive the distribution of deviations from the frontier, and conduct a cross-sectional analysis to determine whether the relationship among the second-, third-, and fourth-order moments predicted by Eq. (2.3) holds. We then test the value of the parameter K_h. Except for conducting this final test, the procedure follows the same steps as the analysis presented in Chapter 5, which was based on the assumption of a vintage model. Therefore, the details of the technical inefficiency estimation and the derivation of the inter-moment relationship given by Eq. (2.6) are omitted.

6.3.1 Relationship Between Moments

The regression models used to estimate the coefficient K_h in the moment relationship

$$M_{4i} - 3M_{2i}^2 = K_h \left|M_{3i}\right|^{4/3}$$

are specified as Eqs. (R1) and (R2) in Sect. 5.4.2 of Chapter 4:

$$M_{4i} - 3M_{2i}^2 = K_1 \mathrm{sign}\left(-M_{3i}\right)\left|M_{3i}\right|^{\frac{4}{3}} + \epsilon_i, \tag{R1}$$

$$\log\left(M_{4i} - 3M_{2i}^2\right) = \log\left(K_2\right) + \frac{4}{3}\log\left(-M_{3i}\right) + \epsilon_i, \tag{R2}$$

Equation (R2) applies only to samples satisfying
$M_{4i} - 3M_{2i}^2 > 0$ and $M_{3i} < 0$.

The log-log OLS regression in Eq. (R2) is employed to mitigate bias arising from the skewed distribution of the explanatory variable. White's heteroscedasticity-robust standard errors are used to estimate the variances of the regression coefficients. In addition, regression models (R1) and (R2) are also estimated as models (R3) and (R4), respectively, excluding approximately 150 industries in which the skewness of the residuals is −0.4 or greater. As shown by the Monte Carlo results in Sect. 2.4 of Chapter 2, when the skewness is −0.4 or greater (i.e., less negative), the noise from the symmetric error term dominates, and the information from the asymmetric technical inefficiency term is not accurately reflected in the moments. [5]

Tables 5.5 and 5.6 in Chapter 5 show the results of the regression analysis. In Chapter 5, the estimated values of K_h shown in these tables were primarily compared and tested against the expected value of approximately 2.381 under the exponential power-type distribution with $p = 0$. In this chapter, they are mainly compared and tested against the expected value of 3 under the square normal-type distribution with $a = 0$. For details of the regression analysis, see Sect. 5.4 of Chapter 5.

The mean of the estimated values of K_h across the variations of (R1) is 3.310 in 1993 and 3.599 in 1995. For (R2), the corresponding values are 4.856 and 4.250; for (R3), 3.311 and 3.621; and for (R4), 3.403 and 3.277, respectively.

6.3.2 *Test for the Presence of X-Inefficiency*

As a first step, we directly test the null hypotheses that the regression coefficients are $K_1 = 3$ and $\log(K_2) = \log(3) \simeq 1.099$ in regressions (R1) and (R2), respectively. For the 1993 data, the Wald statistic for (R1) ranges from 4.53 (IOD) to 9.27 (EWR), and for (R2), from 19.09 (IOD) to 79.66 (IWR). For the 1995 data, the corresponding Wald statistics are 2.62 (EWD) to 5.40 (IOR) for (R1), and 14.84 (EWD) to 42.58 (IWR) for (R1). The results for regression (R2) indicate that the null hypothesis $\log(K_2) = \log(3)$ is rejected in all cases. In contrast, the results for (R1) are less conclusive: some cases reject the null hypothesis at the 1% or 5% significance level (two-sided test), while others do not. These findings are consistent with the observation made in Chapter 5 that regression (R2), which uses log-transformed variables, tends to yield higher estimates of K_h, especially in samples with lower excess kurtosis and smaller absolute skewness, and is therefore more sensitive to such distributional characteristics. The Wald statistics from the tests described above, along with those from the subsequent tests, are summarized in Tables 6.1 and 6.2.

Next, we test the same null hypothesis that the regression coefficients are $K_1 = 3$ and $\log(K_2) = \log(3)$, using the results from (R3) and (R4), in which samples with skewness greater than −0.4 are excluded. These excluded samples are expected to have a larger variance in the symmetric error term relative to the asymmetric one, thereby reducing the ability to retain information about the asymmetric error distribution. For the 1993 data, the Wald statistic for (R3) ranges from 4.42 (IOD) to 8.87 (EWR), and for (R4), from 0.67 (EOD) to 13.96 (IOR). For the 1995 data,

[5] In the Monte Carlo experiments, skewness was also estimated, and an analysis similar to that shown in Fig. 5.6 of Chapter 5 was conducted for the square normal-type distribution. However, because the results are nearly identical to those for the exponential power-type distribution, the details are omitted here.

Table 6.1 Results of Wald Statistics Part I

In 1993		Regression variation			
Model	Hypothesis	IWD	IWR	IOD	IOR
(R1)	Theoretical value	5.895	8.017	4.530	6.381
	Monte Carlo result ($\sigma_v = 0.0$)	0.259	0.542	0.381	0.731
(R2)	Theoretical value	22.190	79.656	19.087	60.256
	Monte Carlo result ($\sigma_v = 0.0$)	51.012	69.952	55.864	66.556
(R3)	Theoretical Value	5.811	7.786	4.419	6.125
	Monte Carlo result ($\sigma_v = 0.0$)	0.260	0.545	0.380	0.728
(R4)	Theoretical value	0.819	15.106	2.514	13.956
	Monte Carlo result ($\sigma_v = 0.0$)	84.493	139.923	105.180	128.268
		EWD	EWR	EOD	EOR
(R1)	Theoretical value	5.575	9.268	7.733	4.687
	Monte Carlo result ($\sigma_v = 0.0$)	0.347	0.654	0.682	0.344
(R2)	Theoretical value	28.362	57.057	64.415	20.373
	Monte Carlo result ($\sigma_v = 0.0$)	53.366	48.770	63.958	43.983
(R3)	Theoretical value	5.444	8.871	7.382	4.571
	Monte Carlo result ($\sigma_v = 0.0$)	0.348	0.663	0.688	0.345
(R4)	Theoretical value	3.076	6.199	8.163	0.671
	Monte Carlo result ($\sigma_v = 0.0$)	98.555	73.197	87.892	63.458

Notes The "Model" column refers to the estimation results reported in Table 5.5 and 5.6. In the "Hypothesis" column, "Theoretical value" indicates that the null hypothesis being tested is whether the estimated value equals the theoretical value of 3.0, which corresponds to $a = 0$. Similarly, "Monte Carlo result" indicates that the null hypothesis is whether the estimated value equals the mean obtained from the Monte Carlo experiments; in this case, the test is conducted using the standard error of the estimate and the standard deviation from the Monte Carlo results. The items in parentheses represent additional conditions

the Wald statistic for (R3) ranges from 2.45 (EWD) to 4.91 (IOR), and for (R4), from 0.00 (IOD) to 9.85 (EWR). The similarity between the results of (R1) and (R3) reflects the fact, as explained in Chapter 5, that the estimated coefficients themselves are nearly identical. In contrast, the results of (R4) differ significantly from those of (R2), showing a notable decrease in values. This is due to the elimination of noisy samples, specifically those with small absolute values of excess kurtosis or skewness. In the variations where the production function is estimated after removing samples whose values for value added and capital fall outside the range of (mean $\pm 4.5\times$ standard deviation), the null hypothesis cannot be rejected in any case.

As confirmed by the Monte Carlo experiments in Chapter 2, estimation bias is unavoidable. Therefore, for each of regressions (R1) through (R4), we conduct hypothesis testing again using the distributional properties of the estimator of K_h under the square normal-type distribution with $a = 0$. These properties are summarized in Tables 2.26 through 2.35 in Chapter 2. As in Chapter 5, we focus on the

Table 6.2 Results of Wald Statistics Part II

In 1995		Regression variation			
Model	Hypothesis	IWD	IWR	IOD	IOR
(R1)	Theoretical value	4.024	4.635	4.731	5.401
	Monte Carlo result ($\sigma_v = 0.0$)	1.404	1.786	1.890	2.291
(R2)	Theoretical value	20.978	42.583	18.328	27.592
	Monte Carlo result ($\sigma_v = 0.0$)	44.395	72.214	33.980	54.687
(R3)	Theoretical value	3.636	4.266	4.203	4.913
	Monte Carlo result ($\sigma_v = 0.0$)	1.366	1.779	1.785	2.240
(R4)	Theoretical value	1.167	6.692	0.003	1.396
	Monte Carlo result ($\sigma_v = 0.0$)	101.893	106.826	66.798	71.486
		EWD	EWR	EOD	EOR
(R1)	Theoretical value	2.615	2.997	3.326	3.622
	Monte Carlo result ($\sigma_v = 0.0$)	0.833	1.092	1.204	1.443
(R2)	Theoretical value	14.842	42.294	15.318	27.008
	Monte Carlo result ($\sigma_v = 0.0$)	57.715	71.209	53.503	63.854
(R3)	Theoretical value	2.451	2.791	3.049	3.343
	Monte Carlo result ($\sigma_v = 0.0$)	0.862	1.143	1.200	1.473
(R4)	Theoretical value	1.515	9.852	1.785	9.516
	Monte Carlo result ($\sigma_v = 0.0$)	96.931	116.584	96.799	113.246

Notes See notes to Table 6.1

case with a sample size of 100, which is closest to the average number of manufacturing establishments analyzed (137.8) and also to the median (72). The results of the tests are summarized in the "Hypothesis" section under "Monte Carlo Results" in Tables 6.1 and 6.2.

Referring to Tables 2.26–2.30 and Fig. 2.4, which present the estimated values and 95% confidence intervals for a sample size of 100 across different levels of σ_v, we observe the following. When σ_v is smaller than σ_u, the estimated values remain stable and slightly exceed the theoretical value of 3. In this range, the distribution of the estimator is asymmetric, with the distance from the mean to the 97.5th percentile longer than that to the 2.5th percentile. As σ_v becomes larger than σ_u, both the estimated values and the percentiles begin to decline. With further increases in σ_v, the mean of the estimator continues to decrease, eventually converging toward zero. Overall, both the mean and percentiles of the estimator decline monotonically as σ_v increases. Therefore, when testing the null hypothesis $K_h = 3$ using the results of the Monte Carlo experiments, it is most conservative to refer to the case where $\sigma_v = 0$, especially given that the estimates of K_h reported in Tables 5.5 and 5.6 for regressions (R1) through (R4) all exceed 3. Moreover, since the distribution of the estimator is asymmetric, hypothesis testing based on percentile intervals is recommended rather than that based on symmetric distributions.

Using the results of regressions (R1) and (R3), we test the null hypothesis $K_1 = 3$ based on the Monte Carlo results reported in Table 2.26 for a sample size of 100 and $\sigma_v = 0.0$, where the mean of the estimated values is 3.095 and the standard deviation is 0.285. The resulting Wald statistics for the 1993 data range from 0.259 (IWD) to 0.731 (IOR) for (R1), and from 0.260 (IWD) to 0.728 (IOR) for (R3). For the 1995 data, they range from 0.833 (EWD) to 2.291 (IOR) for (R1), and from 0.862 (EWD) to 2.240 (IOR) for (R3). In contrast, to test the null hypothesis $\log(K_2) = \log(3)$ using the results of regressions (R2) and (R4), we refer to Table 2.31, which reports a mean of 0.644 and a standard deviation of 0.022 for a sample size of 100 and $\sigma_v = 0.0$. The Wald statistics for the 1993 data range from 43.98 (EOR) to 69.95 (IWR) for (R2), and from 63.46 (EOR) to 139.9 (IWR) for (R4). For the 1995 data, they range from 33.98 (IOD) to 72.21 (IWR) for (R2), and from 66.80 (IOD) to 116.6 (EWR) for (R4). In addition, the estimated values of K_h reported in regressions (R1) and (R3) for both the 1993 and 1995 data fall within the interval between the 2.5th and 97.5th percentiles, 2.667 and 3.803, respectively, as reported in Tables 2.28 and 2.29 for the case with a sample size of 100 and $\sigma_v = 0$. By contrast, the estimated values from regressions (R2) and (R4) for both years exceed the 97.5th percentile value of 0.686, as reported in Tables 2.33 and 2.34 under the same simulation conditions.

As shown in the above test results, when hypothesis testing is conducted based on the outcomes of the Monte Carlo experiments, the conclusions differ substantially depending on whether the OLS estimates or the log-log OLS estimates are used. When using the OLS estimates, the null hypothesis $K_1 = 3$ is not rejected at the 1% significance level in any case. In contrast, when using the log-log OLS estimates, the null hypothesis $\log(K_2) = \log(3)$ is rejected in all cases. As shown in Sect. 2.4 of Chapter 2, the OLS estimates of K_1 are upwardly biased. The estimates of K_h that slightly exceed 3, as observed in the results of regressions (R1) and (R3), are broadly consistent with the Monte Carlo outcomes under the square normal-type distribution with $a = 0$, particularly when the symmetric noise component is small. On the other hand, when using the log-log OLS estimator, the Monte Carlo experiments indicate that the estimated values of $\log(K_2)$ exhibit substantial downward bias. As discussed in Chapter 2, this bias arises because, under log transformation, smaller sample sizes magnify the influence of samples with low absolute values of excess kurtosis or skewness, effectively weighting these samples more heavily in the estimation. In the actual data, the number of establishments per industry varies widely, ranging from several dozen to over 2,000. In industries with a large number of establishments, the estimates are likely unaffected by the downward bias, as suggested by the results in Tables 2.31 and 2.32. When estimating with real data, these industries are sufficiently represented in the regressions. Therefore, unlike in the Monte Carlo experiments, where each hypothetical industry consists of an equally small number of establishments, the estimation may be less susceptible to the bias introduced by the log transformation. Accordingly, it may be more appropriate to test the results of (R2) and (R4) against the theoretical value log(3), rather than against the outcomes of the Monte Carlo simulations. However, this reasoning is not grounded in a detailed examination of the actual distribution of the number of establishments across industries included in the regression analysis. A more thorough investigation of this issue is left for future research.

In summary, when using the OLS estimates based on regression model (R1), the null hypothesis $K_1 = 3$ is not rejected, provided that the test is conducted using the results of the Monte Carlo experiments. In contrast, when using the log-log OLS estimates based on regression model (R2), testing the null hypothesis $\log(K_2) = \log(3)$ against the theoretical value yields mixed results depending on the variation used to estimate the frontier production function: in some cases, the hypothesis is rejected, while in others it is not. However, when the same hypothesis is tested against the outcomes of the Monte Carlo experiments, it is consistently rejected.

It should be noted that, so far, we have conducted two-sided tests for the null hypothesis $K_h = 3$ against the alternative $K_h \neq 3$, not against the one-sided alternative $K_h < 3$. However, given the theoretical upper bound of $K_h = 3$ under the square normal-type distribution, it is also reasonable to consider a one-sided test with the null hypothesis $K_h = 3$ and the alternative $K_h < 3$. This is equivalent to testing the null hypothesis $K_h \geq 3$ against the alternative $K_h < 3$, which, under the assumed distribution, is logically valid. Nevertheless, since all the observed estimates of K_h exceed 3, it is trivially clear that the null hypothesis $K_h \geq 3$ cannot be rejected in such a one-sided test.

On the other hand, these tests do not necessarily reject the hypothesis $K_h < 3$, and therefore cannot completely rule out the possibility that no X-inefficiency exists. If we instead conduct one-sided tests with the null hypothesis $K_h < 3$ and the alternative $K_h \geq 3$, using the 95% percentile value of 3.650 under $\sigma_v = 0$ as reported in Table 2.30, the estimates from models (R1) and (R3) are not rejected at the 5% significance level in any of the eight variations for the 1993 data. For the 1995 data, the null hypothesis cannot be rejected in six out of eight variations for (R1) and in five out of eight variations for (R3). In contrast, for models (R2) and (R4), the null hypothesis is rejected in all variations for both years.

The ambiguity of these results, specifically that the hypothesis $K_h < 3$ cannot always be rejected, is an unavoidable feature of models that incorporate unobserved production factors. This is because the theoretical value $K_h = 3$ represents the maximum value attainable under the square normal-type distribution. When the null hypothesis $K_h = 3$ is not rejected, it is inherently impossible to rule out the possibility that K_h is slightly less than 3 but still sufficiently close to it.

Nevertheless, since all the observed estimates of K_h exceed 3, the most plausible case remains $a = 0$ in Eq. (2.6), which corresponds to the interpretation that the unobserved resource is not controlled. This implies that the most likely situation is one in which inefficiency is not controlled, and thus X-inefficiency exists. If technical inefficiency were instead caused by a controlled but unobserved production factor, the estimated value of K_h would be expected to be less than 3. Although such a possibility cannot be definitively ruled out, none of the regression results obtained from the estimation of the production frontier function is consistent with it. Therefore, assuming that technical inefficiency arises from an unobserved production factor, the most consistent interpretation of the results is that $a = 0$, meaning that the inefficiency is not controlled.

6.4 Conclusion

In this chapter, following the analysis in Chapter 5, we conduct a test for the existence of X-inefficiency based on the definition that emphasizes the absence of control. The test is built on the assumption that there exists an unobservable factor of production whose input level significantly affects productivity. The dispersion of this input across firms generates observable variation in productivity. Because this factor is unobserved, the estimation of the production function suffers from specification error, and the resulting residuals are interpreted as technical inefficiency. If, despite being unable to directly observe or quantify this factor, the firm's management recognizes its existence and importance, estimates its opportunity cost, and controls its input level accordingly, then such control is expected to produce a detectable effect on the distribution of the observed technical inefficiency. According to the framework in this chapter, if the unobservable production factor is controlled, then the observed technical inefficiency follows a square normal-type distribution generated by $ax + bx^2$, where $a > 0$, $b < 0$, and x is a normally distributed random variable. Conversely, if the factor is not controlled despite its significance, the distribution reduces to the special case $a = 0$, corresponding to the chi-squared distribution with one degree of freedom, χ_1^2. Thus, as in the previous chapter, the test developed here is characterized by its explicit modeling of the inefficiency-generating mechanism and by its avoidance of arbitrary assumptions about the distributional form of technical inefficiency.

Furthermore, in this chapter, the proposed testing method is applied to actual data from the Japanese manufacturing industry to examine the existence of X-inefficiency. The method is based on a simple moment relationship derived from the convolution of the technical inefficiency term and the random noise term, as analyzed in detail in Chapter 2. Specifically, it tests hypotheses regarding the distributional form of technical inefficiency by using the ratio of excess kurtosis to the skewness raised to the four-thirds power in the distribution of deviations from the frontier production function. This ratio is designed to characterize the shape of the convolution distribution independently of the variance parameter.

The results of the empirical analysis show that the null hypothesis, under which unobserved production factors causing technical inefficiency are not controlled, is rejected in some cases but not in others. While these mixed results prevent a definitive conclusion, the fact that the null is not rejected in a number of cases provides substantive support for the plausibility of the hypothesis. Although the alternative hypothesis, assuming that the factors are controlled, cannot be definitively ruled out either, the analysis reveals no compelling evidence that would warrant rejecting the possibility that the unobserved factors remain uncontrolled. The parameter value $a = 0$, which is implied by the distributional evidence, is difficult to reconcile with the assumption that the unobserved production factors causing technical inefficiency are acknowledged as important and managed through rational decision-making that takes their opportunity costs into account.

The method presented in this chapter relies solely on the values of the moments up to the fourth order of the regression residuals obtained from the estimation of frontier production functions. As such, it does not depend on the specific functional form of any individual production function. Indeed, entirely different production functions were estimated and used for each industry. This methodological flexibility, however, comes with certain limitations in the interpretation of results. In particular, deviations from the estimated frontier in each industry may arise from industry-specific factors, and the resulting residuals may follow a square normal-type distribution with $a = 0$. As discussed in Section 6.1.3, such a distribution can also emerge when unobserved environmental conditions, such as humidity, affect productivity. While it is implausible that a single environmental factor would influence all manufacturing industries uniformly, it is entirely possible that certain important environmental or production-related factors, unique to each industry, are not adequately accounted for in the estimation. In such cases, if distinct unobserved factors in multiple industries each generate technical inefficiency that follows a square normal-type distribution with $a = 0$, the method used in this chapter may erroneously interpret the result as evidence of a common structural feature across the manufacturing sector as a whole.

This possibility has not yet been examined in detail. Misspecification of production functions is a common source of error, and if such misspecification is widespread across industries, it may partly account for the empirical findings reported in this chapter. However, because the hypotheses concern unobservable factors, there is no direct means of testing them. Nevertheless, both the test developed in this chapter, which is based on the hypothesis of unobserved production factors, and the test in the previous chapter, which is based on differences in vintages, point to the same conclusion: unexplained inefficiencies persist and cannot be readily explained by rational decision-making. Since these results have been obtained independently through distinct analytical approaches, the consistency of the findings lends them a certain degree of credibility.

The most significant concern in evaluating the conclusions of this chapter is that all estimated values of the coefficient K_h, obtained from the regression analysis, exceed 3. If the assumption that technical inefficiency follows a square normal-type distribution is correct, the estimated value of K_h would be expected to be no greater than 3. While the analysis in this chapter proceeds under the assumption that technical inefficiency is observed due to the existence of unobserved production factors, the fact that the observed values of K_h exceed the theoretically expected range calls this assumption into question. However, the methodology employed in this book allows for the possibility that technical inefficiency may result from a combination of several underlying mechanisms. As shown in Proposition 2 of Chapter 1, when multiple distinct mechanisms are present, the estimated value of K_h becomes a weighted average of the values predicted by each mechanism. Therefore, it is possible to interpret the observed values of K_h exceeding 3 as reflecting the combined presence of technical inefficiency generated by a mechanism such as the vintage model analyzed in Chapter 5. Nevertheless, it must be noted that adopting this interpretation makes it even more difficult to reject the possibility that $K_h < 3$.

In conclusion, it is necessary to consider a broader range of possibilities regarding the origins of technical inefficiency. While Chapter 5 addressed its dynamic aspects, the present chapter focused on a static process. When technical inefficiency is viewed as a static phenomenon, it may be interpreted as the manifestation of certain forms of allocative inefficiency that lie along the production frontier, projected onto the observed level of productivity. If this interpretation is valid, then static technical inefficiency may, in fact, be reinterpreted as a particular form of allocative inefficiency.

Note that since the values to be tested are based on the moments of the regression residuals up to the fourth order, it was not possible to analyze the properties of the sampling distribution directly and conduct tests accordingly. Instead, the actual testing procedure relied on the results of repeated Monte Carlo experiments, which were designed to closely replicate the econometric analysis using the Japanese data. As a result, the reliability of the results depends on the quality of the random numbers generated, which constitutes a limitation similar to that discussed in the previous chapter.

References

Amsler C, Prokhorov A, Schmidt P (2014) Using copulas to model time dependence in stochastic frontier models. Econometric Rev 33(5–6):497–522

Amsler C, Prokhorov A, Schmidt P (2016) Endogeneity in stochastic frontier models. J Econometrics 190(2):280–288

Flynn BB, Schroeder RG, Sakakibara S (1995) The impact of quality management practices on performance and competitive advantage. Decision Sci 26(5):659–691

Haschka RE (2024) Wrong" skewness and endogenous regressors in stochastic frontier models: an instrument-free copula approach with an application to estimate firm efficiency in Vietnam. J Prod Anal 62(1):71–90

Phan AC, Abdallah AB, Matsui Y (2011) Quality management practices and competitive performance: empirical evidence from Japanese manufacturing companies. Int J Prod Econ 133(2):518–529

MIX
Papier aus verantwortungsvollen Quellen
Paper from responsible sources
FSC® C105338

If you have any concerns about our products,
you can contact us on
ProductSafety@springernature.com

In case Publisher is established outside the EU,
the EU authorized representative is:
Springer Nature Customer Service Center GmbH
Europaplatz 3, 69115 Heidelberg, Germany

Printed by Libri Plureos GmbH
in Hamburg, Germany